CULTURAL ANTHROPOLOGY

ADAPTATIONS, STRUCTURES, MEANINGS

David W. Haines

George Mason University

PEARSON

Prentice
Hall

UPPER SADDLE RIVER, NEW JERSEY 07458

Library of Congress Cataloging-in-Publication Data

Haines, David W.
  Cultural anthropology: adaptations, structures, meanings/David W. Haines.
    p. cm.
  Includes bibliographical references and index.
  ISBN 0-13-191576-2
  1. Ethnology.   2. Human geography.   3. Ethnobiology.   I. Title.
  GN316.H34   2005
  306—dc22

2004024779

Editorial Director: Leah Jewell
Publisher: Nancy Roberts
Editorial Assistant: Lee Peterson
Senior Marketing Manager: Marissa Feliberty
Marketing Assistant: Jennifer Lang
Prepress and Manufacturing Buyer: Ben Smith
Cover Art Director: Jayne Conte
Cover Design: Bruce Kenselaar
Cover Photos: Top: Keren Su/Corbis; middle: David Young-Wolff/PhotoEdit, Inc.;
    bottom: Philip and Karen Smith/Getty Images, Inc./Stone Allstock
Director, Image Resource Center: Melinda Reo
Manager, Rights and Permissions: Zina Arabia
Manager, Visual Research: Beth Brenzel
Image Permission Coordinator: Debbie Hewitson
Image Researcher: Kathy Ringrose
Interior Design: Kari Callaghan Mazzola
Composition/Full-Service Project Management: Kari C. Mazzola and John P. Mazzola
Printer/Binder: Courier Companies, Inc.
Cover Printer: Coral Graphics

This book was set in 10/12 Palatino.

Pearson Education LTD.
Pearson Education Singapore, Pte. Ltd
Pearson Education, Canada, Ltd
Pearson Education–Japan
Pearson Education Australia PTY, Limited

Pearson Education North Asia Ltd
Pearson Educación de Mexico, S.A. de C.V.
Pearson Education Malaysia, Pte. Ltd
Pearson Education, Upper Saddle River, NJ

10 9 8 7 6 5 4 3 2 1
ISBN 0-13-191576-2

CONTENTS

PREFACE

When I was ten years old and living in Middletown, New York, my parents decided to move to Japan. The morning after arriving in Japan, I walked out onto a small street behind the house where we were staying and into a new world. As a man on a motorcycle zipped by, I managed to get out an *ohayo gozaimasu* ("good morning"). The man had already passed me but he shifted all the way around in his seat and returned the greeting—without, as I feared, crashing into the wall along the road. Much of anthropology for me is in that moment: the feel of a different culture's sights, sounds, and smells; language as the key to crossing into that culture; and the sharp pleasure I feel even now whenever I return to Japan and walk down the narrow, twisting side streets I met over forty years ago.

When I was twenty-two years old, I was out in the highlands of southern Vietnam. I was an interpreter in Vietnamese and a development specialist for the U.S. army, but I found myself in a minority village working on a gravity-pump water system. A woman motioned me into a house. It was a long house with bamboo matting across sleeping platforms, and smoke curled up through the matting from smoldering fires on the floor. It was the home of the village chief, who was extremely ill. My efforts to teach myself their language (from a Vietnamese text) had not progressed very well, but I was pretty sure that this was malaria. Back in the provincial capital, I managed to convince a Vietnamese medical team to move up their periodic visit to the village. It was indeed malaria and the village chief rapidly recovered. Much of the rest of anthropology for me is in that episode: the ever beckoning image of yet another culture and another language as different from the last as the last was from your own; the involvement in practical issues that are sometimes minor and sometimes life-threatening; the strange world of power where an unimportant outsider could mobilize significant resources to achieve a return to health for an important villager.

How do you put that anthropological experience into an academic class? One answer is to use a text and perhaps supplement it with a reader. That approach will work very well in conveying what anthropology has become as a field of study and the range of insights it has produced. Yet, for many of us, the time (and money) spent on such a text divert attention from the heart of the anthropological experience: a connection between the anthropologist and the places and peoples visited. For us, the answer is usually to use a range of case studies that suggest not only the variation in human cultures but also the variation in how we as anthropologists react to those cultures.

However, using only case studies has limitations. After all, there are some general insights that anthropologists have gained that help illuminate the specific case material. For those who choose a case-study approach but also want a text that will outline those general insights, the options are relatively few. The full-length texts—of which there are many good ones—are too time-consuming to permit the incorporation of more than episodic case-study material. Even the mid-length texts—of which there are some very good ones—are hefty enough to limit their use to courses that will use no more than one or two extended case studies. *Cultural Anthropology: Adaptations, Structures, Meanings* is designed specifically to meet this gap. It provides a rough guide to the major insights of cultural anthropology that supports such a case-study approach. This is not, then, a text to be supplemented by other materials but instead is meant to be the supplement itself.

The purpose of this text as a supplement affects its length and its structure. This is a very pruned-down, bare-bones approach. There are many places in the book where most anthropologists (including me) would say: "More needs to be said here"; "This needs more attention to other regions"; or "What about the new theoretical approaches used with this subject?" The issue of length prohibits that. This text is for the building blocks, not for the elaboration of them. That's what the other course materials—whether ethnographies, monographs, or even fiction—are for.

Two other aspects of the structure of the book deserve note. First, I have tried to give equal attention to what I see as the three major strands of anthropological interest. One is ecological and is clearest in Part I. One is structural (or institutional) and is clearest in Part II. The last is more strictly "cultural" and is clearest in Part III, with its emphasis on meaning, its construction, and its expression. In giving equal attention to these three strands, I have also tried to keep the discussions separate. Although there is topical overlap among the three parts, I do not attempt to reconcile them into one approach. The ecological sections are thus unabashedly materialistic, the structural sections show all the virtues and limitations of systemic analysis, and the sections on meaning steadfastly refuse to reduce ideational issues to materialist ones.

Second, I have tried to be inclusive of the issues of theory, method, and practice as they appear to a wide range of anthropologists. Thus, examples may from time to time be more methodological or more theoretical, more academic or more applied. I have taken a very broad notion of what anthropology is about and a particularly broad notion of culture as a kind of buffer (material, social, and ideational) between human beings as biological entities and the environments in which they live. That inclusiveness is particularly important to me since my own work has been as often in the nonacademic as in the academic world. Much of my own research and writing has been not on people in far-off places but on the contemporary United States.

The result of these decisions will not meet the specific needs of all teachers of anthropology but will provide, I hope, a basic framework from which to begin a foray into the riches of anthropology. Those riches are in the extended case material. This book aims to provide students with a foundation for those more in-depth materials ("If this is an agricultural society, what should I expect?"), encourage their use ("It would be interesting to see how this works out in another society"), and serve as a useful reference when reading them ("Now what was that about matrilineal inheritance?").

ACKNOWLEDGMENTS

In developing this text I am greatly indebted to the students in my anthropology classes at George Mason University. Special appreciation goes to my 2003 classes in introductory anthropology, who field-tested this text, and to the several cohorts of students in my graduate seminar on refugees, who have consistently reminded me that academic work and moral commitment can not be separated. Special individual thanks go to the following: Alexander Munoz for insisting on the importance of Aztec *chinampas*; Bettina Guevara for insights on American body-piercing; Erika Tsuchiya and Sam Brase for monitoring my attempts to integrate Japanese language examples into course material; Alison Meyers and Golnesa Moshiri for encouraging my belief that anthropology and information technology are a good fit even for non-IT types; and sociology students Jennifer Myers and Christine Melcher for enduring in sequential semesters my newly developed classes on information technology and on interdisciplinary synthesis—the latter based on the premise that anthropology is indeed the discipline from which to integrate material from the sciences, social sciences, and humanities.

Several colleagues also deserve particular thanks. Sheila Barrows and Fred Conway read and commented extensively on the manuscript as a whole—the former with a clear editor's eye and the latter with a supportive teacher's one. Karen Rosenblum offered invaluable critique of several of the chapters and strong support for the overall intent of this kind of alternative text. Karl Zhang—colleague and teacher—has kept up my spirits as I learn Chinese and thus piece together a broader linguistic and historical understanding of East Asia. Thanks also go to John Whitmore, Ann Palkovich, and Linda Seligmann for support that led to my most recent Fulbright in Korea—an experience that has further enhanced my understanding of Asia from the vantage point of teaching about Southeast Asia to students at an East Asian university. And thanks go to the following reviewers, who provided helpful comments: Donna Coppola Budani of Eastern Michigan University, Barry

Kass of Orange County Community College, C. Richard King of Drake University, and James G. Flanagan of the University of Southern Mississippi. At Prentice Hall/Pearson Education, I am indebted to Nancy Roberts for her interest and support throughout the publication process and to Sylvia Shepherd for invaluable suggestions on how to bridge between my goals for this text and the needs of teachers adopting it. Thanks also go to Kari Callaghan Mazzola of Big Sky Composition for her wonderful sense of design and efficient management of the production process. Finally, this text owes much to Frank Vivelo's venerable *Cultural Anthropology*. That book set a very high standard for those of us who aim for an organized and compact introduction to anthropology.

David W. Haines

Chapter 1

Anthropological Basics

Anthropology has its origins in the late-nineteenth-century attempt to grasp the full range of the human experience: that *all* aspects of *all* people's experience belonged together as an indivisible subject. To that broad sense of inclusion was added an emphasis on direct fieldwork as the best way to understand how other people lived and how they experienced their lives. In North American anthropology, that sense of inclusion and the commitment to field research were applied initially to native Americans (whose lifeways anthropologists feared would soon disappear); to the people whose lives and work were reshaping the North American continent (white and black, native-born and immigrant); and ultimately to the full range of people throughout the world in both technologically simple and complex societies.

Today, anthropology consists of an extensive body of knowledge accumulated by anthropologists and a set of conceptual approaches that help organize that material. Yet anthropology also remains a very personal quest for understanding. That quest hinges on fieldwork that involves a long-term, direct immersion in the cultures being studied. That field experience is structured not so much by formal research methods as by the accumulated experience of other anthropologists, the basic questions they have asked, and the ideas about human interaction that they have "tested" in the field. The quest for understanding also continues to have a strong link to the professional practice of anthropologists as they seek to improve the human condition by addressing how people interact with their environments, how their social organization can be made more effective and more equitable, and how they can more fully achieve their human potential given the context of very intrusive global political forces.

This introductory chapter introduces these anthropological basics in two ways. The first is an overview of anthropological theory, method, and practice. The purpose is to provide a general sense of how anthropologists look at things ("theory"); how they try to gather information about the world ("method"); and the kinds of work they do—and lives they lead—as they do so ("practice"). The second is a review of the early history of anthropology. The purpose is to indicate the major intellectual decisions that have formed anthropology as it is today. The most important of these are a commitment

1

to inclusiveness (anthropology is about all aspects of all people's lives); a recognition that all people have their own distinct histories (just as we do); and a determination to understand other societies on their own terms. The chapter then concludes with a discussion of the way this book is organized around three sets of questions that have emerged in anthropology: how people relate to their environments ("adaptations"), the basic ways in which human society is organized ("structures"), and how people make sense of their lives ("meanings").

BIOLOGY, ENVIRONMENT, AND CULTURE

Although anthropologists have a wide range of general and specific ideas about how things work, there is a common framework shared by most anthropologists. That framework (diagramed in Figure 1.1) includes three major domains: biology, culture, and environment.

BIOLOGY

Human biology is the specific focus for some anthropologists, but all anthropologists recognize and must factor into their analysis what human beings are in physical terms. Often that consideration of human biology is very much in the background. Thus the specific physical characteristics that permit human language need little comment in most anthropological research, since all human societies have that ability. On the other hand, the consideration of human biology may be central in other work. For example, the relative effects of biological sex and the socially constructed issues of gender have long been of concern to anthropologists. Much of the work of Margaret Mead, one of the most widely known anthropologists of the twentieth century, was concerned with exactly that interaction between biology and culture.

ENVIRONMENT

Human beings, however, do not live in a vacuum. They live in a wide range of environments. Indeed, much of the uniqueness of human beings lies in their ability to adapt to a wide range of environments. Thus it is impossible

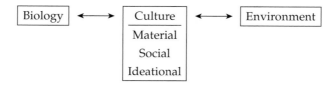

FIGURE 1.1   BIOLOGY, CULTURE, AND ENVIRONMENT

Margaret Mead (1901–1978), the twentieth century's most famous U.S. anthropologist. (*APA/Getty Images, Inc./Hulton Archive Photos*)

to understand the meaning of human biology without studying people in the full range of environments in which they live. This helps explain the anthropological emphasis on the details of the physical places in which people live. Many anthropological case studies begin with extensive discussions of the physical environment: the quality of the soil, the rains, the temperature changes, the kinds of vegetation, the animals. Franz Boas, who held the first university position in anthropology in North America (and who will be discussed in more detail later in this chapter), was originally a physicist. He started out to study the physical environment in the arctic (on Baffin Island) but then found that the human beings who lived there were of rather more interest than the environment itself.

CULTURE

Although anthropologists deal with both biology and environment, their greatest concern has been with the third domain in the diagram—culture. Culture, in its broadest sense, is a kind of buffer that exists between human beings as biological entities and the environments in which they live. After all, if the weather changes sharply, human beings have the options of putting on clothes or taking them off, of heating their homes or cooling them. Culture greatly expands the options that people have. Canadians don't need to migrate south to the United States in winter (although they might like to) and those in the southern parts of the United States don't need to migrate north to Canada in the summer (although some of us do just that). The buffer that is culture is often very physical and very practical. A simple tool, for example, can sharply change the relationship between human beings and their environment: A stone or bone scraper permits the fashioning of hides into clothes; a piece of chipped stone at the end of a big stick (spear) or smaller stick (arrow) permits better hunting; a plow revolutionizes the cultivation of plants.

But culture is not just about tools. It is also about social arrangements. Human beings are not unique in being social and in having families. Yet the human capacity for social groups is impressive in the variation and often in the sheer size of such groups. Those social arrangements provide an additional buffer between human beings as biological entities and their environments. Cooperative groups permit the hunting of big game, fishing with large nets, or even killing whales. Very large groups with hundreds, even thousands of members permit rapid mobilization of people in an emergency, such as war. Very small groups, such as the nuclear family, permit people to spread out across a very large area and be relatively self-sufficient.

Finally, culture is also about ideas, beliefs, and values. This is usually the way the word "culture" is used in everyday life. At its broadest, this aspect of culture can be understood as referring to the core vision that people have of themselves, of the world, and of how they should orient themselves to that world and the other human beings in it. It is what makes them who they are and sets the parameters of what they can accomplish. On a more specific level, culture can refer to ideas that might help people work together (such as a belief in the nobility of sacrifice and service) or that might help people survive against their adversaries (such as a belief in the justness of war). Although much of the importance of this kind of culture is that it is shared among people, it may be helpful to think of this as *ideational culture* to distinguish it from the *material culture* and *social culture* already discussed.

Anthropologists are thus interested in human beings as biological entities, as cultural entities, and as located in specific environments. That makes anthropology a very broad discipline. On the positive side, that broad perspective helps anthropologists avoid simplistic arguments that some aspect of human behavior is "caused" by biology, or "caused" by the environment, or even "caused" by culture. Instead, anthropologists know they must account for the biological, environmental, *and* cultural aspects of human life. As an example, consider race. Whereas many people might accept the idea of race as a simple description of physical differences among people, anthropologists recognize that "race" is, after all, a word with multiple meanings. Understanding race thus requires attention to people's ideas and values—to their culture in the everyday sense. It also requires attention to how supposed racial differences are used in social arrangements. Anthropologists might note, for example, that issues of race in the United States have their origins in a system of slavery that provided cheap labor for difficult work that people didn't want to do themselves. Even though anthropologists know that there aren't clear biological differences between so-called races, they would readily understand how convenient it would be for people who were enslaving others to claim—after the fact—that biology somehow justified it. One of Franz Boas's achievements, for example, was to show that supposed racial differences between northern and southern European immigrants to North America actually disappeared among their children. So much for the durability of racial differences.[1]

FIELDWORK AND PRACTICE

This joint attention to human beings as biological entities, to the environments in which they live, and to their material, social, and ideational culture, has much to do with the way anthropologists go about their work. The "theory" greatly affects the "methods." If anthropologists are to study biology and environment and culture, they will have to locate themselves in a specific place. If they don't, how can they possibly begin to understand the interactions of biology, culture, and environment? So the core methodological rule is "go there." If environment is such an important factor, then the period of time spent in that place will need to be at least a year. Almost all human environments have sharp seasonal changes of temperature or precipitation; those seasons greatly affect the food people are able to obtain, the shelter they will need, and usually their most important ritual events and celebrations. That requires a supplement to the core methodological rule: "and stay there for at least a year." Finally, since much of culture is ideational and hinges on language, the third part of that methodological rule is: "and learn the language." That's just the minimum. Many anthropologists prefer to stay longer than a year and to return later to see if what they found was a relatively durable pattern or a more transient one. This standard of fieldwork is daunting. It is extremely time-consuming, often disorienting, and sometimes dangerous. Yet the result is that anthropological fieldwork is likely to provide more depth and range of understanding than other research approaches. Thus, the anthropologist can often give the richest portrayal of other cultures: what people do, why they do it, and what they themselves think about it.

The broad anthropological theory about the interrelation of biology, culture, and environment and the demanding method of intensive fieldwork greatly shape the way in which anthropologists go about being anthropologists. Their jobs vary greatly. In North America, about half of those with doctorates go into teaching positions where they usually continue their research. The other half go into a range of "real" jobs, many of which are continuations of their own anthropological research. Many work in the areas of international development or humanitarian action, often on behalf of people they already know from their field work. Yet others bring their skills to bear on issues in

---

[1]For the latest round of debate on this aspect of Boas's research, see Clarence C. Gravlee, H. Russell Bernard, and William R. Leonard, "Boas's Changes in Bodily Form," *American Anthropologist* 105 (2003): 326–332, and Corey S. Sparks and Richard L. Jantz, "Changing Times, Changing Faces," *American Anthropologist* 105 (2003): 333–337.

North America. Some focus on populations of immigrants and refugees. Others focus on ethnic or racial minorities—or on those who follow alternate sexual orientations. Finally, a few focus on mainstream elements of the North American population. Some of these have become involved in technological areas, and several are looking at computerization as yet another in a long line of human tools.

In all this range of anthropological work, there is sometimes a tendency to categorize anthropologists as academics (those in full-time university positions); applied anthropologists (usually split between university and research activities); and practitioners (those in "real" jobs). Yet there is often considerable overlap. Even the most academic of the academics are usually involved in research that has quite practical implications. Often the practitioners are working in areas (such as computerization, genetic engineering, and international migration) that have the most challenging theoretical implications. Although they sometimes disagree, all share a commitment to an overarching vision of a rich and varied humanity that demands attention, respect, and—yes—a great deal of effort and time.

THE DEVELOPMENT OF ANTHROPOLOGY

TYLOR AND MORGAN: EVOLUTION, ETHNOGRAPHY, AND HOLISM

The basic theoretical orientations, methods, and practice of anthropology can also be illustrated through a review of the early history of anthropology as a specific discipline. A full review is too hefty a subject for this book, but a short review can provide a basic indication of the three pillars on which the discipline is built: evolutionism, historical-particularism, and structural-functionalism. The labels may seem contorted but they are actually simply descriptive: The *evolutionists* emphasized the importance of evolution in organizing information about different peoples, the *historical-particularists* emphasized the importance of history and of the particular details of how people live, and the *structural-functionalists* emphasized that societies were indeed structured and that the different elements of those societies had practical functions.

The story of anthropology as we know it today began in the latter part of the nineteenth century. The world was rapidly changing. The industrial revolution had given Europe and North America a vastly increased ability to produce new goods, sometimes goods of better quality, certainly goods of increased quantity, and often goods—like weapons—of greatly increased power. This resulted in an enormous power differential between those countries and the rest of the world. That power differential ultimately reduced much of the rest of the world to colonial or near-colonial status. The industrial revolution also resulted in great social dislocations within Europe and North America. Yet this was also a time in which there was hope that the capacity for reason could resolve these social dislocations and create a better world. That belief mirrored the confidence that science had done well in increasing human understanding and promoting great leaps in productive power.

The first anthropologists—the evolutionists—were part of that time of change. They confronted a world that was changing rapidly. They also had an increasing amount of information about an increasing number of people in a world that was being brought more closely together. To their great credit, these first anthropologists recognized the extent of human diversity and decided that this very diversity would be their focus. They would claim all these different human beings as part of one field of study. Further, they would claim that all aspects of these people's lives were within the scope of their new discipline. Thus anthropology was at its very creation the study of all people (any time, any place) and of all aspects of their lives. As Edward Tylor (1832–1917), the most eminent of the evolutionists, put it, the focus of anthropology was to be culture, for which he offered the following definition:

> Culture or civilization taken in its wide ethnographic sense is that complex whole which includes knowledge, belief, art, morals, law, custom, and any other capabilities and habits acquired by man as a member of society.[2]

This is a broad definition indeed. Two of the words he used deserve underlining because they continue to be so important for anthropology. The first is *ethnographic*. Its literal meaning is simply the study or description (*~graph*) of a people (*~ethnos*), but it conveys the need for that study to be detailed and thorough. Tylor's use of the phrase *complex whole* is echoed to this day in the anthropological emphasis on *holism*, which means that all the different pieces of what people do add to a comprehensive, complex whole, and that you cannot understand the pieces without understanding that whole.

That very inclusiveness, however, posed a problem. Even in Tylor's time, there was a very broad and growing amount of information on different human societies. There was thus an organizational problem: how to sort all this information into a meaningful structure. Influenced by the new popularity of evolutionary theory in biology, Tylor and others began to sort the information they found into general stages of development—of social evolution. It is for this they are called evolutionists. As two examples of the attempts of evolutionists, consider Tylor's own work on religion and the work of Lewis Henry Morgan on technology.[3]

---

[2]E. B. Tylor, *Primitive Culture* (London: John Murray, 1871).
[3]The discussions that follow are drawn from E. B. Tylor's *Anthropology* (London: MacMillan and Co., 1881) and Lewis Henry Morgan's *Ancient Society* (University of Arizona Press, 1985 [originally 1877]).

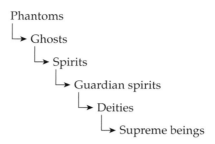

FIGURE 1.2   TYLOR'S SEQUENCE OF RELIGIOUS IDEAS

Tylor was interested in religion and attempted to reason through how human beings developed their sense of the supernatural (see Figure 1.2). His argument began with the mystery of death. Clearly when someone died the body was still there, but the something that made them who they were was gone. That the spirit of the person simply disappears instantaneously without a trace would, on the face of it, be unreasonable. Surely there is at least some brief passing phantom of that person. If people have a notion of that residual something of the person, then they might develop a more elaborate notion of a spiritual entity that retained much of the personality of the dead person—what we would call a ghost. Surely, Tylor reasoned, if people have the notion of an enduring spirit of a dead person, they might also develop the notion of an independent spirit that had *not* previously been a person. Perhaps the spirit that is the living person, in fact, comes from somewhere else and enters the child at conception or birth, and then leaves the body again at the time of death. From such notions of spirits, Tylor reasoned that notions of guardian spirits, deities, gods, and ultimately a supreme being would develop. Tylor's thoughts on religion remain valuable, especially because they highlight the practical logic underlying many religious beliefs.

Lewis Henry Morgan (1818–1881) was an American who had spent much time with the Iroquois. He developed a framework for understanding societies based on their material culture. His reasoning was that technology had pervasive effects on societies. The items he chose as critical advances were fire, fishing, the bow and arrow, pottery, domestication of plants and animals, iron tools, and writing. Surely these things make a difference. Rather than simply note them as important factors, however, Morgan organized them into an evolutionary scheme (see Figure 1.3). Thus those societies that had fire and fishing, but lacked the bow and arrow, were at the middle stage of "savagery." Those who had pottery made it into the "barbarian" category. Iron tools put you at the top of the barbarians, but only a written language let you enter the ranks of the civilized.

Morgan's evolutionary scheme has much merit. The control of fire, the domestication of plants and animals, iron tools, and writing do indeed yield

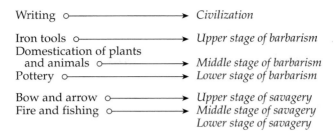

FIGURE 1.3   MORGAN'S EVOLUTIONARY STAGES

potential benefits for a society. If this were only a kind of technology rating, it would be hard to object to it. However, this three-fold categorization of savagery, barbarism, and civilization has a potentially smug and nasty tone to it, and it was indeed used for many aspects of human behavior that had little to do with technology. It was also used to justify the enormous inequalities of the time. As these evolutionary schemes became more grandiose and self-serving, they also became more inconsistent and sometimes factually inaccurate. Thus in the area of marriage, one set of people saw the sequence from "savagery" through "barbarism" to "civilization" as involving a shift from group marriage to polygamy to monogamy. Another set of people, however, saw the sequence as moving from promiscuity through matriarchy to patriarchy. Unfortunately for all of them, there wasn't much correspondence between these stages of marriage and Morgan's more defined technological ones. For example, people with very simple technology often had monogamous marriages. For religion, a similar pattern developed. One set of people argued that the "savagery" to "barbarism" to "civilization" progression was seen in the shift from magic to religion to science. But how could they themselves, who were supposed to be "civilized," still be religious and attend church each Sunday? Another set of people argued that the transition was from animism (a general belief that there are spirits) to polytheism to monotheism. As with marriage patterns, however, these sequences did not directly match what was found in the field. Technologically simple cultures often had what appeared to be monotheistic views.

BOAS: CULTURAL RELATIVISM

Although the specific arguments of the best of the evolutionists—such as Tylor and Morgan—had much merit, the degradation of their ideas into crude stages of savagery, barbarism, and civilization caused a reaction. This strong reaction created North American anthropology as we know it today. Central to that reaction was Franz Boas. Boas (1858–1942) was originally trained as a physicist in Germany and went to Baffin Island in 1883 to study the effects

Franz Boas (1858–1942), pioneering North American anthropologist. (*Image #2a5161, American Museum of Natural History Library*)

of its arctic environment. He thus came to anthropology through his interest in the environment. However, once on Baffin Island he became more interested in the people. From his journals there, he wrote:

> I often ask myself what advantages our "good society" possesses over that of the "savages." The more I see of their customs, the more I realize that we have no right to look down on them. . . . We have no right to blame them for their forms and superstitions, which may seem ridiculous to us. We "highly educated people" are much worse, relatively speaking. The fear of tradition and old customs is deeply implanted in mankind, and in the same way as it regulates life here, it halts all progress for us. I believe it is a difficult struggle for every individual and every people to give up tradition and follow the path to truth. . . . As a thinking person, for me the most important result of this trip lies in the strengthening of my point of view that the idea of a "cultured" individual is merely relative and that a person's worth should be judged by his [heart]. This quality is present or absent here among the Eskimo, just as among us. All that man can do for humanity is to further the truth, whether it be sweet or bitter. Such a man may truly say that he has not lived in vain.[4]

Thus at the very beginning of his career, Boas set the tone. As with the evolutionists, all aspects of the lives of all people were to be included, but their lives were to be understood not as stages in some grand evolutionary scheme, but rather as the common attempt of all people to achieve their full humanity.

---

[4]As quoted in George Stocking's *Race, Culture, and Evolution* (New York: Free Press, 1968), p. 148.

Boas's phrase "merely relative" should be underlined, for it, like Tylor's invocation of "that complex whole," is now a standard assumption of anthropology: Cultures must be understood on *their* terms, not ours. Thus to the invocation of holism is added that of *cultural relativism.*

Here with Boas lay a new commitment to human diversity and to human equality. Here also lay the anthropological emphasis on fieldwork. No longer was information to be processed into self-serving schemes by "armchair" anthropologists. Rather, anthropologists were now to go to where the people lived to understand the details of their histories and the wealth of their material, social, and ideational culture. Boas, after all, did not have his great insight at home, but out in the field. He would, in his later career, personally train two generations of anthropologists who would spread out across North America to document the Native-American experience that they all feared might soon disappear entirely. They would then move more broadly throughout the world to document other cultures and to consider what lessons those other cultures might have for us. But here, with the young Boas, the commitment was already made. As with the evolutionists, all aspects of all people's lives were included. However, that inclusion was to be based on the premise of equality and achieved through detailed fieldwork. The odd title "historical-particularist" thus rings with two invocations as relevant today as then: "All people have their own history" and "the details matter."

RADCLIFFE-BROWN AND MALINOWSKI: STRUCTURAL FUNCTIONALISM

Boas and the other North American anthropologists were not the only people who reacted against the evolutionists. The British structural-functionalists had a similar response. They too were wary of grand evolutionary schemes and they too emphasized detailed fieldwork. A. R. Radcliffe-Brown and Bronislaw Malinowski, the two most important of the structural-functionalists, provide an interesting contrast. Radcliffe-Brown (1881–1955) was very much the theoretician while Malinowski (1884–1942) was very much the field worker. Indeed, Malinowski's work in the Trobriand Islands during World War I is often considered the model for modern anthropological fieldwork. The personal styles of the two men were quite different. Radcliffe-Brown was a rather proper, native-born Englishman who wrote books with titles like *The Natural Science of Society* and *The Andaman Islanders.* Bronislaw Malinowski was a flamboyant Pole who subsequently moved to England. His titles included *Argonauts of the Western Pacific, Coral Gardens and Their Magic,* and *The Sexual Life of Savages,* and, just in case you didn't know enough about sex already, *Sex and Repression in Savage Society.*

Despite their differences, both Radcliffe-Brown and Malinowski saw societies as working systems that were logical on their own terms. For them, history was less important than it was to the Boasians. It was not that all

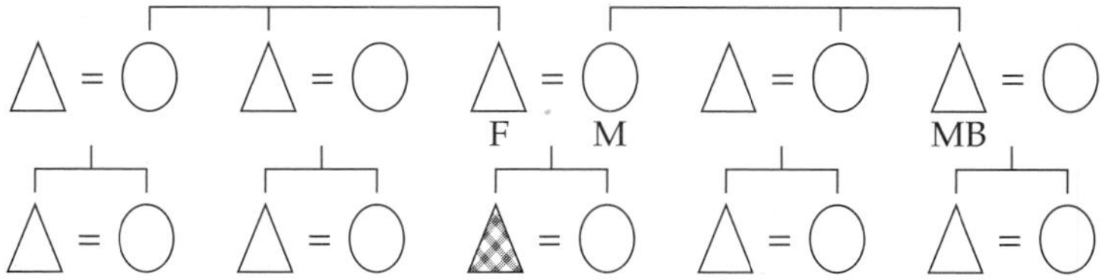

FIGURE 1.4   THE MOTHER'S BROTHER

cultures had their own histories but that all societies were working systems. Those systems needed to be understood on their own terms as they existed in the present. The classic example of their approach involves "the mother's brother" (see Figure 1.4). At the time they were doing their research, the relationship between sons and fathers was frequently described as innately tension-filled. Freud's view, for example, was based on issues of repressed sexual feelings toward the mother and consequent competition with the father. What both Radcliffe-Brown and Malinowski immediately observed, however, was that these ideas were based on the particular structure of European society. In European society, inheritance is generally patrilineal (i.e., the line runs through the father). Thus sons inherit from their fathers. Yet in other societies, they noted, inheritance is not from fathers to sons. In matrilineal societies, much inheritance is from mothers to daughters. However, there is also inheritance between males. A young man in such a society usually inherits from his mother's brother rather than from his own father. When the structural-functionalists looked at matrilineal societies, they found that relations between fathers and sons were not at all what they were in European societies. Instead, the relationship between the two was relatively warm and flexible while the relationship with the mother's brother reflected stress and competition. For the structural-functionalists, there were two main lessons from this consideration of the mother's brother: First, always consider the full range of options in different kinds of societies and, second, examine the simple things (such as who inherits from whom) before launching into grand psychological theory.

From the evolutionists, then, comes the basic sense of inclusion: that all aspects of all people's lives belong on the record. From both the historical-particularists and the structural-functionalists come the emphases on fieldwork and understanding societies on their own terms. For the historical-particularists, "on their own terms" emphasized the history of a people, and for the structural-functionalists it emphasized the practical logic of their social arrangements. The subsequent history of anthropology rests on these foundations. Many current debates can be anticipated from this early work. One is the problem caused by the broad scope of "all aspects of all people's lives." How do you manage that amount of information? Another is the problem caused by the length of fieldwork. Over that period of time, an anthropologist will inevitably become personally involved and not simply an objective outsider. That will benefit the research but it will also introduce problems of how to analyze information that is so strongly and personally channeled.

ADAPTATIONS, STRUCTURES, MEANINGS

This chapter has introduced anthropology as a broad, cross-cultural, integrative discipline that is concerned with human biology, the environments in which people live, and the material, social, and ideational culture that serves as a buffer between human biology and the environment. Out of that broad framework come three general sets of issues. These are addressed in the three parts of this book.

The first part, "Adaptations," focuses on the issues of how human societies can be understood in terms of their adaptation to the environment. The chapters in Part I introduce the basic variations of foraging, horticulture, agriculture, pastoralism, and industrialism. The central premise is that each adaptation creates societies with particular tendencies: large kinship groups for some but nuclear families for others; peace for some but frequent war for others; relative equality for some but sharp disparities for others. Part I should give you a sense of the variation in human societies and to what degree that variation reflects a people's relationship to their environment. You'll find a bit of Lewis Henry Morgan's interest in technology here, and much of Franz Boas's early fascination with the environment and how people adapt to it.

The second part, "Structures," focuses on the issues of social organization, thus focusing on the social aspects of culture. For anthropologists, the most important organizing principle of human society is probably kinship. Ties of blood and marriage are, for most people, the most reliable of human ties. The anthropological record shows immense variation in how kinship ties are created, perceived, and used. Yet anthropologists also look at other ways in which human beings are wound and bound together. Some are political, some economic, and some a combination of these. Religion is also included here since much of its effect is to provide a structure for relationships among people—and between people and a wide range of spirits and other supernatural entities. Part II should give you a sense of the basics of human social relations and what the options are in organizing people by kin, political, economic, and religious ties. You'll find many echoes in Part II of the structural-functionalists, including discussion of matrilineality, patrilineality, and the now familiar "mother's brother."

The third part, "Meanings," addresses the issues of how people perceive the meaning of their lives and how they create and recreate that meaning through thought and deed. It thus focuses on ideational aspects of culture. The discussion begins with cognition (some basics about how our minds organize the world) and then turns to language (some basics about how our speech and writing organize the world). Part III then considers how people develop a reciprocal relationship with their bodies, physical places, objects, and events. That reciprocal relationship involves drawing meaning from each of these and also infusing them with revised or simply revitalized meaning. Part III concludes with a discussion of the ways anthropologists are engaging in action with the contemporary world. That action is one way that anthropologists work their own meaning of things back into the world in which they live. This very last chapter on action suggests some ways you can view the world and act in it based on the material presented in all three parts of this book.

SOME WARNINGS

In reading this book, a few warnings are in order. First, in order to meet the specific purpose of this volume as a supplement to courses that emphasize case studies, the approach is indeed very abbreviated. I cannot do justice to the complexity of many issues nor can I invoke more than a little of the vast anthropological literature that now exists. My decisions about what to include generally have been to emphasize the basics of anthropology rather than anthropological debates about those basics. It is not that the debates aren't important, but simply that they provide a relatively poor place in which to begin an introduction to anthropology.

Second, I have aimed to introduce key ideas first, and only then—and sparingly for reasons of space—to give case studies. I saw no other choice without lapsing into a more extended narrative format leading to a longer (and more expensive) book. The purpose here, after all, is to try to provide some basic guidance, so the specifics of the case studies (ethnographies if you prefer) can take center stage. The result is that you may need to slow down somewhat for these chapters. I have done my best to streamline the presentation and keep the arguments as jargon-free as possible, but some occasional pauses to think things through may be needed.

Third, despite that need for conciseness, I realize that this book may also be used as a reference guide—a kind of concordance for terms and ideas. Toward that end I have tried to provide reasonable backup. The extra sources listed at the end of the chapter should help you to the next level of detail on each subject. There is also a glossary that will help in identifying terms. The usual textbook style convention of italicizing significant words is also used.

I hope that helps. I have also occasionally added footnotes with special terms or references that may be useful but are probably not essential in most introductory classes.

Good luck. Anthropology is a terrific field—and a terrific undergraduate major. It is a terrific field because it helps illuminate people's lives and because, since it is such a personal discipline, it also helps activate the minds and spirits of the people who do the research. So enjoy learning about how really interesting people can be. But also learn from anthropologists as they attempt to do the impossible: to be objective, to be fair to the people they study, to be true to themselves, and to write it up in a reasonably engaging way.

SOURCES

As would be expected, there is a very large literature on anthropological theory, method, and practice. For general overviews of theory, three useful volumes are Marvin Harris's *The Rise of Anthropological Theory: A History of Theories of Culture* (Thomas Y. Crowell, 1968; Alta Mira Press, 2001), which is both detailed and argumentative; Philip Carl Salzman's *Understanding Culture: An Introduction to Anthropological Theory* (Waveland, 2001), which is a more recent and succinct approach; and H. Sidky's more detailed *Perspectives on Culture* (Prentice Hall, 2004). L. L. Langness's *The Study of Culture* (Chandler and Sharp Publishers, 1987) is especially useful for the extensive quotations that give the flavor of early theoretical arguments. For more detailed historical work on anthropology as a discipline, the work of George W. Stocking is essential, especially his *Race, Culture, and Evolution: Essays on the History of Anthropology* (Free Press, 1968). Adam Kuper's *Anthropology and Anthropologists: The Modern British School* (Routledge, 1996) is an entertaining look at anthropology across the Atlantic. There are various compendia on methods, but the heart of anthropological method is probably clearest through autobiographical accounts. For example, Hortense Powdermaker's *Stranger and Friend: The Way of an Anthropologist* (W. W. Norton, 1966) and Margaret Mead's *Blackberry Winter: My Earlier Years* (Kodansha, 1995) provide classic accounts that will take you into the heart of the anthropological approach to field research. Finally, a good sense of anthropological practice can be gained from *Practicing Anthropology,* a career-oriented publication of the Association for Applied Anthropology and from the volume *Careers in Anthropology: Profiles of Practitioner Anthropologists,* edited by Paula L. W. Sabloff (National Association for the Practice of Anthropology, 2000).

The film series *Strangers Abroad* provides very good introductions to six of the major figures in early anthropology. All the segments are sound, but the ones on Margaret Mead and Bronislaw Malinowski are especially useful in introducing, respectively, the flavor of American anthropology and the issues of fieldwork. The segment on Franz Boas is also useful, but the film on Boas from the earlier *Odyssey* series is more informative. Watching the first half (30 minutes) of the film will help underline the range of Boas's contributions.

PART I

(*Keren Su/Corbis*)

ADAPTATIONS

CHAPTER 2

INTRODUCTION TO
PART I, ADAPTATIONS

Anthropologists have always been concerned with the interaction of our own biology (what we are capable of); the environment (which facilitates and constrains what we do); and our culture (which through its tools, social arrangements, and beliefs serves as a buffer between us and the environment). Human beings share roughly the same biological capabilities, but they live in a range of environments. One key set of anthropological questions is how human societies vary in terms of their adaptation to these different environments. From that examination, we can learn what is common to all people and also better appreciate the full range of human possibilities.

That issue of adaptation to the environment is the subject of Part I. This brief overview introduces the range of human environments, four key themes that appear in this set of chapters, some basics about people that emerge in all of these adaptations, and the general plan for how the examination of adaptations will be organized.

THE RANGE OF HUMAN ENVIRONMENTS

The environments in which human beings live are extremely diverse. They range from the arctic to the tropics in terms of temperature, from the desert to the rain-forest in terms of precipitation, and from the heights of the mountains—the Andes and Himalayas, for example—to the seas. Most of those human environments also have seasonal variation in terms of temperature and precipitation. Those seasonal variations, in turn, affect the kinds of plants and animals in the environment at different times of the year, further influencing the way human beings can live in that environment.

In examining human beings in a wide range of environments, anthropologists divide the way people live into five major kinds of adaptation.

With *foraging* (or hunting and gathering), people largely live off what the environment provides. Whether in the desert or the forest, the arctic cold or the tropical heat, they move widely through an environment whose plants and animals provide their food and whose raw materials provide their shelter—whether in caves, huts made from trees, or shelters made from animal skins.

With *horticulture,* human beings make some adjustments to the natural environment. They domesticate a variety of plants, and usually some animals as well—especially pigs. This reorganization of nature into gardens permits a more sedentary[1] lifestyle and larger social groups. However, declines in the productivity of gardens over time often require clearing new fields and sometimes moving to new territory entirely.

With *agriculture,* human beings further develop the domestication of plants, usually specializing in a few crops (especially grains such as rice and wheat) that respond well to more intensive agriculture. With irrigation and use of a plow, the land can produce at a consistently high level. The result is a very sedentary society with a surplus that permits the growth of towns and larger urban areas.

With *pastoralism,* the specialization is in terms of animals. Although pastoralists often grow some crops, their emphasis is on a few animals (cattle, sheep, and goats in particular) that provide a broad range of products: from meat and dairy for food, to hides for clothing and shelter, to bone for tools. Unlike agriculturalists, pastoralists are usually very mobile as they accompany their herds on the search for grazing land and water.

With *industrialism,* human beings are involved in more varied work that produces a wide range of products. Some of these, such as agricultural tools, tractors, chemical fertilizers, and new crop varieties, enhance the productivity of the agricultural work on which industrial society is based; others underpin a new, increasingly urban society. Here, people must adapt to a new kind of environment: one that is to a large degree made by people themselves.

FOUR KEY THEMES

Part I of this book will examine each of these five adaptations in more detail. The issues at stake will range from kinship to ecology, from social control to war. There are, however, four key themes that will emerge in discussing all of these different kinds of society. A preview may be helpful.

CONTROL

The first theme is control. Different societies take differing degrees of control over the environment. Hunters and gatherers, for example, make only modest changes to their environment, while industrial societies extract resources from the earth that can never be renewed. Increased control over the environment may make greater productivity possible, but it may also put a society at risk if that control is mishandled or any mistakes are made in foreseeing

---

[1]"Sedentary" for anthropologists refers to people who live in one place and are thus not migratory. It does *not* mean that they are just sitting around!

its effects. Specialization in a particular kind of food, for example, may initially make more calories available. Yet that specialization may make it easier for disease to spread among plants or animals, raising the possibility of lack of food—perhaps even famine. Generally speaking, there is an increase in control from its minimal level among foragers to its maximum among industrialists.

DENSITY

The second theme is density. With increased control over the environment, there is usually increased density in human settlement. The presence of more people makes a profound difference in human interaction. With relatively small groups, for example, frequent face-to-face interaction yields a society in which people know each other very well on a personal basis. In larger, denser settlements—such as modern cities—that personal contact is replaced by frequent interaction with strangers. The denser the population, the more human activity must be directed toward managing the affairs of the people rather than managing the relationship to the environment. Generally speaking, there is an increase in density from foragers to industrialists, but with two important exceptions: pastoralists (with relatively low density) and agriculturalists (with far higher *rural* density in many cases than is true in industrial societies).

COMPLEXITY

The third theme is complexity. With increased control over the environment and increased density of settlement, there is usually an increased complexity in social organization. Simple, common-law understandings of what is proper behavior, for example, yield to complex legal codes. Face-to-face exchanges of goods and services yield to impersonal catalog and Internet sales. Even building one's home becomes enmeshed in governmental regulations about zoning, insurance, taxation, and various kinds of building, plumbing, and electrical codes. Generally speaking, there is an increase in general societal complexity from foragers to industrialists, but with a caveat. Some aspects of life among foragers and horticulturalists are quite complex (marriage and kin systems, for example).

MOBILITY

The fourth theme is mobility. Some adaptations put a premium on stability and others on mobility. For example, if there is intensive investment in agricultural land, there is a decided tendency to not move. On the other hand, should there be resources in other places that are either necessary or better, then there is at least an incentive to move. Unlike the other themes, mobility does not increase in a linear way from foraging to industrialism. Horticulturalists, for example, are sometimes quite mobile and sometimes quite sedentary. Furthermore, it is one of the great ironies in the contemporary world that as we search for good comparisons to the mobility of our lives in an industrial (or postindustrial) society, we look not to the agricultural societies that provided the basis for industrialization, but to foraging societies that in most other ways differ sharply from us.

SOME HUMAN BASICS

In considering how these four themes of control, density, complexity, and mobility play out in different human adaptations, it is also important to factor in some basics of human nature. Human beings have essential, biological features that affect how they adapt to all environments. For example, human beings *age*. They require enormous care in their early years, spend many additional years completing their physical growth, and yet longer in achieving their full intellectual and social development. Any society will include different kinds of people in different age groups, and members of the society will view these people in different ways. People in one's parents' generation, for example, are viewed very differently from people in one's own generation or in that of one's children.

Equally important is *sex*. Although societies differ greatly in the extent to which they structure separate male and female roles, no society that wishes to endure can escape some division of labor based on sex. Women, after all, will produce the society's children and almost always will have primary responsibility for children during their early years. Thus, in order to understand any human adaptation to any environment, it is necessary to consider the biological differences of sex and how they are organized in a particular society—especially how biological differences of sex are constructed into socially based notions of proper *gender* roles. In most societies, the socially accepted gender roles for women and for men go far, far beyond the basic biological distinctions between them.

It is also important in looking at all human societies to consider the bases on which people group together. Perhaps most important is *kinship*. Human beings require an extensive period of nurturing as they grow and a strong bond is formed between children and those who take care of them. The initial caretaker for the child is almost inevitably the mother. That mother/child group is usually supplemented by a father, producing a *nuclear family*. Ties of kinship, however, go well beyond the immediate nuclear family of father, mother, and child. When a child is born, he or she has not only parents but also grandparents, brothers and sisters, uncles and aunts, and cousins.

Another option for creating links between people involves *location*. People who live near each other usually come to know each other. Through cooperation, they may become friends or work partners. Indeed, they often have to work together. If their fields are irrigated from the same river, for example, they will have to agree on how that water flows into each of their fields. Furthermore, in larger societies in which people cannot trace their kin relations, physical location itself becomes an alternative way to decide who belongs to what group. In industrial societies, location becomes a major basis for social organization. A political border between two nation-states, for example, can determine whether a set of kin on opposite sides of the border live together or even visit each other.

One more element must be added to human variation by age and sex and to the organizing principles of kinship and location. That is *skill*. Individual people have different capacities: Some have better physical skills, others have the ability to absorb new information, yet others are adept at social interaction. Those individual skills are often very important to the society as a whole. Depending on the particular adaptation, a society will need to have a way to identify skills and often to develop them.

Understanding Human Adaptations

The process of understanding the relationship of people to their environments necessarily hinges on two steps. The first is an appreciation of the specific environment, what it requires and what it permits. The central questions are what resources are available and what are the most effective ways to obtain and use those resources given the constraints imposed by that environment. There may well be options. Thus, for example, a river valley might be a very good place to hunt and fish, but it might also be a good place to grow crops.

The second question is how the human basics of age, sex, kinship, location, and skill relate to that particular environment. For example, in an environment that requires considerable mobility to hunt wild game, the elderly may have a far more limited role than they would in a society that stayed in one place. Gender roles might be quite flexible in a society in which men and women frequently cooperated in their work but sharply divided in societies where men may be gone for long periods of time—grazing herds, for example, far from home. Location might be a very crucial aspect of social organization in a society that stayed in one place to till its fields, but a very poor second to ties of kinship when people are on the move among different fields in the course of a year.

Having completed those two steps, and made a general match between environmental constraints and options and human constraints and options, it is possible to discuss more broadly the material, social, and ideational aspects of any given society and to generalize (but with caution) about kinds of adaptation to the environment. There are many questions that might be asked, but consider the following questions that an anthropologist might ask about a society on first acquaintance. They serve also as a check-list that might help us address many pressing issues in our own societies: issues of gender roles, of power and social inequality, of war and peace. The anthropological record is, after all, the broadest base of knowledge we have of human beings in their full range of lived experience. It is our best bet for answering fundamental questions about what we are as human beings and what we can be—for both good and ill.

What is the basic division of labor? For example: Are there sharp differences between the work of men and women? Are there specialists for particular economic tasks? Without knowing who does what work, we cannot know how much of a society's social interaction is based on practical issues and how much on tradition or force.

What is the importance of territory to the society? For example: Are people free to move during the course of the year? Are their ties to land very strong? Without knowing the nature and strength of such ties, we cannot predict what will happen when people are displaced—which is very frequently in the contemporary world. We also cannot know how much of the social tie to territory is "hardwired" in human beings.

What are the specific kinds of kinship ties and groups? For example: Are there large, formal kin groups in the society? Are certain kin more important than others? Without knowing about the specifics of kinship, we cannot assess what happens when particular relatives are lost or kin groups are split by war, natural disaster, or economic need—all these are also very frequent in the contemporary world.

How is social conflict resolved? For example: Are there formal authorities to resolve disputes? If people resolve problems themselves, how do they do so? Without knowing this, we will certainly misjudge the people in question. But we will also miss the opportunity to examine how much of in-group human conflict rests on human psychology and how much on the specifics of a particular way of life.

What is the degree of equality? For example: Are men and women relatively equal? Are there class distinctions between people who have property and people who don't? Without knowing this, we run the danger of creating social programs—or political interventions—that may actually decrease the degree of equality in a society.

What kinds of religious beliefs are there? For example: Do people's religious beliefs include the natural environment? Do their beliefs focus on their own ancestors? Without knowing this, we cannot sense that broadest spiritual aspect of people's lives. Furthermore, we cannot assess our own spiritual views for what they may tell us of ourselves, the ways we live, or the very nature of the spiritual world.

Is the society ecologically sound?   For example: Does the society do permanent damage to the environment? Does the return from the environment match the efforts people put into it? Without this, we cannot assess what kinds of economic changes both match the ideology of a global economic system and also provide models for sound coexistence between humans and the environment overall.

Is the society secure?   For example: Can people make it through periods of seasonal shortages? Are they protected against catastrophic events such as floods? Without this, we cannot assess the longer-term risks that a society faces and perhaps also will fail to understand the kinds of risks we ourselves run.

Is the society prone to peace or war?   For example: Does the society have to fight off outsiders? Can it avoid conflict with others? Without this, we cannot assess how societies will act when provoked. For our own societies, this question provides an invaluable mirror for whether we ourselves are prone to war or peace—and why.

STRUCTURE OF THE CHAPTERS IN PART I

Each of the chapters in Part I discusses one of five major human adaptations: foraging, horticulture, agriculture, pastoralism, and industrialism. Each chapter begins with a consideration of the environment in which the people live and their basic strategy in adapting to it. The central questions are, as noted, what resources are available and what are the most effective ways to obtain and use those resources. Each chapter then considers how the human basics of age, sex, kinship, location, and skill relate to that particular strategy. For example, what are the implications of age in a horticultural society? How are gender roles structured in pastoralist societies? What is the influence of physical location on ties between neighbors in agricultural villages? The emphasis in the early part of each chapter is thus on how the known biological and social features of human beings mesh with a particular kind of adaptation to the environment. The next section of each chapter then addresses the above-listed nine questions about the nature of that society. The questions are the same in each chapter and will be presented in the same outline format. After consideration of these nine questions, each chapter in Part I concludes with two brief case studies. The case studies are chosen to represent the variation in how a particular adaptation works under different conditions. A "Sources" section then provides brief suggestions on further readings and films.

What you should gain from these chapters is an understanding of the variations in human societies as they adapt in different ways to different environments. That, in turn, should help you understand what is predictable and what is unexpected about particular societies. It may also help you consider how alternate human societies might be created with new environments, new ways of extracting resources, or new arrangements of the human basics of age, sex, kinship, location, and skill.

CHAPTER 3

FORAGERS

Foraging societies rely on what is available in their environment. Although they may have an impact on that environment, they do not make the extensive changes that are involved in other types of adaptation. Instead, in their search for food, they use the wide range of plants and animals that already exists in their environment. They thus exercise relatively little control over the environment and are spread out in relatively sparse settlements. Their social and cultural organization reflects the specific opportunities and constraints provided by this adaptation to the environment, especially its requirement for flexibility and mobility in the search for food—whether by hunting or gathering.

This chapter provides an introduction to foraging societies. The discussion begins with the nature of the relationship to the environment, then turns to general social organization, and finally considers the nine key questions that will be addressed in each of the chapters in Part I. The two case studies for this chapter are the Mbuti of Central Africa and the Yolngu on the northern coast of Australia.

RELATIONSHIP TO THE ENVIRONMENT

Natural environments vary greatly around the globe. Human beings have managed to survive and often prosper in environments ranging from the arctic to the tropics, from the jungle to the desert, from good soil to poor, from reliance on the land to reliance on the sea. Foragers respond to what is available in these varied environments. They may hunt anything from the very largest animals to the smallest, whether on land or in water. They may gather anything from fruits and berries to wild roots and tubers. As they hunt and gather, they will also have to protect themselves from the elements, keep predators at bay, and raise the next generation.

MOBILITY

These varied environments are often abundant in what they provide—often surprisingly so even in such harsh environments as deserts. In most environments there is a wide range of animals to hunt, nuts and berries to gather, and roots to dig up. Fish are often plentiful in rivers and along coasts. Insects, grubs, and worms also have their place—and a very nutritious one. However, that abundance is not in a single place but spread out broadly over the land. Thus the first requirement for most foraging societies is mobility. The food isn't coming to you; you are going to it.

This requirement to go after the food raises two problems. The first is that all the food is unlikely to be in one place. Thus you have something of an organizational problem for the daily food quest: You have to figure out an itinerary that takes you to the different places where the different foods are. The second problem is that you may not even know before the fact exactly where those places are. Whether you are hunting game, finding ripe berries, or locating beehives for honey, you will need to devote time and effort just to figure out what these places on your daily itinerary should be. You may need to assess your odds carefully. Part of the problem is that what is abundant and good today may be gone or rotten tomorrow. Fish that run plentifully in spring are absent in the other seasons. Nuts that are plentiful one day may have been eaten by game the next, berries that were plentiful yesterday have gone bad—or to the birds—today. Thus the requirements of hunting and gathering will vary from day to day and through the seasons.

FLEXIBILITY

Even when particular foods are available, they often pose some organizational constraints on how to gather or hunt them. If there are large numbers of nuts or berries that need to be gathered quickly, it may make sense for people to function as something like an agricultural labor crew that conducts a harvest of the nuts or berries. In other cases, such large group efforts would make little sense. Honey, for example, is usually distributed widely, so that the best strategy would be to spread people out over a very large area to find the hives. If the berry bushes or the nut trees are not in patches or groves, then it probably also makes sense to spread people out in small groups or as individuals. Thus, depending on the food, people will modify how they work together to match the requirements of that particular food source.

Such demands are particularly clear in hunting. Compare, for example, hunting game (such as deer or antelope) in a forest and larger game (such as elephants or buffalo) on the plains. With bow and arrow—or even spear—the hunting of forest small game is likely to require considerable stealth, cunning, and patience. It is likely to be most efficient when done by individuals or very small groups. A single person can easily bring down the game, and the presence of other people would probably make the hunt more difficult. In the pursuit of big animals on the plains, the situation is rather different. A single individual—no matter how patient, skilled, and tireless—is unlikely to bring down a large animal, such as an elephant, on his own. Here, then, the most efficient hunting method requires a larger group. If the hunt is not for a single

Spear fishing along the coast of Queensland in Australia. (*Cary Wolinsky/Aurora & Quanta Productions, Inc.*)

animal but a herd, the requirements change again. If the hunt is to be conducted as a drive with the goal of running a set of animals over a cliff, into a pit, or into a net, an even larger number of people will be needed. These people will have to be very well-coordinated in what will be almost a military maneuver.

The crux of hunting and gathering as an adaptation to the environment is this combination of mobility and flexibility. To utilize the full range of the natural resources in their environment, foragers will have to follow those resources to different places and according to a schedule that will vary across the seasons and often from day to day. Depending on the specific resource, hunters and gatherers may need to work alone, in small groups, or in larger groups. On any particular day, members of the community may find themselves wandering off in small groups to gather fruits and roots or going out in a large group to take advantage of a big harvest of berries or nuts. Men and women, the old and young, might well be cooperating—or they might be separating for different tasks. During any particular season, that range of daily options will also shift. Spring may find men and women cooperating on group fishing with nets. An arctic winter may find men alone at their ice holes fishing for seal. Fall may find all together—men and women, the oldest and the youngest—harvesting acorns.

SOCIAL ARRANGEMENTS

This low-control, low-density adaptation to the environment thus requires great mobility and great flexibility. How would you structure a human society that meets these requirements and also permits the raising of a new generation? Much of the answer lies with how the human basics of age, sex, kinship, locality, and skills are organized. These are discussed in turn in the text that follows.

Age is an essential feature of human biology. Much of the interrelationship of age and the foraging adaptation is readily apparent. Because of the frequent need to move from place to place, people of *all* ages need to be physically self-reliant. The young are likely to be encouraged to be self-reliant at a very early age. Carrying them around while gathering, or especially while hunting, is a waste of effort. The alternatives to taking them along aren't very good either: Leaving them on their own is dangerous and leaving a caretaker with them robs the community of an extra pair of hands. Likewise, even the elderly will need to be physically self-reliant. If the entire group moves some distance—which is very likely on at least a seasonal basis—the elderly must also be able to move. If people cannot move under their own power and with good speed, they become a serious liability. Although their wisdom may be appreciated, their physical limitations preclude their full participation.

Differences by *sex* will also be important. Women are the ones who give birth and, because of nursing, are almost inevitably the primary caregivers for children's early years. Women are thus less mobile in a society in which mobility is important. Much hunting, for example, precludes bringing along very small children, so young mothers are likely to be excluded from those activities—especially if they involve extensive time in travel. Furthermore, the group as a whole would want women to avoid any dangers in hunting. Women are, after all, the future of the society. Men are far more expendable. In a foraging society, then, one can expect some division of labor between men and women. Men are likely to do the longer distance and more dangerous part of the food-gathering and women are likely to do food gathering that involves shorter distances, permits the addition of children (gathering berries, for example), and is less dangerous. Thus there is a predictable split between men as hunters and women as gatherers.

On the other hand, the core requirement of flexibility suggests that with foragers strict distinctions by sex (and by age) make little sense. While the pursuit of one food source might result in a predictable difference between men and women, in other cases the inclusion of both sexes is important. Thus, while women certainly hunt less than men, they are often not precluded from it, especially when there is a need for a larger group. If a hunt involves chasing animals into a net or over a cliff, for example, women may be included with men. The more people, the more noise to drive the animals in the direction you want them to go. Conversely, men will also participate in gathering. If they are on their way somewhere, there is no reason they too shouldn't be gathering what the environment offers. In foraging societies, then, there may well be significant overlap of tasks. Men may be more the hunters and women more the gatherers, yet men also gather and women also hunt.

These issues of age and sex suggest something of the character of foraging societies, but they don't quite explain how the need for flexible groups will be handled. Here, however, human biology suggests an option: the relationship between people based on blood. People know who at least some of their relatives are. And it makes sense that they should draw on those relatives for the tasks at hand. If a hunting party is needed, who better to trust than a relative? Thus *kinship* is likely to be very important in foraging societies. On the other hand, the different tasks required on different days and in different seasons may require different numbers of people and different skills. One older aunt might be a very good companion in a search for a beehive—since she can read the forest signs very well. Yet on another occasion, a set of cousins might be a better choice: for example, to go berry-picking. You already know where the berries are, need more people, and your cousins are just more fun. So although all these kin are important, the dictates of foraging suggest that you might want to keep your options open about exactly which kin to use for which task.

There is, however, a bottom limit on how small a kin group you might need, and that involves the immediate family. For procreation, of course, it takes two—or at least it does the good old-fashioned way. It makes sense to keep that couple together for child-rearing—but it also takes two for daily life. If there is some difference in what men and women do—what resources they can produce—then a man or woman alone lacks access to the resources produced by the other sex. In a foraging life, that lack can be decisive. So the minimum structure for kin groups is the nuclear family as we understand it: Husband and wife need each other, the children need the parents, and the society needs the children.

Another human basic introduced in the last chapter was *location*. Many human relationships are built from ties of shared locality. For hunters and gatherers, however, the very extent of mobility limits the effectiveness of ties of locality. A move in camp means that a former neighbor may not be a neighbor any more. The kind of relationship that lasts through such geographical moves is, instead, kinship. Move two miles—or a hundred—and your brother is still your brother, your mother still your mother. Blood ties carry well over distance; ties of locality less so. Thus with a foraging society that depends on mobility, kinship is a far steadier basis for relationships. Shared locality is not unimportant, but unless those living next door are your kin, you probably shouldn't count on them for very much.

THE NATURE OF SKILL

The final human basic is *skill.* There are three crucial aspects of skill in foraging society. First, most skills need to be held by virtually all people. If the size
of groups is so variable and the tasks so flexible, everybody needs to have
most of the basic skills needed to survive, including extensive knowledge of
the environment. Second, most of these skills are apparent to everybody else.
There's very little hidden about what people can and cannot do. These people know you and you know them. Third, the need for special skills (beyond
those held by everybody) is generally episodic and task specific: a good leader
for a hunting party one day, a knowledgeable healer the next day, perhaps a
prophet sometime, and certainly a midwife. This means that in foraging societies, all people (or at least all men and all women) are learning much the
same skills, know quite objectively how good they are at things, and, when
they do have special needs, seek out somebody they know who has that specific skill.

NINE KEY QUESTIONS

Overall, then, foragers are relating to a largely natural environment that requires them to be mobile and have flexible group size, depending on the task
and the season. The basic relations of age and sex reflect that, as do the reliance on kinship, the relative lack of reliance on ties of locality, and the trans-
parency of people's skills. The answers to the nine key questions about this
adaptation follow from those key characteristics and appear below in the format that will be used in all the chapters of Part I.

> *Division of Labor:* All human societies have some division of labor.
> In hunting and gathering societies, however, that division is relative-
> ly simple and task oriented. There are important differences in men's
> and women's work and, to a lesser extent, between that of younger
> and older people. There are also likely to be a few specialized roles.
> However, the varying requirements of the day and season suggest the
> need for flexibility. Thus the division of labor is likely to be neither
> harsh nor rigid.

> *Territoriality:* Because resources are spread out over a large area,
> foragers are highly mobile. They may return to a favorite area but,
> even then, they may well have to make new shelter. There is thus no
> sharp commitment to a particular piece of territory or to the im-
> provements made to a particular piece of territory. Instead, foragers
> are likely to have a diffuse commitment to a broad range of territory.
> This gives them some advantages over people who are tied to place
> and to property that can't be moved from that place.

Kinship: Foragers are largely organized on the basis of kinship ties. On the one hand, the need for small, mobile groups puts a particular emphasis on the nuclear family. Husband and wife are not only a reproductive unit but the smallest group that has access to most of the basic skills of the society. On the other hand, the need for larger groups on some occasions suggests the need for a broader pool of kin from whom to draw as needed. The result of these two pressures is usually an emphasis on the nuclear family combined with flexible relations with a broader range of kin.

Social Control: Because foragers have shifting needs from day to day and season to season, it is vital that they be able to draw on other people for cooperative efforts. It is thus essential to avoid any enduring conflicts. When conflicts do arise, they are usually resolved through informal means. These people, after all, know each other well, interact on a daily basis, and are frequently kin. The solution is usually to talk problems through. Since people are mobile, there is also the possibility of simply going off somewhere else for a while, letting issues cool, and then returning later. Good time for a fishing trip.

Equality: There is some division of labor in foraging societies. Nevertheless, all people need to have roughly the same skills to survive in the environment. That implies a basic equality. That basic equality of skills is enhanced by the fact that people generally have equal access to resources. More game, more plants, and more space are usually available. Access to equivalent resources is a fundamental basis for equality. The result in foraging societies is usually a general equality among women, a general equality among men, and at least a relative equality between men and women.

Religious Beliefs: The religious beliefs of foragers—as of all people—are highly variable. Yet two central points stand out. First, foragers live very close to the natural world. This often leads them to sense a spiritual power in nature itself. Second, since foragers are self-reliant and relatively egalitarian, their access to the spiritual world is likely to be very personal, rather than mediated through others.

Ecological Soundness: Foraging societies make good ecological sense. They rarely deplete the environment, since their very survival depends on the environment continuing to replenish itself. Since they generally depend on a very wide range of food sources, their effect on any one resource is likely to be limited. Furthermore, the relation with the environment also works well for the people. Studies of the time spent in the food quest by foragers tend to indicate relatively modest expenditure of effort. At its best, foraging is thus an adaptation that is hard neither on the environment nor on the people.

Security: Although foraging societies have often been pushed to extinction by other kinds of societies, on their own terms they are relatively secure. The pressure they place on the environment is usually low and the environment itself thus remains as their "surplus." Their reliance on a broad range of food sources makes them relatively immune to the disappearance of a single food source—which also means a diet that is nutritionally well-balanced. Nevertheless, since food resources are usually not spread evenly across the year, some parts of the year may indeed be difficult.

External Conflict: Since foraging societies have a broad territorial range through which they move, they may well come into contact with other groups. Since they have little valuable property to defend, and can generally find other sources of food, such contact does not necessarily lead to serious conflict. The foragers can simply move on. This does not mean that foragers are always peaceful. Because of their mobility, they can be very effective raiders. Nevertheless, foraging societies probably have more options for peace than do the societies to be discussed in later chapters.

Case Study
The Mbuti: In the Forest and of the Forest

The Mbuti are often described as "pygmies" in early accounts. They live in the central part of what is now called Congo-Kinshasa, formerly Zaire. Like most other foragers, they live in relatively small groups that vary over the course of the year in size and location. Sometimes they move out into clearings where they are, at least temporarily, much like the horticulturalists to be described in the next chapter. Yet they also move from those clearings deep into the forest to gather fruits, berries, and nuts, and to hunt. Hunting relatively small animals—like several of the antelopes—can be a solitary pursuit for men armed with bows and arrows. Usually, however, men cooperate in small groups. On other occasions, larger groups of men and women will beat the bushes driving animals forward into nets. That flexibility in group size and composition is perhaps the most distinguishing feature of foraging societies.

That flexibility in group size and structure is matched by a relative equality of the people. All have access to roughly the same resources of the forest and all live roughly the same life. The frequent movement means that the Mbuti have very few material possessions—by definition no more than they can easily carry. Their shelter is constructed rapidly from available materials, especially the large *mongongo* leaves. There is a clear division of labor by

A group of Mbuti in Central Africa. (*Wendy Stone/Getty Images, Inc./Liaison*)

sex: Men do the majority of the hunting and women do the majority of the gathering. Women are also in charge of "the home." If there is a leak through the *mongongo* leaves during the night, it is they who get up to fix it. Yet there is also much overlap in tasks. Men sometimes gather and women sometimes help in hunting. The result is a relative equality and mutual ease between the sexes.

The feelings of the Mbuti toward their environment are positive and deeply held. Although they are deep in a forest that the neighboring villagers view with distrust and even fear, the Mbuti see the forest as a place of light and beauty. Indeed the forest is imbued not only with life in the natural sense but also in the spiritual sense. If things are bad, they only need to wake up the forest. The forest is innately good. The Mbuti love of song is directly tied to the forest. The *molimo*, the trumpet-like instrument that accompanies their singing, is itself heard as the voice of the forest. The Mbuti and the forest thus sing together.

One of the first things the Mbuti did when they began to accept Colin Turnbull—who went to live with them a half-century ago—was to cut lines in his forehead and place dirt from the forest floor into those cuts. That simple ritual—conducted extemporaneously with a razor—meant that Turnbull now carried the forest with him and would inevitably return to it. Such a mixture of blood and dirt, implanted within the body, is a powerful image of the union of people with their environment.

Case Study
The Yolngu: Foraging, Dreaming, and Reconciliation

"Yolngu" means "people" in the languages used by the aboriginal peoples along the northern coast of Australia. Prior to colonization, they—like other aboriginal Australians—earned their living by foraging from an often difficult land. Along the coast where the Yolngu lived, however, were bountiful ocean resources: crabfish, squid, octopus, whale, cuttlefish, stingrays, and sea cucumber—the last such a valuable delicacy that in precolonial times fleets of ships from Sulawesi would come each year to trade for them. The importance of the sea was marked in all aspects of people's lives—even in such personal names as stingray, squid, and coral reef. But there were also marshes and swamps (with crocodiles whose skins would become an important trade item) and fresh water streams and springs with yet other food resources. Life on the coast was thus less harsh than on the interior. Population density was correspondingly higher and life more settled. With a settled life, technology was somewhat more developed because, among other reasons, there was less need for everything to be easily portable. The Yolngu, for example, used a wide variety of nets and fish traps as they utilized these different salt and fresh water resources.

The social life of the Yolngu was elaborate. Society was divided into two major marriage groups with numerous clans. Religious life was rich and strongly integrated into daily life. Spiritual forces could be seen both in the living animals of the sea and in the marks on the land made by the beings who existed at the beginning of time. Central to religious life was what is usually translated as the Dreaming, a kind of reenvisioning of the world as it originally was. That reenvisioning permits the contemporary world to be reformed and reordered according to that primal world. What emerges in the Dreaming is thus "a charter of absolute validity" that allows people to stand outside current events (to see them for what they are) and to "find some purpose in the whole human situation."[1]

The Yolngu did not live an isolated life. They were actively interacting with other peoples. Their experience with traders from Sulawesi was reflected in their technology (for example, the ready availability of iron). It was also reflected in their Dreaming. One particular being who emerged in their Dreaming was Birrinydji, the man of iron, who represented both the Yolngu and the Sulawesi traders who visited them each year. Here was a being who could bridge the divide between aborigines and outsiders. As Ian McIntosh studied the general nature of reconciliation in Australia between whites and aborigines, he found that the Yolngu thus had their own indigenous basis for such

---

[1]W. E. H. Stanner, as quoted in Ian S. McIntosh's *Aboriginal Reconciliation and the Dreaming* (Needham Heights, MA: Allyn & Bacon, 2000), pp. 38–39.

a reconciliation. While the new masters of Australia might, like the Sulawesi traders, have great material resources and wealth, still there was a bond between them and the Yolngu, a spiritual charter through which reconciliation could be pursued. Sometimes this Yolngu view of reconciliation was portrayed in graphic ways. Thus one Yolngu leader devised a new flag for a united Australia that included on it both the Union Jack and a picture of Birrinydji. If both the indigenous people and the *balanda* (the nonindigenous people) were bound together through Birrinydji, then other more practical kinds of reconciliation could also take place. Adoption was one such option. The Yolngu would adopt *balanda* into their clans, giving them a full Yolngu social identity. The person adopted, in turn, could be a valuable ally for the Yolngu by helping them navigate the broader Australian society.

As McIntosh observes, the situation of the Yolngu is not fully typical of Australian aborigines. The Yolngu were spared much of the worst of Australian policy toward indigenous groups. They retained much of their land when other aborigines were losing theirs. Their children were not taken from them when other aborigines saw their children disappear into government-run boarding schools that separated them socially and linguistically from their parents—what has come to be called the "stolen generation." In addition to being spared the worst of such problems, the Yolngu also had the positive advantage of some experience with the broader world. Thus when Australian society moved toward reconciliation with indigenous groups, the Yolngu were able to make a strong contribution to that process. Their contribution had much to do with practical matters, but it also rested on a spiritual view of the world that was broad enough to encompass black and white, forager and farmer, Yolngu and *balanda*.

SOURCES

Hunters and gatherers have generated great interest and great debate among anthropologists. Much of that debate has been about the relative importance of meat and plants to their diet and the relative contribution to the food search by men (who do the majority of the hunting) and women (who do the majority of the gathering). A good summary of the range of foraging adaptations is provided in Robert L. Kelly's *The Foraging Spectrum: Diversity in Hunter-Gatherer Lifeways* (Smithsonian Institution Press, 1995). Or try browsing the *Cambridge Encyclopedia of Hunters and Gatherers*, edited by Richard B. Lee and Richard Daly (Cambridge University Press, 1999).

For the Mbuti, the classic source, and an excellent volume for class use, is Colin Turnbull's *The Forest People* (Touchstone, 1968). As an alternative, Elizabeth Marshall Thomas's *The Harmless People* (Vintage Books, 1989) considers the related !Kung who live not in the forest but in the great Kalahari desert. That book can be supplemented by any number of excellent films on the !Kung. The Yolngu example comes largely from Ian S. McIntosh's *Aboriginal Reconciliation and the Dreaming* (Allyn & Bacon, 2000). Two useful comparative sources on more traditional aborigine society (including the Yolngu) are W. H. Edward's *Traditional Aboriginal Society: A Reader* (Paul and Co., 1998, 2nd edition) and Ian Keen's *Aboriginal Economy and Society* (Oxford University Press, 2004). The 2000 feature film *The Yolngu* (Australian Children's Television Foundation) uses an all-indigenous cast in exploring coming of age in contemporary Yolngu society.

CHAPTER 4

HORTICULTURALISTS

Horticulturalists often deal with the same kind of plants and animals as do hunters and gatherers. However, there is a fundamental difference. The horticulturalists take increased control. They rearrange those resources in a more convenient, productive, constructed environment: the garden. Plants and usually some animals are domesticated, meaning that they are brought within one's own control; the "wild" plants and animals are tamed. The basic logic of horticulture is thus different from that of hunting and gathering. Human control over the environment is greatly increased. This increased control produces good yields and permits a far more sedentary lifestyle. That, in turn, increases the density of settlement, which, in turn, has implications for the complexity of social organization.

This chapter describes horticulturalism. As in the previous chapter, the discussion begins with a description of the basic relationship of horticulturalists with the environment. There is then a discussion of the basic social arrangements in horticultural societies, followed by answers to the same nine key questions posed about foraging societies (division of labor, dispute resolution, ecological soundness, and so on). The two case studies for this chapter involve the Hmong, a very mobile people of highland Southeast Asia (many of whom have moved to North America as refugees), and the Trobriand Islanders, a more settled horticultural people living off the East Coast of New Guinea.

RELATIONSHIP TO THE ENVIRONMENT

Anyone who spends much time in the natural environment will notice the diversity of plant life. They will learn from their own personal experience and from other people in their society that certain plants are edible, where those plants grow, and something of how they grow. They might note that some plants seem to thrive with more sun or perhaps with occasional shade; some grow best in wet ground while others do better in dry or well-drained soil. They would certainly note when plants were best for eating. They would also have seen plants sprouting from other plants or growing where seeds or nuts

had been dropped. Finally, they would probably also note that plants do especially well when they have the benefit of nutrients such as decaying vegetation or excrement.

Given such observations, the question might arise whether the way plants
grow could be duplicated and perhaps improved through human intervention.
One important advantage of doing so would be to locate plants more cen-
trally, thus avoiding the constant daily and seasonal movement that characterizes most foraging societies. If people can grow the plants—if they can
duplicate nature—then they can also decide where those plants will grow. It
may also be possible to improve the way the plants grow. Either the new
planned location might itself be better or it could be made better. That requires control of sunlight, water, and soil. The horticulturalist adaptation
hinges precisely on these three variables.

SUN, WATER, AND SOIL

On a small scale, managing the three elements of sun, water, and soil might
not seem difficult. But there are potential problems and many of them are serious. Too little *sun* and plants won't grow; too much sun and they may with-
er and die. Exposure (north, south, east, or west) may be critical. Preservation
of some shade from a top canopy may be essential. This is probably the easiest issue to resolve. After all, forests can be cleared for more sun or partially
preserved for some shade. In hilly terrain or partially forested land, it may
also be possible to create the proper kind of sunlight for particular crops:
morning sun, for example, but afternoon shade. *Water* also presents problems:
Too little water or too much water may be fatal to the plants or sharply affect
yields. The choice of site will be essential but so also will be accuracy in pre-
dicting when rains will come. Flood and drought remain great dangers. Finally, good *soil* is essential. Although the consistency of the soil is important
in itself, the crucial issue involves such nutrients as nitrogen, potassium, and
potash. In some cases, soil is naturally rich. Certainly, animals droppings have
a good effect. Many horticulturalists also use a very good fertilizer that is excellent at leaching rapidly into the soil. It's ash. Why not, then, burn the forest, thus clearing the land, letting in light, and laying a very nice layer of good,
fast-acting fertilizer on the ground just before you plant your crops?

SLASH AND BURN

Many horticulturalists use exactly this "slash and burn" type of cultivation,
which is technically called *swidden*.[1] They pick an area of forest that is in a
good location and conduct a controlled burn. These controlled burns clear

---

[1]The term *swidden* derives from the old English word for "to singe."

Slash-and-burn horticulture: The Akawaio of Guyana clear a field. (*Bruce Coleman, Inc.*)

out the undergrowth but usually leave the larger trees. Those can either be cut down or—perhaps with some additional pruning—left in place. The burn leaves a layer of ash that will leach into the ground fairly rapidly. The field is then ready for planting. Sometimes horticulturalists will plant only a few crops, but usually they will plant a very wide range of crops, which will mature at different times. Thus the gardens are not like agricultural fields where a large crop has to be harvested at one time. Instead, different crops become available at different times and can be harvested as needed or as desired. Some root crops—such as manioc—may survive for long periods of time in the ground and provide a useful food reserve if other, more desirable foods aren't available. Depending on the crop, the process of planting may involve scattering some seeds, or sticking a piece of a root in the ground, or poking a hole in the ground with a stick (usually called a *dibble stick*), dropping in a seed, and then kicking some dirt over the hole. These gardens may subsequently require some weeding, but since the crops get a head start in the newly cleared fields, that weeding is often fairly limited. Some effort up front has thus yielded a garden that will last for many, many months with relatively little need for upkeep.

BETTER CROPS, MORE PIGS

Horticulturalists thus rearrange nature into gardens over which they exercise some control, particularly in preparing the ground and planting the chosen plants. As they do so, they can also often improve those crops. They will see which plants grow the best and can select seeds or roots for next year from those. Furthermore, since they are now located in one place, they can domesticate some animals as well. After all, if they have created their own rearranged nature in the gardens, why shouldn't they also have animals? Animal excrement is useful on the fields and the animals might benefit from grazing on the remains of the fields after crops have been harvested. Pigs are a particularly good choice. They are good scavengers, good to eat, and can bulk up very nicely as a sort of walking food reserve. Pigs are often the major ceremonial food in horticultural societies and indeed often the best measure of a person's wealth.

SOIL EXHAUSTION AND MOVING ON

The slash-and-burn version of horticulture has much to recommend it. As long as the burn is controlled, there is little damage to the land and the fields will eventually regenerate. The gardens themselves are an efficient combination of a wide range of foods in a better, more convenient location. That combined and convenient location means that people can be more sedentary. That increasingly sedentary life permits some domestication of animals as well; that, in turn, permits a more predictable access to protein and an effective food reserve "on the hoof." There is, however, one fundamental limitation. The fertilizer that made this all possible begins to lose its value over time. The effect of that ash will be strong in the first year, less so in the second year, and in continuing decline thereafter. It will be a long time before the forest regenerates enough for a second burn—or at least for one that will produce a significant layer of ash. So new fields are needed every few years. In some cases, it may be possible to rotate the fields. However, as fields become more scattered and it takes longer to reach them, it may be time to move on to an entirely new area and begin again, abandoning the old gardens to their regeneration.

Horticulturalists, then, extend their control over nature by making selections of particular plants and animals, domesticating them, and rearranging them into gardens. The result retains some of the advantages of foraging (especially a diverse diet and a lack of environmental damage) but adds some new benefits. Relocating plants to a garden, for example, provides much convenience and the possibility of a more settled life that does not require frequent moves. It also provides the basis for larger populations and increased density. The limitation lies only with the length of time that the fields remain productive. Lacking full control over water and especially lacking alternative fertilizers, horticulturalists may well have to periodically sacrifice their sedentary life for a move to new territory.

SOCIAL ARRANGEMENTS

INCREASED COMPLEXITY OF SOCIAL ARRANGEMENTS

This expanded control over the environment has important social implications. Since the food is now more centralized in the gardens, horticulturalists are not required to be as mobile as hunters and gatherers. They do not
need to move as far on a daily basis and they do not usually need to shift residence with the seasons. The gardens themselves are multiseasonal. Thus
the foraging requirement for small, mobile, flexible groups does not apply.
Groups need not be small and they need not generally be mobile. The steadier, more repetitive pace of horticulture also reduces the requirement for
flexibility in group size. The requirements for this more sedentary society—
aside from the possibility of large-scale moves in search of new fields—are
thus different. A more settled social order is needed. Furthermore, because
gardens are so productive and so centralized, there will also be greater density of people. That density in itself will increase the complexity of social
relations.

Finally, that more sedentary lifestyle will inevitably result in more material goods—goods that would simply be too cumbersome for foragers.
Houses are likely to be more elaborate. There will be fences for gardens, pens
for animals, and more tools. There will thus be far more physical *property*
than there is for foragers. The gardens themselves are property and their harvests belong to those who planted the fields, not to anybody who happens
to wander by. And, of course, there are the pigs. All these kinds of property
may be good and valuable, but they are inevitably the sources of conflict.
They can be an especially raw source of conflict when the owner of the property dies. Property inevitably raises the issue of *inheritance*. When somebody
dies, who gets those pigs?

Horticultural societies thus have more people living together, living together more closely, and with more to argue about. Yet this kind of society also
requires cooperation. Burning the fields, for example, needs to be a cooperative effort. The labor may be done by the young but the practical experience of the older people is vital to synchronize the timing of the burn with
the rains. Too early means the ash runs off before crops can be planted; too
late means the crops are not in on time. Too damp means no fire; too dry
means a fire out of control. If nothing else, all need to be available in case—
despite all precautions—the fire starts to get out of control. Cooperation is also
needed to resolve the many kinds of conflict that can arise: who has the right
to the best land; who decides when and where to move the entire village;
whose pig wandered into somebody else's house and perhaps ended up as
their dinner. With the increased gravity of the disputes, the increased number of people involved, and the decreased ability to avoid each other, it is
harder to resolve issues simply by talking them through.

EXPANDED AND FORMALIZED KINSHIP SYSTEMS

Horticultural societies thus face many of the more complex problems of social organization that we ourselves face. The result, for them as for us, is a society that has more formal organization and clearer indications of who is "in charge" than do foraging societies. Yet horticulturalists resolve such problems of social organization without the creation of separate economic, social, political, and religious organizations. Instead, the equivalent of such separate organizations are all hung largely on a single framework: that of *kinship*. For kinship to work as such a framework, however, it must be far more defined than it is among foragers, with their separate nuclear families and a rather diffuse set of other kin. Kinship needs to be both more extensive and more structured.

If there is to be a more extensive and structured kinship system, which can serve as the overarching framework for a society, then there must be some rules about two issues: first, who is related to whom and, second, who has authority over whom. Part II of this book will discuss such issues of kinship in far more detail, but some brief comments are needed here on these two issues of membership (who belongs where) and seniority (who's in charge of whom among the members). In terms of membership, the basic options are that a child belongs either to the group of the father or to that of the mother. The former is *patrilineal* (the line of the father); the latter is *matrilineal* (the line of the mother). Both systems work very well in establishing membership and both systems are used by many, many horticultural societies.[2] Seniority must also be determined. Here the influence of age is almost universal: Those of an older generation have priority over those of a younger generation. Within a single generation, those who are chronologically older have seniority. The question of the relative seniority of men and women is somewhat more difficult. Certainly in patrilineal societies, males have seniority over women, usually even if those women are older. In matrilineal societies, women's relative seniority is usually higher.[3]

With rules for membership and seniority decided, kin groups are a clear and effective means of organization. Everybody knows in which group they belong and who within that group has the authority to make decisions. Such a structure has added value in horticultural societies that have to make

---

[2]Both systems also have a difficult point of transition when people are married. Should one of them give up their membership in their own kin group to be part of the spouse's group? This issue is discussed in some detail in Part II. It is a critical issue and the one that makes patrilineal and matrilineal systems rather different in tone even though they are so similar in their logic.

[3]The relative age of the connection in the prior generation may also be a factor. For example, it may be more important that your mother was older than her sister than that you are younger than your mother's sister's child (your matrilateral parallel cousin). You may be considered "senior" because your mother was.

large-scale moves. Horticulturalists may live in relatively clustered settlements, so the possibility of developing ties based on close residence—as neighbors or co-villagers—exists. However, if the entire village is to move, then kinship is a better and surer basis for that organizational task. Kinship, after all, is portable and enduring. Neighbors may come and go, but blood ties continue to exist. Thus in those horticultural societies that move the most frequently, there is often a particularly complex and formal kinship organization—usually patrilineal for reasons that will become clear in Part II.

NINE KEY QUESTIONS

Overall, horticulturalists have some sharp differences from foragers. With increased control over the environment come increasing density and increasing social complexity. Most of the complexity is dealt with through expanded and formalized kinship systems. Those kinship systems tend to have relatively clear rules about who belongs to what group and who has relative seniority within those groups. Such kinship groups are especially helpful in addressing one of the most distinctive features of many horticultural societies: the alternation of a rather sedentary lifestyle with periodic moves in search of new fields. These key characteristics of horticultural societies reappear below in response to the nine key questions raised for each of these adaptions.

Division of Labor: In horticultural societies, the division of labor is somewhat sharper and more extensive than it is in foraging societies. Differences between men and women may be heightened, particularly if some gardens are relatively distant and tended by men. The daily lives of men and women may become more separate. Beyond such basic divisions of gender and some increased effects of seniority, especially for those who head kin groups, there is likely to be relatively little in the way of special roles except—as with foragers—for such tasks as healing, midwifery, and contact with the spirit world.

Territoriality: Horticulturalists are linked to the land they cultivate and the places in which they live. However, since the exhaustion of the soil may force them to move on, those links are not unbreakable. Even today, in some parts of the world, horticulturalists have the opportunity to move on to new land that has not been claimed by others because it is too mountainous, inhospitable, or remote. As long as there are such new opportunities, horticulturalists are not likely to be highly territorial. In that sense they, like foragers, have the option of moving on.

Kinship: With increased density of settlement comes an increased need for cooperation and coordination. Kin are the most reliable resource for such mutual assistance and large kin groups make practical sense, especially if they are relatively tightly organized. Furthermore, since there is considerable property (pigs, houses, tools), there is also a need for rules about how that property is passed on when people die. Again, a tightly organized kinship system has distinct advantages—whether matrilineal or patrilineal. Kinship among horticulturalists tends to be central to the society, highly structured, and extensive.

Social Control: In horticultural societies there are more people with more to argue about. Land itself may not necessarily be of long-term value, but certainly current gardens are. Disputes that arise might be resolved between the people themselves but if not, resolving them will be of direct interest to their broader kin groups. Leaders of those groups may not have any formal authority beyond their status as kin seniors, but that is likely to be enough to enforce their decisions. Social control through kinship is thus the hallmark of most horticultural societies.

Equality: With horticultural systems, the access to resources is no longer as broad as it is for foragers but, unless land is scarce, people have the option of starting their own individual gardens. There is thus relatively equal access to resources and, in that sense, relative equality among people—or at least equality among men and equality among women. The degree of equality between men and women, however, is highly variable and has much to do with the structure of the kinship system. In matrilineal horticultural societies, for example, women's access to resources is likely to be enhanced—thus producing a greater relative equality between men and women. In patrilineal societies, the prospects for relative equality between men and women are dimmer.

Religious Beliefs: In horticultural societies, people are likely to acknowledge a wide range of spiritual forces. With larger kin groups that are more formally structured, ancestors are likely to be more clearly remembered for longer periods of time. Since horticulturalists are dependent on the land for its productivity, spirits of the land are likely to be important as well. Rain, and the timing of it, are crucial, so spirits of the sky or rains will probably also be recognized. In most cases, religious specialists will be people who have had individual experiences with these spirits. Yet in some cases, a person's more formal position may be important: For example, contact with the ancestors is likely to be the responsibility of the senior person in a kin group.

Ecological Soundness: Horticulturalists make a variety of changes to their environment, but the effects are usually not permanent. The burning of the forest itself does little (if any) long-term damage and the fields will generally regenerate into forest. Horticulturalists may even aid this process by leaving some mid-size trees alone, thus speeding that process of regeneration. As with hunters and gatherers, there is the added benefit of relatively moderate working hours. Studies of the time used for growing food suggest that horticulturalists are efficient and thus have the benefit of considerable time for other activities. Horticulture thus appears as a sustainable adaptation from the perspectives both of the environment and of the people themselves.

Security: The horticultural adaptation is generally quite secure. The cultivation of a range of crops, for example, provides good nutritional balance. That range also provides protection against the loss of any single crop from disease or theft. Even if someone or some animal raids a garden, for example, they are likely to take only what is currently ripe. The result may be hunger today but not famine tomorrow. The range of crops (especially root crops that will last a long time in the ground) and the domestication of animals (especially pigs) provide good buffers against lean times.

External Conflict: Horticultural societies are likely to be of limited interest to outsiders because they usually have little of value to those outsiders. It wouldn't make much sense, for example, to take over somebody's gardens because you would then have to wait around for each crop to ripen. From the horticulturalists' point of view, there is limited value in conflict with outsiders and they, like foragers, have the option of moving on. However, there are potential problems. One is raiding. Another problem arises if additional land is no longer available. Their land, which did not seem very valuable, now is. Even more dangerous, however, is when the land of horticulturalists becomes of interest to others who think they can use it for "better" purposes. Sometimes that means growing a valuable export crop, such as rubber or opium. Even more dangerous is the arrival of agriculturalists who, as the next chapter will demonstrate, can make rather more intensive use of the land.

Case Study
The Trobrianders: Matrilineality and Women's Wealth

The Trobriand Islands, which lie off the coast of Papua New Guinea, became famous as a result of Bronislaw Malinowski's writings from the period when he was "stranded" there during World War I. Malinowski was enormously lucky in finding himself in the Trobriands. The elaborate *kula* exchanges of ritual necklaces and bracelets is one of the most influential images in anthropology and sociology. The Trobriands also have a rich array of magical practices, a relatively relaxed standard of sexual relations among the young, and a matrilineal kinship system. Malinowski made the most of these advantages in his writing. The Trobriands made Malinowski famous, and he made the Trobriands famous.

The Trobriand Islanders are horticulturalists. Their main gardens are for yams. The basic approach to the yam garden is a modification of the swidden ("slash and burn") system. Here, the undergrowth is cut first, along with the branches of the larger trees. Then that undergrowth and branches are burned, providing the necessary nutrients for the soil. Compared to other crops, yam cultivation is relatively demanding. The soil needs to be worked well before planting, the plants need to be staked as they grow, and a solid fence must be built around the field to keep the pigs out. Most of the work is done by men. However, during the most difficult part of the preparation of the fields, men and women work together—often putting in very long days. Although these yam gardens are the main gardens, there are also general household gardens, which, unlike the yam gardens, are generally the responsibility of women. The yam gardens are relatively specialized. They yield, much like the agricultural fields to be discussed in the next chapter, a large harvest of a single valuable and storable crop. Piles of yams in a field are the sign of a good garden. When the yams are put in a yam house for storage, they are then a sign of wealth.

Perhaps the most interesting thing about the growing of yams in the Trobriands is the way in which yams are used in social relations. Although men do most of the work in the yam gardens, neither the gardens nor the yams belong to the men who grow them. Instead, the gardens are owned by women and are inherited from women in the previous generation. Since the women own the gardens, the product of those gardens is also theirs. The men who work the fields are not, however, the husbands of these women. Instead, their brothers do the work. A man thus works the fields of his sister and gives to her the yams that are the products of those fields. Those yams are largely consumed by the sister, her husband, and their children. The man himself, then, is not eating the yams he himself produced, but is eating those that belong to his wife and that were grown by *her* brother. This is a typically Trobriand way of doing things. Instead of eating their own food, they find a way to make food itself into a complex system that weaves people together in ties of exchange.

Annette Weiner, who studied the Trobriand Islanders some fifty years after Malinowski did, analyzed these patterns of kinship and gender in detail. While men were hardly insignificant in this matrilineal society, women did have their own wealth and it was often considerable. Particularly when death occurred, it was women who organized the large mourning feasts and themselves competed for status based on their wealth. That wealth was evidenced by how much they could give away. Those gifts included large numbers of bundles of banana leaves and skirts they could either produce themselves or obtain from others. In their quest for status, their husbands were obliged to aid them. After all, a Trobriand man's identity rested on the women in his life: his mother and sisters for the land they had, his wife for the food produced on her land by her brothers, and his mother's brother for any formal titles he might inherit.

Case Study
The Hmong: Patrilineality and an American War

The Hmong are a highland people whose ancestral home lies in China but who have moved over the centuries along the mountains into Southeast Asia, particularly into the mountain areas that form the boundary between Vietnam and Laos. The Hmong are shifting cultivators who use controlled forest burns to clear the fields and then plant a variety of crops. Their practices mirror those described earlier in the chapter. Unlike the Trobriand Islanders, however, the requirement for new fields is a persistent demand in the rugged highlands and results in frequent moves.

Given the great mobility of the Hmong, it is not surprising that the Hmong kinship system is very extensive and highly structured. That tight structure has been valuable to them not only in managing their movement along the hills but also in interacting with a wide variety of other horticulturalists in those hills and with the politically stronger peoples of the lowlands: the Thai, Lao, and Vietnamese. As is true of most very tightly organized kinship systems, the Hmong base kinship membership on the relationships among men—and their patrilineal system includes very large clans that have powerful clan leaders. A Hmong man is thus who he is because of his relations to, and descent from, other men.

The Hmong are in some ways relatively typical shifting horticulturalists. However, as is almost always the case in the contemporary world, the

A Hmong woman with her children in Laos. (*Jorgen Schytte/Peter Arnold, Inc.*)

Hmong do not live in isolation. Two outside factors—one economic and one political—greatly changed their fate in the second half of the twentieth century. The economic factor was opium. Horticulture far off in the mountains is an ideal way to grow a crop that requires considerable attention by its growers but considerable isolation from political authorities. Thus the Hmong, who themselves use opium only moderately, found themselves with an extremely valuable cash crop. The political factor was what Americans calls "the Vietnam war" and what the Vietnamese government calls "the American war." Suddenly these isolated areas on the border between Laos and Vietnam became strategically significant. Since the highlands were inhospitable territory for both Americans and Vietnamese, they inevitably turned to the highland groups themselves as a military presence along the border. To the Americans, then, the Hmong were a well-organized people in a strategically located area. Consequently, many of them were recruited into the war on the U.S. side. They worked particularly with the U.S. Central Intelligence Agency in the so-called "secret war" and were, by all accounts, very effective fighters.

With the collapse of the American-supported government in Vietnam in 1975, the situation of these Hmong shifted. Once again, their strong kinship system came into play as they moved again, this time not for new fields but for safety, across the Mekong River into Thailand. There they remained for several years until a combination of pressure from Thailand and lessened hope for return to Laos propelled many of them to the United States. Others attempted to return to Laos and some remained in temporary asylum conditions in Thailand. Even in 2004, some 15,000 Hmong were still living "temporarily" and in very poor conditions on the grounds of a temple in Thailand. Belatedly, the American government has agreed to resettle the majority of them in the United States.

The fate of the Hmong in the United States has not always been a kind one. Despite some attempts, it has generally not been possible for them to recreate their horticultural lifestyle. Yet the ability to rely on a kinship system—rather than a territorial arrangement—has enabled them to move in large numbers from place to place in the United States just as they moved from place to place in China and Southeast Asia. Initially large numbers of Hmong moved to California's Central Valley with more modest numbers moving to such places as North Carolina and Minnesota. Most recently, increased numbers have moved to Minnesota. These migrants of the mountains have thus become international migrants to the United States and now regional migrants within the United States.

SOURCES

There is some debate in anthropology about the extent of the difference between horticulture and agriculture. I have emphasized the difference because the two have become such clearly competing ecological adaptations in many parts of the world. For more general discussion of horticulture and agriculture, see Daniel G. Bates's *Human Adaptive Strategies: Ecology, Culture, and Politics* (Allyn & Bacon, 1998) and Bernard Campbell's *Human Ecology* (Aldine, 1995).

For the case studies, see Geddes' *Migrants of the Mountains* (Clarendon Press, 1976) as the standard source on the Hmong. It may also be useful to look at Gerald C. Hickey's *Sons of the Mountains* and *Free in the Forest* (both from Yale University Press in 1982) for information on other highland groups in that same general area.[4] Anthropologists have been greatly interested in

---

[4]It may be worth noting how important highland Southeast Asia has been in shaping the early views of anthropologists about how relatively large, kin-organized groups can shift in political identity and action—as seen particularly in Edmund Leach's *Political Systems of Highland Burma* (Athlone Press, 1986).

the experiences of the Hmong in America. Anne Fadiman is not an anthropologist but her *The Spirit Catches You and You Fall Down* (Farar, Straus, and Giroux, 1997) is so exceptionally well-written and so intuitively synchronized with anthropological interests that it is well worth reading (I regularly use it in upper-division classes). The film *Becoming American* is somewhat dated but provides a sound introduction to the Hmong in Southeast Asia and in the United States. For the Trobriand Islands, there is a particularly useful pairing of the classic works by Malinowski and the more recent work of Annette Weiner. For the former, *Argonauts of the Western Pacific* (Waveland, 1984) is the most frequently read, but *Coral Gardens and Their Magic* (Routledge, 2001) gives more of the detail of horticulture itself. Weiner's *The Trobrianders of Papua New Guinea* (Holt, Rinehart, and Winston, 1988) is essential reading and the film, *The Trobriand Islanders* (from the *Disappearing World* series) is very useful (Weiner was the consultant for the film and appears in it). Some sense of Malinowski in the Trobriands is provided by the Malinowski segment of the *Strangers Abroad* film series.

CHAPTER 5

AGRICULTURALISTS

Agricultural societies share many of the features of horticultural societies. Both horticulturalists and agriculturalists rely on a range of domesticated plants and, usually, some domesticated animals as well. For both, the domestication of plants in set gardens and fields permits a more sedentary life and a greater density of people. Compared to horticulturalists, however, agriculturalists have increased control of water and fertilization and tend to specialize in a very few major crops—often only one. This increased control and specialization yields a surplus that can support additional economic and political activities in the agricultural communities and in the towns and cities that they support with this surplus. Since agricultural land becomes very valuable, issues of ownership are crucial. If land is limited, the result is likely to be social differences between those with land and those without it.

This chapter provides an overview of agricultural societies in terms of basic adaptation to the environment, core social arrangements, and key characteristics. The major theme of the chapter is that with increasing control over the environment, there are improved agricultural yields, greater density of settlement, greater complexity in social arrangements, and a far more sedentary society. There are more people living together continuously with more to cooperate about—and more valuable property over which to compete. The two case studies at the end of the chapter concern Vietnamese villages practicing wet rice cultivation and an Aztec cultivation system that, despite the absence of a plow, had very high agricultural yields.

RELATIONSHIP TO THE ENVIRONMENT

The story of agriculture involves the same elements as the story of horticulture: a range of plants that benefit from varying amounts of sunlight, water, fertilizer, and attention. For all of these, the difference between agriculture and horticulture lies with sharply increased control. In the swidden garden already described, crops are in gardens, with somewhat better predictions about water and an initial layer of fertilizer from the forest burn. With agriculture, however, there is better management of water, longer-term solutions to the need for fertilizer, and increased specialization in crops.

IRRIGATION

With predictable rains, horticulturalists may fare rather well. But the unpredictability of rainfall may cause crops to fail from lack of water, from too much water, or simply from the timing of rainfall. An early rain, for example, may cause the ash from a swidden burn to run off the field. A different, more promising situation occurs along the banks of rivers where seasonal flooding may bring water to fields. Later, receding water levels drain the fields. If annual flooding replenishes the soil, such seasonal flooding can spare even horticulturalists the need to rotate fields. The crucial improvement is to control this flooding and extend its benefits farther up and down the river, and ultimately to fields more distant from the river. Upstream, the development of irrigation channels enables water to be brought to new fields that were not previously flooded. Downstream, irrigation dikes help control the timing of the flooding and reclaim agricultural land from the marshes that characterize many river deltas. Such riverine situations are at the heart of the early development of agriculture.

FERTILIZATION

With swidden systems, the initial ash from a burn provides an excellent immediate supply of fertilizer, but the effects wear off. Rotation of fields without burning is an option. However, if the land is to be used year after year with high productivity, additional fertilizer is essential. One solution is to put organic material on the soil and let it leach in. Previous crops, animal droppings, or even the special mulch used by the Aztecs will help. However, a more convenient solution lies with the river flooding already described. Water flowing downstream contains silt. When the river water flows out onto the riverbank fields, it slows down, and the silt then settles out of the water. As irrigation systems control the direction and speed of the flow of water, they also provide an important new mechanism for ensuring the continuing fertility of the fields.

SPECIALIZATION

Experience with a range of crops shows that some grow more easily than others and often require little human care after planting. Some grow more reliably, producing roughly equivalent yields year after year. Some provide a bigger payoff at harvest, store more easily without rotting, and respond more dramatically to increased water, fertilizer, and sun. Finally, some crops respond more readily to attempts to domesticate them. A crop that is hardy,

Terraced rice fields on the island of Bali in Indonesia. (*Rick Sherwin/ Photolibrary.com*)

reliable, easy to grow, storable, and improvable is thus a good candidate for specialization. The result of that quest for an ideal crop is usually a grain. In the Middle East, it was wheat or barley, in the Americas it was maize; and in Asia it was rice.

THE PLOW

One further improvement completes the agricultural picture. Although flooding of fields may bring in fertilizer, getting the fertilizer into the soil requires additional effort. Hoes may be used, but that is a slow and laborious process. If soil is compacted as a result of a long dry season, hoeing may be virtually impossible. With a plow, the ground can be tilled more deeply and under less than ideal conditions. As a result, both fertilizer and air can be worked deep into the soil. Since a plow is very hard to pull, draft animals (such as oxen, horses, and water buffalo) are invaluable.

LARGER, MORE PREDICTABLE YIELDS

The implications of this increasingly intensive agriculture can be seen from data on three ways to grow rice. In Southeast Asia, rice is a very good crop when grown in a variety of ways. It can be, and is, grown in exactly the kind of swidden gardens described in the previous chapter. It can also be grown by plowing fields and then scattering ("broadcasting") the seed. Finally, rice can be grown through the more intensive process of transplanting seedlings into paddy fields where the level of water can be controlled, letting the water not only seep into the soil but also physically support the plants as they grow. The paddy fields and connecting canals and ditches also provide a special environment in which fish and microorganisms grow and in turn enrich the soil.

Historical data from Southeast Asia provide useful information on yields for all three types of fields. All are productive. *Swidden* cultivation shows a yield of about .65 tons per acre—although this declines over the years as the soil becomes exhausted. *Broadcasting* is actually less productive per acre (.59 tons) than swidden but requires only about a fifth of the effort to plant an acre. It is thus far more efficient in terms of human labor. Furthermore, it isn't necessary to rotate fields. Finally, *transplanting* requires somewhat less work per acre than the swidden system[1] but results in a yield per acre (.98 tons) that is far higher than in the other two systems. It is thus, by far, the most efficient system in terms of land.[2] The results are clear in terms of population density. The swidden system provides a population density of 31 people per square mile, the broadcasting system a density of 255 people per square mile, and the transplanting system a density of 988 people per square mile.

The key to agricultural societies is the ability to use fields continuously and to produce a crop that is hardy, reliable, relatively nutritious (at least in raw calories), and storable. Increased efforts on irrigation and drainage systems produce higher yields. Additional labor increases per-acre yields. Transplanting, for example, requires much more labor but produces a larger harvest. The result is that agriculturalists win the numbers game. There will ultimately be more of them.

SOCIAL ARRANGEMENTS

THE IMPORTANCE OF LAND

Agriculturalists are highly sedentary. As they improve the fields, and the fields respond with better yields, there is little incentive to move and much to stay. Since good agricultural land can produce indefinitely, people don't have to leave their land. Consequently, existing agricultural land is unlikely to become "vacant" and available for other people. The only ways to expand fields are to develop new land or to displace people from existing fields. There are usually limited options for moving somewhere else and starting again. Much of the world's best agricultural land has been taken up for over two thousand years, some of it for much longer.

---

[1] If all infrastructure costs—especially maintaining irrigation systems—are included, transplanting takes much more effort than the swidden systems.

[2] As will be noted later in the text, contemporary yields are higher by a factor of two to three. That reflects improved rice strains and the increasing use of fertilizer.

The value of agricultural land and what it produces shape the social relations of agricultural societies. As land is so valuable, there is likely to be
conflict over it. Rules are needed about who has the right to the land. With concerns about *ownership* and *rights of use* also come questions about *inheritance*.
Since the improvements to a field are permanent, then the right to the fields
should be permanent as well. That requires a mechanism to transfer that right
to the next generation. Within a family, it must be decided which of the children gets how much of the land. In the broader community, it must be decided how much of the land should be collectively owned and how
responsibility for that should be passed on over time.

The nature of the agricultural product from this land also has implications. The harvest for a grain crop, for example, is a large quantity of food
that is storable and transportable. Most grains dry readily and will remain
viable for long periods of time (at least with modest attempts to avoid mois-
ture during storage). These bags of grain can be used for a variety of purposes. Some will be saved for consumption but, at least in a good year, some
can also be exchanged for other foods, for tools, for paid labor to help at
harvest time, or perhaps even to buy land from someone whose fortunes
have fallen. This agricultural *surplus* is also of interest to those outside the
immediate area. A raiding party might find it of interest, as would outsiders
trying to build their own economic or political power. These bags of grain
could support their own communities and feed their workers. The development of agriculture is thus interlinked with the growth of cities and political states. It is the misfortune of agriculturalists to be locked into land
that is valuable both to them and to others. They live out in the open, usually in accessible river valleys and plains. They are vulnerable precisely because they can't leave their land. Their friends and enemies know exactly
where they are, the value of what they produce, and the long-term value of
the land that they inhabit.

AGE AND SEX, KINSHIP AND LOCALITY

This highly sedentary lifestyle, increased population density, valuable property, and storable, transportable agricultural surplus together have implications for social relations in agricultural societies. At the most basic level,
relations of age and sex, generation and gender, shift somewhat from horticultural and foraging societies. Although men and women may, on occasion, work together, agricultural life tends to create separate male and female
work domains. Even the increasing importance of property may force a distinction between male and female rights to land ownership. If women end
up owning land and passing land to their daughters, then female preroga-
tives may well be protected. However, the very density of settlement mili-
tates toward more structured kin groups and, as will be discussed in Part II,

patrilineal structures tend to be more capable of expansion than matrilineal ones, and they tend to predominate in agricultural societies. With a sharper division of labor between men and women and differences in rights of ownership, there are likely to be social differences as well. Relations by age may also become more hierarchical. The elders of the community have not only accrued a great deal of practical and social knowledge that makes them useful experts, but also may well hold the property on which all depend. As family elders, they will hold private land; as village elders, they will control access to public land.

Relations of kinship are as important in agricultural societies as in horticultural and foraging societies, but the size of kin groups may be greater and their formal structure more rigid. After all, there is greater population density and thus a greater need for social control and organization. Since people do not move, large sets of kin are likely to accumulate over time in particular localities. Those kin groups help organize and protect their own members. They may also serve as the core of local political structures. If one's neighbors are also one's kin, for example, kin organization and local community organization may be one and the same. Such ties of blood in agricultural societies, however, are often complemented by ties of locality. Whether related by kinship or not, neighbors are crucial. They are vital to one's own success and well-being. Their cooperation is essential in developing land, allocating water to it, and managing times—such as harvest—when extra labor is needed. Furthermore, disputes with them can be dangerous. Irrigation systems, for example, almost always require collective effort to build and collective restraint to administer in an equitable way.

SPECIALIZATION OF LABOR

In some ways, the issue of skills is similar in agricultural societies to the other societies already discussed. As with foragers and horticulturalists, virtually all people need a common set of skills. In agricultural societies, however, the issue of skills has two additional wrinkles. First, because of the density and social complexity of agricultural societies, and their frequent need to deal with outsiders, some special assigned political roles are likely to be necessary—such as village head or chief. Second, because of the increasing technological complexity of agricultural life, there is also a need for people trained for particular jobs, whether that involves iron-working, trade, accounting, or engineering. Agricultural villages will need plows, goods from other places, a way to count for tax and inheritance purposes, and the ability to develop and maintain disaster-proof irrigation systems. For these tasks, it is necessary to anticipate and train for future needs. The production of a surplus will make it possible for people to engage in such nonagricultural activities as education and training.

NINE KEY QUESTIONS

Overall, agriculturalists not only adapt to a particular environment but actively change that environment through their irrigation systems and the very act of plowing the soil. They are highly sedentary and the increasing yields from their fields make their settlements dense, and they often become increasingly dense over the generations. Ownership of land is a crucial issue that is likely to introduce social divisions into the society. Kinship often involves very large and tightly structured groups. However, since non-kin living nearby are also very important, other kinds of social organization will develop based on ties of locality. The dense, sedentary settlements of agriculturalists thus show mixed and overlapping ties of blood and land. The productivity of the land produces useful surpluses, but differential access to land may make those surpluses more the property of some people than others. These characteristics underlie the answers to the nine key questions posed in each of these chapters.

> *Division of Labor:*   In agricultural societies, the division of labor becomes sharper and more extensive. Differences between the sexes may be heightened as the flow of activities and rights of ownership shift. Differences in activities and property rights may sharpen by age. In addition, there is also division of labor by occupation. At the village level, specialized occupations may be only part-time: for example, a farmer who also repairs tools or does some trading in the agricultural off-season. Beyond the village, the possibilities engendered by an agricultural surplus almost inevitably result in such "jobs" as builder or engineer, tax collector, soldier, bureaucrat, and teacher. For such tasks, an ad hoc emergence of competence over time is inadequate. Instead, people will have to be specifically trained for jobs through either formal education or apprenticeship.

> *Territoriality:*   Good agricultural land is an immensely valuable resource. It will not be easily or often given up. So agriculturalists are strongly linked to the land. Indeed, the resource of land may become more valuable than the resource of people. More people can be easily produced, but more land cannot. With agriculture, then, people become locked into the land. The land is not only their past and present, but their future as well. Without ownership of land, one's children will be destined for poverty and perhaps one's family line for extinction. Only the combination of poor land at home and new opportunities elsewhere is likely to dislodge people from their homes.

> *Kinship:*   With increased density of settlement comes an increased need for cooperation and coordination. Kin remain the most reliable resource for that and thus large kin groups make practical sense. Furthermore, with increasingly valuable property comes the need to

determine who will have future rights to that land. As a result, kinship tends to be more strictly defined and frequently takes on a patrilineal structure. Kinship among agriculturalists thus tends to be important, highly structured, and extensive—*unless* new land elsewhere lures people away and the advantages of the mobile nuclear family again become relevant.

Social Control: There is much to argue over in agricultural societies. Land is valuable but there are also houses, agricultural tools, and draft animals. Disputes that arise may be resolved within the kin group. However, since there are likely to be different kin groups in agricultural communities, some bridging authority is needed. Frequently this will be a set of village elders drawn from the main families of the village. They are likely to have formal authority and some ability to enforce their decisions. One of the functions of those elders will be to deal with outside political forces that wish to control the local community for their own purposes.

Equality: With agricultural systems, the access to resources is no longer as broad as it is in foraging and horticultural societies. Land—especially good, improved land—is likely to be in short supply. Consequently, some people will have more or better land than other people. Those other people end up with little or no land. They may work as laborers or tenants on the land of those who are better off. There is the potential for serious social inequality between the "haves" and the "have-nots"—including formal systems of control over labor such as slavery. However, the "haves" usually need the "have-nots" for extra labor so attempts will be made through personal patronage or communal land to ensure that all members of the community have at least a marginal livelihood.

Religious Beliefs: In agricultural societies, people are likely to acknowledge a wide range of spiritual forces. With kin groups in the same place over many generations, the ancestors have a lasting presence. The fields they improved, the houses they built, and their burial grounds are a part of the everyday scenery. Spirits of land and water are also likely to be important. In larger agricultural societies that are more formally organized, there may, as well, be spirits representing the political order. Finally, since agricultural societies are inevitably involved in trade and in state formation, they are likely to be exposed to major world religions.

Ecological Soundness: Agriculturalists, unlike foragers and horticulturalists, make changes to the land that are often permanent. With plowing, irrigation, and deforestation, the natural world is changed. The breaking of the land by the plow (as in the American West), may permanently change the landscape. The drainage of marshlands results in the loss of wetlands. Conversion of highland areas to agriculture creates soil runoff. Agriculture also imposes burdens on people. Agriculturalists usually end up working far harder than do foragers and horticulturalists—although they may benefit from a lull in work after harvests are in.

Security: One of the great advantages of agriculture is its ability to make yields both larger and more predictable. However, as population increases and the infrastructure becomes more complex, any failure in the system has catastrophic implications. Drought and flood take a horrendous toll, even in modern-day agricultural societies. Crop disease can also have catastrophic effects. Specialization in a single crop thus puts the population at great risk. It also tends to reduce the nutritional balance of the diet in favor of raw calories.

External Conflict: Agricultural societies are of interest to outsiders because of the value of their land and because they produce a harvest that is storable and transportable. Bags of grain can feed other people: enemies, friends, and one's own government. Agricultural societies are also easy to find and relatively easy to control. It is virtually impossible for agricultural societies to be free from external conflict. As they become part of state systems, they will be acutely aware of the trade-offs between the protection they receive from the government and the taxes they must provide to it.

Case Study
Vietnamese Villages: Strings and Clusters

Agriculture in Vietnam's Red River delta developed some 2,500 years ago along the middle stretches of the river, exactly where there was some annual flooding but not marshy conditions that required drainage. The first capital of an identifiable Vietnamese state (Van-lang) was built precisely along this stretch of the river. From these initial footholds, rice cultivation began a long process of expansion. For the Red River, most of that effort involved draining a marshy delta. Hanoi itself, for example, is located down the Red River from the original settlements. Only many centuries after that was the land drained all the way to the coast and such port cities as Haiphong.

The Vietnamese villages that developed in the Red River delta were compact and usually surrounded by tight bamboo hedges. The production from the fields, supplemented with other vegetables from gardens and a smattering of chickens and pigs, permitted a well-settled life. What we know of village life in the past indicates a kinship nucleus to the village, with the leaders of dominant kin groups functioning as the village elders. Those kin groups were patrilineal. The orderly inheritance of this land was so important that it often generated imperial edicts stipulating, for example, that sons were generally to get equal shares of the land and daughters and widows to get half-shares. As another example, one portion of the land was to be put aside as "incense and fire" money for the veneration of the ancestors. That portion went to the eldest son. Although kinship was crucial, the village was itself an important social unit beyond the kin groups that comprised it. The village as a whole held a portion of its land collectively. That land was used to support general village activities and—at least ideally—was to be used by those whose personal land holdings were limited. The village had its own spiritual entities represented in temples and its own founding ancestors were recognized by tablets in the village community hall. Usually prominent in that hall was the imperial edict that had officially established the village many centuries in the past.

Inevitably, over the centuries the density of the population increased. As new land was wrenched from Cham and then Khmer control to the south, many from the overpopulated northern areas sought new lives farther south, first along the narrow coastal strip near Hue, and then in the vast delta of the Mekong River. There again, the irrigation problem was as much one of drainage as of getting water to the fields. In these southern areas, villages took on a different shape. They were not compact, secluded, and bounded by a bamboo hedge, but instead were strung out along the rivers and canals that formed both an irrigation and transportation system. Indeed, it was not always easy to distinguish villages. Sets of houses would spring up in the middle of fields, at a road crossing, or a waterway. These small hamlets would then be organized together as a village. The scenery of rice, houses, tombs, and clumps of trees is similar in the north and south, but in the southern areas it has a distinctly scattered and open look. In the south, kinship was also vital in village structure. Sometimes hamlets and sections of bigger villages might include neighbors who were all close kin. Yet in other places, neighbors might not be kin. For these Vietnamese, life on the "frontier" often meant smaller family groups and, many have argued, a less rigorous imposition of patrilineal rules.

Yet neither the dense villages of the north nor the string villages of the south existed in isolation. Whether it was the dikes that prevented flooding of the Red River or the extensive canals that controlled the backwash of the more tidal Mekong, public works enabled the cultivation of wet rice. While both kinds of village had strong self-government, both were also subject to outside government. The outside government, for example, frequently had a hand in designating the village chief, since that person had to function both as representative to the central government and as a representative from it to the local community. The government—whether under the ancient Vietnamese kings, the current socialist republic, or the former South Vietnamese republic—always understood the need for the agricultural produce of the villages and for the labor of the people as farmers, and as soldiers.

Case Study
The Aztecs: Agriculture without a Plow

In the Americas, a wide range of horticultural societies existed before the European onslaught. Central to most of those societies was maize. Extensive archeological work has documented the domestication of wild maize and its gradual development from a very small ear to the large ears of corn that we know today. None of these societies was agricultural in the specific sense of using plow agriculture, yet several developed exactly the kinds of state systems and urban settlements that we generally associate with fully developed agricultural systems. A consideration of how they managed that process is instructive. The most fully developed of these agricultural systems in the New World were those in central Mexico. Both before the Aztec period and during it, fields were capable of producing good yields of maize continuously over time, thus meeting the essential requirements of fully sedentary life and a significant agricultural surplus.

Historical accounts suggest that these agricultural systems reached their fruition under the Aztecs in roughly the two centuries prior to the Spanish

The floating gardens of Xochimilco, Mexico. (*Severin/SuperStock, Inc.*)

conquest. Tenochtitlán, the major Aztec city, was itself situated on an island in the middle of a large lake. The city had to be protected from flood waters from other lakes during the rainy season, so a ten-mile dike was built along the exposed eastern side of the city. The agricultural fields themselves were often along the borders of the lake and also directly in the lake itself. This required reclaiming shallow waters by adding sod brought from the mainland with soil piled up from the shallow basins themselves. The result was a series of ditches that separated field areas from canals that both brought in water and allowed transportation. Most of the maize was grown in seed beds (often on floating rafts) and then transplanted to the fields themselves. (Those floating seed beds are, historians believe, the cause of the erroneous impression that the fields themselves were "floating"). At least for the Lake Texcoco area of Tenochtitlán, the salinity of the water also required aqueducts that brought in fresh water from the mainland. Farmers thus had to simultaneously resolve problems of drainage, protection against saline water, and access to fresh water.

The result was a kind of field called *chinampas* that depended on multiple kinds of fertilizer. Some nutrients could be expected from the water itself. To this was added extensive organic fertilizer in the form of water plants growing in the canals that were used as a heavy mulch. Finally, mud from the bottom of the canals, which contained a range of good nutrients (including fish feces) was also placed on the fields. Thus, even without a plow, the soil was sufficiently rich and replenished frequently enough to permit good, continuous yields. As in the rice paddies of Asia, water systems provided not only water itself but also a full environment in which fish and microorganisms could grow and in turn enrich the soil.

Some *chinampas* continue to be used in selected areas today, particularly in Xochimilco, a few miles south of Mexico City. The Mexican government has spent considerable funds to protect them and maintain what is a significant tourist draw for Mexicans and, increasingly, for ecotourists interested in the *chinampas* as a model for sustainable, organic agriculture. The fields are still very productive although they have increasingly been turned toward growing flowers rather than maize. Their effectiveness is thus clear from current information. However, even the historical record suggests how efficient that plowless agriculture was. At the time of the Spanish arrival, Tenochtitlán was one of the world's major cities. It supported an extensive nobility, a wide range of craft specialists, a large army, and a highly developed religious system, including an estimated 5,000 priests. The Aztec state was able to sustain a large government and extremely active military campaigns that, among other things, furnished the large numbers of people who were sacrificed as part of Aztec rituals each year.

SOURCES

The literature on agriculture ranges in topic from the origins of agriculture to the very latest in genetically engineered crops. For the classic discussion of the political implications of agriculture and irrigation, see Karl Wittfogel's *Oriental Despotism* (Yale University Press, 1957). *Rice and Man* by Lucien Hanks (University of Hawaii Press, 1992) remains a wonderfully accessible introduction to the subject (and is the source for the Southeast Asian data on rice yields); Robert McC. Netting's *Smallholders, Householders* (Stanford University Press, 1993) provides a broad overview of the implications of intensive agriculture; and a visit to the Web site of the International Rice Research Institute (www.cgiar.org/irri or www.riceweb.org) will yield a wealth of information about the enormous improvements in yields that have been made for the world's single most important food crop. Daniel G. Bates's *Human Adaptive Strategies: Ecology, Culture, and Politics* (Allyn & Bacon, 1998) and Bernard Campbell's *Human Ecology* (Aldine, 1995) were noted in the last chapter and would be useful here as well.

For further information on the Vietnamese case study, see Keith Taylor's *The Birth of Vietnam* (University of California Press, 1983) for the essential review of early Vietnamese society. Gerald C. Hickey's *Village in Vietnam* (Yale University Press, 1964) remains the crucial source for the southern areas of the country. A very interesting compilation of work on various northern Vietnam villages is provided in *The Traditional Village in Vietnam* (The Gioi, 1993). For the Aztecs, a good introduction is provided by Frances Berdan in *The Aztecs of Central Mexico* (1997; orig 1982), and more detailed discussion is available in Michael Smith's *The Aztecs* (Blackwell, 1998) and Richard F. Townsend's *The Aztecs* (Thames and Hudson, revised edition, 2000).

CHAPTER 6

PASTORALISTS

Unlike horticulturalists and agriculturalists, who expand and refine the use of plants, pastoralists expand and refine the use of animals. Usually choosing one or two animals that are hardy, herdable, breedable, and the source of multiple products (meat, milk, bone, skin), they organize their lives around the lives of those animals. In many ways they are like foragers, except that they are foraging for food for their animals and not for themselves. Like foragers and many horticulturalists, they are also inevitably on the move in this search for food and water for the animals. Finally, like agriculturalists, pastoralists have a kind of property that has great value to others. Unlike an agricultural commodity, however, herds are themselves mobile and can, for example, simply be led away by would-be thieves.

This chapter reviews the basic characteristics of pastoralist societies, emphasizing the logic of building a life based on the needs of one's animals. The first section of the chapter concerns the basic pastoralist relationship to the environment. That is followed by a consideration of the social arrangements that make sense given that relationship to the environment: particularly the issues of mobility, property, and skills. That, in turn, is followed by a consideration of the nine key questions asked in each of these chapters of Part I. The first case study at the end of the chapter is about the Nuer, a cattle-herding people living in the southern Sudan. In recent years they have been drawn into one of the world's worst and most-enduring civil wars; as a result, many Nuer have come to the United States as refugees. The second case study concerns the Sarakatsani, herders of sheep and goats, who make a long annual trek from the lowlands to the highlands of Greece.

RELATIONSHIP TO THE ENVIRONMENT

THE VALUE OF ANIMALS

The logic of pastoralism is in one vital way similar to that of agriculture. Pastoralism hinges on specialization. Just as agriculturalists tend to specialize in a few crops, so pastoralists specialize in a few animals. The reasons for choosing the crops or animals in which to specialize are also similar. For agriculturalists, a good crop is one that is hardy, responds well to cultivation, and has a good yield. Likewise, pastoralists seek an animal that is hardy, breedable, and has a good yield.

An animal is a good candidate for specialization if it is *hardy.* It should not easily sicken and should be able to endure at least some hardship. It should be hardy both when young and as an adult. An animal should also be *breedable,* both in the general sense that it breeds easily and in the sense that improvements in the stock can be made by controlling that breeding. The animal should also have a good *yield,* much like a crop does. Furthermore, because of the specialization in one or two animals, it is helpful if the animal has a good yield in a variety of ways. Certainly animals should be good as meat, but their ability to provide dairy products may be more important. Their by-products—such as skin (hide), hair (wool), and bone—are also important. Many pastoralists go beyond those basics to other by-products: hair as brushes, blood as food, urine for washing (since it is sterile). Finally, there is one additional requirement. The animal must also be *herdable.* Often intelligence is less important than docility, but it might be nice to have both.

The agricultural search for a good specialized crop usually results in some kind of grain. For pastoralists, the answer usually narrows to some combination of three animals: cows, goats, and sheep. All three are good as meat, all three provide dairy products, all three provide hair and hide. The value of wool is an extra bonus for sheep; horns are a bonus for cattle. This doesn't mean that pastoralists don't raise other animals, but generally these are for secondary purposes. Thus, in raising cattle, it would be good to have another animal that would help you herd the cattle (thus the value of horses). In raising sheep, riding a horse might be valuable, but a well-trained dog might also do very well. Horses and dogs are thus part of the human team that is herding the animals—and, in many societies (but not all!) are quite specifically off-limits as food.

MANAGING HERDS

In caring for their animals, pastoralists must come to terms with their environment in a new way, not for their own direct needs but for those of the animals. Like foragers, they will probably have to move on a seasonal basis. Those seasons may be characterized by temperature. Thus the herds can be taken farther up in the hills during the summer and back to the valleys during the winter. Sometimes the seasons are characterized more by precipitation. Thus it may be during the rainy season that the herds move to higher ground, and in the dry season that they move down along the rivers in search of water. Even in the absence of such seasonal changes, movement

A shepherd and his flock in Provence, France. (*Peter Bowater/Alamy Images*)

will be needed. Most animals, at least in relatively large herds, require extensive grazing land.

One particularly important aspect of pastoralist life is the relatively large size of the herds. Animals for pastoralists are not—as they are for foragers, horticulturalists, and agriculturalists—simply an extra source of food or prestige. Instead they are the core food and the center of attention. There are practical advantages in herding relatively large numbers of animals together but also difficulties. One is that during the seasonal round a particular resource, such as water, may become limited. The larger the herd, the more pressure there is on that resource. These large herds are thus vulnerable not only to a lack of food or water in general, but to the specific lack of food and water at specific times and specific places during the year. This is the central dilemma in the lives of pastoralists: They may not need any particular food or water source very often, but when they do need it, they often really need it. Consider the potential clash with agriculturalists. The agriculturalists would probably want to fence off their fields near the river so cattle don't trample their corn. The pastoralists may not care about that for eleven months of the year, but during the dry season, when their cattle are thirsty, they will not shrink from cutting those fences and trampling that corn if that is the only way to get the water. That debate about fencing or not fencing was a fierce one in the shaping of land use in the western parts of North America.

SOCIAL ARRANGEMENTS

MOBILITY AND ORGANIZATION

Pastoralism is thus an adaptation quite distinct from those already discussed, yet it resembles them in certain ways. Like foragers, pastoralists are almost inevitably on the move but, unlike foragers, their movements are more on the behalf of their animals than for themselves. Like agriculturalists, pastoralists have a useful commodity that may raise covetous sentiments among their neighbors but, unlike agriculturalists, they themselves are mobile and can thus move more aggressively and often very quickly to protect their interests. Pastoralists, then, are unique in this combination of mobility and large, well-organized groups for herd management and protection. That has important implications for pastoralist society. As would be expected, the high degree of mobility is accompanied by reliance on kinship and, since the need for formal order is high, reliance on patrilineal kinship systems. More problematic, however, are the pastoralist relations to territory, to property, and to equality.

THE DEFENSE OF TERRITORY AND PROPERTY

In terms of *territory*, pastoralists are in the unfortunate position of having to assert rights to multiple places at different times. They may have, for example, relatively settled homesteads during one season of the year (say, winter) but more scattered camps during another season (say, summer). They don't need the summer camps in winter but they do need to know that the summer camps will be there and available the next summer. They cannot afford to have someone else move into that area during the winter and stay the next summer. Likewise, they may have little interest in a river that is on the way to the summer camps except for a brief period on their way to the summer camps when their herds are thirsty. Yet they cannot afford to have someone take control of that river during the time they are not there and then deny them that water next year. They must protect their rights to future use of places and resources that may, right now, be far away and of little concern. Likewise, when they are at the summer camp, they cannot afford to have someone move into their winter quarters. This is not just a matter of physical property, since it may well be that women and younger children have remained there for some time after the men have left. Pastoralists must therefore defend places where they aren't now but will be at some time in the future. In that impossible task, they will need the ability to move rapidly and to work effectively in large groups.

In terms of *property*, pastoralists have a very valuable commodity in their herds. That commodity itself is mobile. Most of their money is, so to speak, on the hoof and self-propelled. Theft is thus a constant danger. If some other group is quick enough and daring enough, they can have your herd on its way before you can react. To counter that threat requires an ability to react quickly and in well-organized force. Animals can also be lost. For example, individual herds are likely to be merged at some times during the year. The result may be that it is difficult to tell which animal belongs to which person—or at least to prove which animal belongs to whom. That requires not only some organization but also some trust. You can't afford to work with anybody who might steal. If anybody does try to steal your animals, it is vital—and usually a matter of personal honor—to make sure they don't succeed or, if they do succeed, that they are punished so severely they won't ever try it again. In the code of the old West, then, cattle rustling is a hanging offense.

EQUALITY AND INEQUALITY

Finally, pastoralists tend, in some ways, to be very egalitarian. As men work with the herds, they must rely on each other. Each man must be able to do almost all tasks and, when necessary, to actively help defend the herds from outsiders. This tends to breed a rough equality and independence among men even though they must also cooperate well together. On the other hand, the very nature of the life tends to separate men from women during much of the year and to allocate to them very different tasks. Men may take care of the herds while women watch the home—and perhaps cultivate some crops. Or men may take care of one set of animals and women the other. In either case, men are likely to be the most mobile. Although a sharp division of labor by sex does not necessarily rule out equality, it certainly doesn't foster it. Thus, among pastoralists, there is often simultaneously a great degree of equality among men yet very sharp inequality between men and women.

NINE KEY QUESTIONS

Division of Labor: In pastoralist societies, the division of labor is minimal in some ways yet very sharp in others. Differences between the sexes are usually great in terms of the flow of daily and seasonal activities. Such differences may also sharpen by age. Men beyond their prime physical years, for example, are likely to have a harder time in pastoralist than in agricultural societies. Aside from such division of labor by age and sex, little other formal specialization is likely.

Territoriality: Pastoralists are in the difficult position of requiring rights to use a great deal of land, though not all of it at the same time. They must thus maintain access to a broad range of territory. There are likely to be times of the year when resources, water for example, are limited and pastoralists must have access to them. Thus pastoralists will be committed to a range of territory even though they are only using part of that range at any particular time. Pastoralists will be fierce in their defense of that range.

Kinship: With increased mobility and larger groups to manage the herds, there is a strong need for cooperation and coordination. Kin remain the most reliable resource for that, and large kin groups make practical sense. Since patrilineality provides a surer basis for particularly large and tightly organized kin groups, pastoralists are usually patrilineal. Furthermore, pastoralists have valuable property that requires clarity of ownership and inheritance. A well-defined kinship system also helps resolve such problems.

Social Control: There is much to argue about in pastoralist societies. The herds themselves are valuable and there may also be other kinds of property. Many disputes that arise can be resolved within the immediate group. However, since various kin groups will be interacting during at least some times of the year, some additional authority is needed. This might be a group of the heads of major kin groups working together as a kind of leadership council. There may also be intermediaries—perhaps religious leaders— who can help arbitrate disputes but who probably have limited formal authority.

Equality: With pastoralist systems, the access to resources is often relatively similar for most males. Thus pastoralist societies often show remarkable equality among men. However, the very nature of those resources and the need to move frequently tend to create very separate lives for men and women. Such separateness does not inevitably cause inequality, but it can have that effect. Although some pastoralist societies have relatively balanced relations between men and women, many pastoralist societies have extremely sharp control by men over women.

Religious Beliefs: Pastoralists are likely to acknowledge a wide range of spiritual forces. As with agricultural societies, the importance of large kin groups would suggest an important place for the ancestors. On the other hand, the extent of mobility and the rough equality that pervades relations among men suggest the relevance of a more individualistic and universalistic religion—a religion that will travel well. Shamanistic practices are likely to exist based on individual connections to spirits. Broad-ranging gods (for example, gods of the sky) are especially appropriate. It seems also to be the case that there is a tendency for conversion among pastoralist groups to Islam and Christianity. Both provide a universalistic vision that indeed travels well and allows for individual access to spiritual strength.

Ecological Soundness: Pastoralists, by definition, need the same resources in the coming year that they have this year. Thus, like foragers, they cannot afford to exhaust any of the resources they use. In that sense, pastoralism is eminently ecologically sound. It may be particularly so in using land that is poorly suited for other purposes. Furthermore, the intensive use of animals ensures that there is little waste. In theory, then, pastoralists—unlike agriculturalists—make no permanent, severe changes to the land. Nevertheless, extensive grazing may well cause changes and overgrazing may occur if herds become too large or are confined to areas that are insufficient for them.

Security: One of the greatest disadvantages of pastoralism is exactly its specialization. Thus, as with agriculture, specialization raises the risk of catastrophic loss. A drought, for example, may put the herds at risk for water. Even worse, disease can wipe out major portions of the herd. Aside from that catastrophic possibility, and the frequent threat from other human beings, the pastoralist adaptation has much to recommend it. The "surplus" is on the hoof and—at some risk to the future of the herd—can be eaten if necessary.

External Conflict: It is the misfortune of pastoralists to be at risk for two main reasons. First, their herds are themselves valuable. Other pastoralists might wish to take the herds and might have the speed and enterprise to do so. Agriculturalists would be interested as well: They have a relative lack of livestock, since their land is too valuable to be used for grazing. Second, pastoralists must protect a range that includes places that may be far away from their current location. If any of their range is suitable for agriculture, for example, they run the risk of permanently losing access to that land. In that kind of conflict with agriculturalists, they will have the initial advantages of speed and organization. But the agriculturalists will, sooner or later, have the numbers.

Case Study
The Nuer: Cattle on the Upper Nile

The Nuer are cattle herders who live in the upper reaches of the Nile River in the southern part of the Sudan. The twentieth century was difficult for them, beginning with a great loss to the herds from rinderpest, the penetration of British colonialists, and—at the end of the century—one of the world's longest civil wars, pitting the Nuer and the related Dinka, who have largely converted to Christianity, against the Islamic northern part of the country. That war has taken its toll on the people, on the cattle, and on the lifestyle that hinged on both. Nevertheless, the basic structure of the Nuer life appears to remain.

For the Nuer, pastoralism revolves around cattle. The cattle are used for their full range of possibilities: from milk to blood to meat for nourishment, and from hides to hair to bone for tools. The cattle are the focus of much Nuer imagery and the currency through which social arrangements are made. They are also the focus of the yearly round, which, for

Near Akobo, Nuer boys lounge among cattle, their tribe's most precious possession. (*Abbas/Magnum Photos, Inc.*)

the Nuer, is largely determined by water. There are distinct wet and dry seasons in the Sudan; the wet season largely corresponds to our summer and the dry season to our winter. During the rainy season, the Nuer move to higher ground to avoid the flooding in what becomes a very marshy area. On that higher ground—think of very low elevations of barely rolling countryside—the Nuer plant some crops and place their cattle in byres (corrals). During this time of the year, the cattle are fed rather than let out to graze. After the rains end, the rivers gradually recede, and wild grasses grow. At this time, some of the Nuer—especially young men—begin breaking camp and moving the cattle to lower ground where they can graze and have access to water. By the middle of the dry season, larger and larger groups of Nuer begin congregating at the diminishing number of places where there is adequate water. Finally, as light rains begin, the Nuer move back toward higher ground in order to have crops in the ground by the time the heavier rains begin.

These Nuer movements across the land and through the seasons require a variety of social and political interactions. During the wet season, when the Nuer are in place on higher ground, they live in settled clusters of houses. During the dry season, however, the Nuer first break apart into smaller groups to graze. Those smaller groups are initially male. Later on, the Nuer will coalesce into larger groups around water sources. All members—men and women, old and young—will once again be together. Thus the Nuer social system must be adequate to the demands of relatively dense, village-like interaction in the wet season; more dispersed, and often age-specific and sex-specific groups in the early dry season; and large concentrations at the height of the dry season.

The Nuer answer to that call for a portable, flexible, social framework is an extensive patrilineal kinship system. Since the groups vary so much in size and structure at different times of the year, that structure is expansive enough to include all Nuer but also flexible enough for smaller groups to function independently at different times of the year. The size of the resulting kinship framework of the Nuer, which includes hundreds of thousands of people, has generated the phrase "headless government." The argument is that the Nuer kinship system accomplishes many of the purposes of formal government but without any actual "leaders." The flexibility of that kinship framework has also been noted among Nuer who have come to the United States as refugees from the civil war. Although many of the Nuer are without relatives in the United States, and without the pastoralist lifestyle of the Upper Nile, they have proved very adaptable—including putting their expertise with cattle to effective use in meat-packing plants.

Case Study
The Sarakatsani: Men and Sheep, Women and Goats

In the northern part of Greece live a large number of people often called Vlachs (shepherds) or Sarakatsani. Their life revolves around their flocks of sheep and, to a lesser extent, goats. For them, the seasonal round is largely one of temperature. In the summer they move their flocks high into the mountains, grazing in the 3,000- to 6,000-foot slopes. In the winter they return to the lowlands, eking out what they can for their flocks on more limited pasturage. That life requires considerable self-reliance. Shepherds may often be on their own in the dark on steep slopes high on the hills. The Sarakatsani life also requires cooperation. Herds are fairly large and include animals from different—although related—households. Finally, Sarakatsani life requires integration with the wider society. Dairy products must find a buyer, men must serve in the Greek army, and the seasonal migrations up and down the slopes must negotiate their way through sometimes hostile agricultural villages.

Some sense of the difficulties of the full annual round can be gained by considering the management of the flocks in winter in the lowlands. With grazing land at a premium and the temperature a danger to the animals, the flocks are split into three groups of sheep and a fourth group of goats. The first group includes the pregnant ewes; they will be grazed on relatively good ground—although the very best ground will be saved for them until they have actually lambed. The second group in terms of priority is the relatively small group of the previous year's lambs. The third group includes the rams and those ewes that have not successfully mated and are thus not pregnant, and the fourth group includes the goats. The animals are individually owned and marked, but the need to reserve the best grazing land for the pregnant ewes and to maximize the labor of the shepherds creates important economies of scale in merging animals into these four combined herds.

There is much in Sarakatsani life that keeps the worlds of men and women separate. On practical grounds, for example, it is predictable that the Sarakatsani on the steep slopes after dark are men. Likewise, it is reasonably predictable that it is men who negotiate the mixing of different families' herds and men who negotiate passage and exchange of goods in a trek through sometimes hostile territory. As with other pastoralists, the need to follow the herds and to manage them through multiple social and political structures tends to take men far from home. When men and women live such separate lives, it is likely that their views of life and of each other will tend to diverge. Thus it is with the Sarakatsani. While there is a relatively high degree of equality among men and among women, there is a very high degree of separation and inequality between men and women. That separation is seen not only in activities but in the very symbolism of Sarakatsani life. That symbolism is woven into the views they have of the animals on which they depend. The characteristics of the animals become the imputed characteristics of the genders. Thus men are symbolically linked to sheep and women to goats.

Although goats are a relatively small proportion of the herds, it is they who provide the crucial symbolic alternative to the sheep. From the Sarakatsani perspective, sheep have a number of impressive features. They are very hardy and can endure the cold. When in pain, they make little noise—thus appearing stoic. They are also reasonably restrained eaters. Goats, on the other hand, are less resistant to cold weather and, indeed, very prone to pneumonia in the wet winter months. When in pain, they make a great deal of noise and are also regarded as greedy—even insatiable—eaters. To that basic contrast is added the religious symbolism of Christianity. Thus sheep are pure and of God; goats are impure and thus—despite their taming—still at least partially of the devil. That sharp contrast provides a ready framework for the discussion of gender as well. Men, who tend the sheep and would take for themselves these attributes of endurance and restraint, take on that holy role of the pure ones. Women, tenders of the goats, are assigned some of the attributes of goats. Their sexuality and menstruation are considered threats to the purity of the sheep and thus contact between the two is avoided—unless that is, the sheep become sick and are brought into the house where the ministrations of women, as mothers, provide their only hope for recovery.

SOURCES

Pastoralism is an intriguing adaptation and rather more varied than I have been able to present here. Some sense of the diversity of pastoralism can be obtained by looking at such edited volumes as *The World of Pastoralism: Herding Systems in Comparative Perspective* (Guilford, 1990; John Galaty and Douglas Johnson, editors) or *Changing Nomads in a Changing World* (Sussex Academic Press, 1999; Joseph Ginat and Anatoly Khazanov, editors). A good pairing of case studies might be Fredrik Barth's classic *Nomads of South Persia* (Waveland, 1986) and Dawn Chatty's *Mobile Pastoralists* (Columbia University Press, 1996). *The Kirgiz*, a segment of the *Disappearing World* series, is a reasonable film introduction to a nomadic group, especially valuable on the nature of political leadership and the implications of being denied the full extent of a traditional migratory range.

Regarding the case studies, see E. E. Evans-Pritchard's *The Nuer* (Oxford University Press, 1969) for the classic discussion of their livelihood and their politics. Sharon Hutchinson's *Nuer Dilemmas* (University of California Press, 1996) provides a more recent view of the Nuer, and Jon Holtzman's *Nuer Journeys, Nuer Lives* (Allyn & Bacon, 2000) discusses the Nuer as refugees to the United States. The film *The Nuer* is a beautiful portrayal of traditional village life. It is long and mercifully free of narration. Even watching a short segment will provide some sense of the physicality of Nuer life. For the Sarakatsani, see J. K. Campbell's classic *Honor, Family, and Patronage* (Oxford University Press, 1964). Located in the hills, the Sarakatsani are credited with having kept alive much of Greek culture during the onslaught of the Ottoman Turks. The seasonal migrations described by Campbell for the 1950s continue—although they are somewhat reduced.

CHAPTER 7

INDUSTRIALISTS

Industrialism is a very broad label that applies to a very wide range of technologically complex societies that have developed in different ways. Technology and society have also changed sharply since the early days of industrialism. Indeed, many people would argue that we are now in a postindustrial society. Nevertheless, certain broad patterns emerge in all these societies that differentiate them from other kinds of society, including the agricultural societies on which they were initially based. With industrialism, control over the environment is greatly expanded—expanded so much that most of our lives are spent in what we might call "engineered environments" rather than the relatively "natural" environments in which nonindustrialized societies live. That extended control over the environment is associated with enormous increases in the density of urban life and in the general complexity of social organization. It is also accompanied by significant mobility.

This chapter provides an outline of industrial societies with emphasis on their differences from the other kinds of adaptation already discussed. The first section discusses the very different relationship to the environment that characterizes industrial societies—especially their span of control and the mobility of their populations. The following sections outline the general social relations of industrial societies and how such societies fare in terms of the same nine questions asked of other kinds of society. The first case study at the end of the chapter concerns China, a country that is now undergoing massive industrialization. The second example is a personal one and concerns the new relationship between people and computers.

RELATIONSHIP TO THE ENVIRONMENT

RESOURCES, TECHNOLOGY, AND LABOR

Industrialism is about new tools and more advanced technology. Those tools and technology permit the manufacture of new, more powerful, and more numerous products. Those products may range from simple consumer goods (clothing, for example) to military goods (better guns and more of them) to machines themselves (from the small ones that run household appliances to the large ones that run nuclear power plants). These tools and technology are based on a degree of power that shifts the logic of producing things. It is horse-power without the horses, manpower without the men.

The changes wrought by industrialism may be most clearly seen by considering an example of something that other kinds of societies also produce. As such an example, compare crop production as described in the last chapter with crop production as it develops in industrial societies. In agricultural societies, a mix of technology, resources, and labor are combined in the production of the crop. Agricultural societies are not, after all, without *technology*. They have plows and those plows usually have iron tips. That means the surplus from the goods produced—let's say bags of rice for the moment—is being exchanged in some fashion for these tools. Somewhere then, must be *resources* of raw materials to make the plows, including a source of iron, a mining operation to extract it, some smelting process, and some smithing to forge that iron into the desired tool. The main resource in an agricultural society, however, is land. Improvements to that land—especially with irrigation—make it far more productive. To that improved land and the basic agricultural technology of the plow is added the *labor* of the people themselves and of their field animals. A distinctive feature of intensive cultivation is that additional labor on the land can produce a bigger harvest. Thus investments in further labor can achieve increased yields.

The situation is thus as diagramed in the top part of Figure 7.1. Resources (land) are utilized by people (using human and animal labor) through technology (plow) to produce an agricultural crop. If there is more land, productivity can increase by cultivating that new land. Generally speaking, however, most of the good agricultural land was taken up very, very long ago. Thus further improvement must be through technology or labor. If technology is limited or itself involves labor (for example, digging drainage ditches), then further improvements are made almost entirely through labor. Thus agricultural societies can and do become very dense in population.

A more industrialized version of agriculture is also possible. It involves changing the relative input of technology, resources, and labor, as shown in the bottom part of Figure 7.1. One way to do that is to use the machinery to transform the land so that it can support agriculture. Hills can be leveled, swamps drained, land reclaimed, or water diverted across large distances through canals or even pipes. Alternately, there can be direct improvements in how fields are cultivated. Some of that is achieved by using agricultural machinery to replace animal or human labor. Other factors might include better fertilizers (produced in factories rather than gathered from the local outhouses or deposited directly by the pigs); further development of plows (high-grade steel plow tip); or improvement in the crop itself through research and, ultimately, genetic engineering.

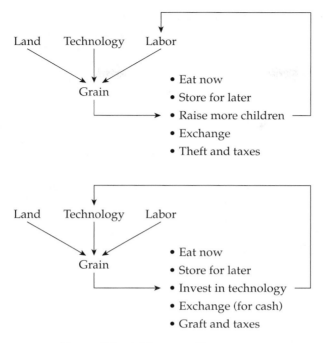

FIGURE 7.1   A MODEL OF PRODUCTION

What industrialism provides is not simply a modest change in this for-
mula, but a huge one. Some of that change has to do with yield: for example, better fertilizers and new strains of crop that can use those fertilizers. Yet
the bigger part of that change probably involves the enormous increase in
the productivity of human labor. If human labor and animal labor are no
longer alone in the fields but joined by machine labor (tractors, threshers,
harvesters), then far, far less human labor will be needed and perhaps no animal labor at all. The net result—although it will take time—is that the same
fields are producing at least as much per land unit with only a fraction of the
human labor.[1]

_____

[1]The amount produced per land unit may increase as well. That is not central to the basic argument here, but it may be worth noting how great that increase in production per land unit can
be. In the discussion in the chapter on agriculture, for example, rice yields per acre approached
1 ton for the transplanting system. These days, however, rice yields per acre are higher in almost
all countries and are far higher in countries that have switched to new crop varieties and have
mechanized rice-growing: for example, Japan and the United States (both at a 2.9 tons per acre);
and South Korea (3.1 tons per acre).

Aging steel plant on the Nervon River in the Basque region of Spain. (*Joanna B. Pinneo/Aurora & Quanta Productions, Inc.*)

The agricultural example thus shows sharp changes in the relative importance of technology and labor. That technology, in turn, hinges on some other kind of production. Just as resources (especially land), labor, and technology go together in producing the crop, so they also go together in producing the things that make it possible to produce the crops. While an iron tip for a plow might be hammered out by a local blacksmith, a tractor, its oil and gasoline, and a high-grade steel plow are probably not going to be locally produced. That means that resources (many of which are nonrenewable) will have to come from other places. Those places may be relatively close or very far off.

INCREASED RANGE OF CONTROL AND MOBILITY OF LABOR

This changed balance of inputs has many implications. Two are of particular importance because of their implications for how society is organized. First is an increase in the range of control. For industrial societies, it is necessary to have access to the full range of "production," whether it involves crop products or machine products. If you are running a farm with tractors, harvesters, and threshers, you need gasoline. This is not an optional luxury. You cannot afford to have somebody else deciding whether you will or won't have gasoline to run your tractor. That would mean that you were no longer independent. Furthermore, you have to make sure that the supplies of gasoline will exist in the future. When war comes, for example, you now have a more complicated rule: The war can't occur in your rice fields, or in your oil fields, or in any other place that will disrupt any of the things you now need to run your farm—or factory, or business. Therein lies much of the history of the twentieth century, including problems in the Middle East and the Japanese attack on Pearl Harbor—the Japanese were desperate to secure access to oil in Southeast Asia.

Second, in industrial societies labor is almost always in the wrong place. In an agricultural society, it makes perfect sense that most people are working the land. Their effort is productive. Once human labor is supplemented and eventually largely replaced by machinery in agricultural production, then that logic changes. There will then be too many people on the farm. At the same time, however, the factories producing the tractors will be expanding and thus more people will be needed there. If a tractor factory happens to be in a rural agricultural area, people could switch from one to the other relatively smoothly. That has been the argument for locating new production facilities in rural areas. However, there are likely to be many reasons to locate the factories elsewhere: closer to raw materials, closer to transportation, closer to markets, closer to other factories that use their products or furnish them with goods that they need. Labor—people—will thus have to move. Some of that movement will be from region to region. Initially, almost all of it will be from the country to the city, from predominantly agricultural jobs to predominantly industrial jobs. This movement is not, however, simply a one-time event. It continues throughout the industrializing process.[2]

SOCIAL ARRANGEMENTS

These two factors—degree of control and mobility of labor—have pervasive implications for how industrial society is organized and how people organize themselves within it. These two factors give rise to two rather different stories: one for the society as a whole and one for the people within it. The society as a whole becomes more extensive, with greater integration and greater needs for stability in its resources. The people, on the other hand, become less deeply rooted in place and move frequently into different geographical areas and sometimes into different work. For the society as a whole, there is an ever-widening expansion of the nature and kinds of links that hold it together. For the people as individuals, however, their personal links narrow as they lose their roots in both local physical communities and in extended kin groups. For the people, then, this highly complex, integrated society recreates something of the life style of foragers: people who move in relatively small groups

---

[2]The arguments for a "postindustrial" society are an extension of this argument. For industrialism, there is a displacement of labor from agriculture to industry, from countryside to city. That occurs, to simplify, because human labor is largely replaced by machine labor on the farm. The postindustrial shift has exactly the same logic. Human labor is replaced by machine labor in the factories. Once again labor is in the wrong place. The fact that a different kind of labor may be needed, makes the transition more difficult.

from place to place in search of shifting resources. Some further consideration of the issues of control and of mobility helps illuminate these two rather
different perspectives on industrialism: that of the society as a whole and that
of the individuals within it.

Industrial society is, as would be expected, operating at a much higher level
of control over the environment. Yet it is not only the overall degree of control but the different kinds of control that make a difference. Industrial society can not be characterized as a single way of adapting to the environment
but as a set of adaptations that must, in turn, be effectively integrated. Both
the individual adaptations and the integration of them must be controlled.
One problem with that level of control is that you have to create and then
maintain it. As with agriculturalists, so with industrialists. In agricultural societies, the very success of irrigation, for example, lays the basis for catastrophic famine if those irrigation systems collapse. Likewise the very success
of systems built in industrial societies creates the basis for catastrophic failure.
If power fails more than temporarily and the machines don't run, societal collapse is inevitable. So all the different parts of the system (agriculture and
mining, tractor production and food processing, power lines and transportation networks) have to work, they have to work together, and they have to
work reliably.

That requirement for the maintenance of control requires specialists who
know those different systems individually and collectively. That very degree
of specialization means that people will not understand other people's work
very well (it's too specialized). The task for the people in charge is to control
things that they do not fully understand. How do you control something that
you don't understand? Here, industrial societies have taken different roads.
Some, like the United States, have taken a relatively loose approach to economic matters, only to find that they needed to control more directly at least
some parts of the economic and financial system. Others, like China, have
stressed the need for central control by the government, only to find that they
needed to loosen that control to increase overall productivity.

The span of control in industrial society requires specialization. As different areas within that broad span of control become increasingly complex
and specialized, so will the training and education of those who conduct
the work. People will thus be different from each other in occupational
terms. These different occupations are likely to have very different characteristics: some more manual and some more mental; some more people-
oriented and some more machine-oriented; some with control over other
people and some that require following other people's orders. It is not
then, as in agricultural societies, that a few people are specialized, but that
in industrial society potentially everybody is. This removes one of the most

important commonalities that binds people together: a shared experience with their environment and their adaptation to it, whether in gathering food, gardening, hunting, or herding.

MANAGING MOBILITY

The second major theme stressed here is that with the process of industrialization, labor ends up being in the wrong place. In the early stages of industrialization, extra labor is largely in agriculture where it is no longer needed, and it consumes food resources that could be used elsewhere. In later stages of industrialization, labor may be in an industry that was once a vanguard but has now become yesterday's news: coal and steel in the central and eastern parts of Canada and the United States, textiles in the U.S. South, computers in the high tech zones around Boston, San Francisco, and Toronto. On the other hand, labor is usually *not* in the places where it is needed: wherever that new place is where the new products are being designed and developed. So, in industrial societies, people move. Even when companies move production facilities across borders to find cheaper labor, those new factories—whether in new Chinese cities or maqiladora plants on the Mexican side of the Mexico-U.S. border—also cause labor mobility as people are drawn to these new employment opportunities from other places in those countries.

It is possible to imagine cases in which this movement could be handled in a relatively organized fashion. A factory owner might, for example, choose an area that had sufficient numbers of the correctly trained people. The bigger and more specialized the business, however, the harder that is. One alternative is build an entire town around a new plant and advertise for workers in areas that have excess labor to come to this new place and settle down with their families. But there are potential problems. Perhaps it is not clear how fast production will develop and thus exactly how many workers will be needed. Perhaps those people coming with their entire families will want good wages for that move and, precisely because they have families, want such extras as good schools for their children. Think of a company that offers great benefits, including the down payment on your house, and has just given your local community ten million dollars for a new park. That's great but it will, directly or indirectly, raise costs for the business owner.

A different management approach—and one that is becoming far more common in the private sector—is simply to acknowledge that individual people are needed as labor. You don't, after all, really need families and communities, you just need people to work. Those people might sometimes be men (especially if the work is heavy) and perhaps sometimes women (especially if you believe that they will either be better at the work or perhaps do equivalent work for less money). You want that labor to be available when you need it and want it out of the way when you don't need it. (No guaranteed employment; no unions!) You want the work done well, done your way, and done as cheaply as possible. If somebody wants a raise, or gets sick or old or pregnant, you want to just be able to get rid of them and bring in somebody new who is younger, cheaper, and more tractable. This approach was—and is—frequently used. Think of the millions of undocumented workers who provide agricultural and construction labor in the United States without "requiring" fringe benefits, job security, union-level wages, or community services for their families.

MOBILITY AND THE FAMILY

While these two approaches yield a rather different tone to society, they do both address the fundamental issue of mobility. That mobility varies. It may range from a one-time move to frequent moves. A person might move from a rural home to a city, might follow a chain of migrant agricultural jobs each summer, or might move among major global cities in a career in business management. In industrial societies, it is hard to avoid such moves. If those moves are inevitable, then the logic of the forager applies: the smaller and more flexible the groups, the easier to move. The advantages of the nuclear family are impressive. It is the smallest possible unit that bridges the genders and the generations. It is thus not surprising that the kinship systems of industrialized societies resemble those of hunters and gatherers rather than those of horticulturalists, agriculturalists, and pastoralists. Yet the force exerted on people to move can fracture even the nuclear family. If both the husband and wife work, for example, their current jobs or future career development may well pull them in different directions. If they live in two separate places—and commute between them—they may well postpone having children or choose not to have them at all.

In the face of such mobility, the family itself may start to look like a liability both to the people themselves and to those who employ them. From the perspective of the person who faces a job move, family obligations are expensive, the ability to meet those expenses may be unpredictable, and the negotiations on who will move where (or commute for how long) may be aggravating. Consider it from the employer's perspective. Why effectively hire a family by paying one person enough to support a family when you can hire an individual at a sort of discounted rate. Even if you can't reduce the salary, you can save substantially on additional costs (health insurance, days lost to family business) and probably have employees who will give you more of their attention—and might even be more willing to work unpaid overtime.

This potential loss of family ties has important implications for the society: both in terms of marriages that end (divorce and its effects on children) and of marriages not made (and thus children not born). This would seem to be self-destructive to the society since the very labor force of the future is not being created. There is, indeed, concern and sometimes outright panic in many industrialized countries about exactly this decline in having children. For many countries it is immigrants to the rescue, whether as short-term workers (especially common in Europe, the Mideast, and parts of Asia) or as permanent new settlers (largely in Australia, Canada, New Zealand, and the United States). Thanks to these various forms of international migration, declines in fertility can be a cause for much hand-wringing but result in little damage to the economic future.

NINE KEY QUESTIONS

Division of Labor: In industrial societies, the division of labor is sharp and pervasive. For the vast range of specialized jobs, an ad hoc emergence of competence over time is likely to be inadequate. Instead, people will have to be specifically trained for specific jobs through formal education and structured experience on the job. Such occupational specialization may be structured around age and sex, particularly in early industrialization. However, the logic of assigning different jobs by age and sex is enormously reduced in advanced industrial societies. Thus while the division of labor is far more complicated and pervasive in industrial societies, the division of labor by age and sex is lessened.

Territoriality: Good agricultural land continues to be an immensely valuable resource. However, it is joined in importance by other kinds of natural resources. Previously unimportant kinds of land may suddenly become very important if they have resources either above or below ground. Even access to resources beyond one's own territory becomes vital: petroleum and shipping lanes, for example. For industrial societies, the link to territory is a combination of the different kinds of territoriality seen in other societies: actual full-time occupation of some territory in addition to periodic access to a broader range. Industrial societies as a whole are fiercely territorial. On the other hand, for individual people the link to specific pieces of territory may not be very strong at all.

Kinship: With mobility of the kind needed in industrial societies, kinship is greatly narrowed in scope. As with foragers, the nuclear family tends to predominate. Furthermore, the experience of the highly industrialized countries of Europe, North America, and East Asia suggests that the nuclear family itself may be fracturing: increased divorce, decreased marriage, fewer children. Such a narrow and often fractured kinship system provides limited support for people in times of need, thus the importance of general societal "safety nets." One of the dilemmas is that kinship and ties of locality are both narrowing at the same time. Thus the two prime components of human "community"—ties of blood and ties of place—are weakening concurrently.

Social Control: There is an enormous amount to argue over in industrial societies. Land continues to be valuable but there also are other kinds of valuable property. That property can usually be converted into money, which is portable and can be accumulated in large amounts. Disputes that arise, whether about property or other matters, may be among those who know each other well, but the disputes are far more likely to involve strangers or people with whom interaction has been very limited. There is thus very little informal basis for resolving disputes—nor are there the larger kinship or locality groups that could help. Instead, there is a range of specialized institutions and specialized roles for social control. Those institutions will have their own power to enforce decisions. Laws, police, judges, jails! And, of course, the lawyers to explain this unexplainable system to you.

Equality: With industrial societies, the issue of access to resources—which is fundamental to equality—is complicated. On the one hand, the sheer variety of useful resources and ways to attain them suggests that people may have expanded options for improving their lives. Furthermore, much of the rationale for differences by age and gender disappears. On the face of it, job qualifications for most jobs would not seem to require men rather than women, or the younger rather than the older—as long as the candidates happen to have equivalent preparation for the jobs. All that argues for equality. On the other hand, much of the work of industrial societies is done by machines and could not be done without them. Getting the resources to produce and fuel those machines is expensive. Capital (money) is important and that tends to give an advantage to those who already have it. In that sense, access to resources is not equal, separating those with "property" from those who have only their labor to sell.

Religious Beliefs: In industrial societies, people acknowledge a wide range of spiritual forces. However, localized kinds of spiritual forces are likely to be on the wane. Relatively unstructured nuclear families, limited memory of earlier generations, and simple distance from family grave sites all suggest that ancestors are unlikely to be very important. Likewise with spirits of land. If you are relatively mobile, such spirits are an inconvenient way to address religious issues on a day-to-day basis. Thus, much like pastoralists, those in industrial societies need a religion that travels well and that can be with them as individuals as well as members of families or other groups. World religions make sense. They provide a social connection that is broader than kin groups (although they support them), an ever-present and everywhere-present deity, and nicely portable scriptures.

Ecological Soundness: Industrial societies exact a harsh price on the environment. Like agriculturalists, industrialists make changes to the land that are often permanent. Industrialists, however, actually exhaust resources. Water from aquifers, minerals and metals from mining, and even ozone from the atmosphere are depleted in ways that can never be remedied. These things won't grow back. Unlike other human adaptations, then, industrialism is not self-sustaining on its current resources and must always find new sources of energy. Actual contamination of the planet is also occurring. One political problem with that contamination is that much of it occurs somewhere else and is thus relatively invisible to us in North America, whether it is our exported garbage or the pollution created by the factories whose products we import.

Security: The great advantage of industrialism is that it can produce almost anything, whether those goods are agricultural or industrial, necessities or luxuries, nurturing of the human spirit or just cheesy. However, as the infrastructure becomes more complex, any failure in the system has catastrophic implications. Furthermore, since the system is largely powered by nonrenewable resources, it can continue only if it finds new resources of a different kind. The worst problem is that there is, effectively, no "Plan B." Like agriculturalists, industrialists can't go back to a simpler, lower-density lifestyle. Yet as long as things do work, the physical well-being of most people in advanced industrial societies is relatively good—because of better public health and sanitation if nothing else.

External Conflict: Industrial societies are likely to be of interest to outsiders because of the value of their resources and the wide range of products that they produce. What makes the relations of industrial societies so different, however, is that with industrialism the range of resources that are of value is greatly extended. Things that once had little value, or had been buried so deeply they couldn't be mined, or had been in places that couldn't be reached, now have value. Thus industrial societies will be ever vigilant in protecting every little piece of territory that they have. Borders will be finely drawn and fiercely protected. At the same time, industrial societies will be alert to opportunities to expand beyond their own borders for resources and markets. They will always be watching to see where other resources may lie and how those resources can be controlled—no matter how far beyond their own borders those resources lie.

Case Study
China: Industrialization and Labor Migration

On a recent trip to China, I decided to get out of Shanghai and visit Nanjing, reputedly one of the most pleasant of China's big cities. I thought this might be a useful break from Shanghai with its masses of cranes and construction. Yet Nanjing was also in turmoil. As I walked down one street, workers were carefully dismantling, brick by brick, the houses that had taken up a full city block. The usable bricks were stacked up carefully on the edge of the street. That's the way things used to be done, especially since building materials have tended to be in short supply in China. As I walked south on a smaller road, there was a modern plaza area where several other small roads converged. Looking around, I noticed that all the buildings were new. In fact they were very new. A multi-story department store lay ahead. Towering above the department store—and built on it—was an office building or hotel (or perhaps a combination of the two). It was impossible to tell because they hadn't yet finished the upper stories. Yet the department store, directly below the construction, was already open. That's the new way. Somehow China was using two systems at once: hard manual labor to pull down old buildings brick by brick; huge cranes to put up new skyscrapers—and opening them before they were even finished.

China is not without an industrial base, but its progress over the last decade has been phenomenal. While growth has lagged in North America and Europe, has been almost stagnant in Japan, and has been subject to sharp fluctuations in much of the rest of Asia, China has surged forward. That growth has been in heavy industry, in raw infrastructure development (for example, a dam along the Yangtze river that will be the world's biggest; a gas pipeline across the country that will be one of the world's longest), and in science (for example, the decoding of the genetics of a major rice strain). Whether China is successful in this enormous process will be one of the most important questions of the twenty-first century. Whether it is successful quickly enough to avoid total ecological collapse is also an issue. Think of everything you know about the smoke and waste and pollution of early industrial development in Europe and North America, multiply that by ten or so, and condense it into a twenty-year period.

One of the inherent problems of industrialization is that people are in the wrong place. Originally they are rural when they need to be urban. Then they are one kind of urban (steel workers, for example) and they need to be another kind (electronics assembly or software design, for example). China is confronting both problems at the same time. It is still a country that is only about 30 percent urban. (North America, by contrast, is approximately 75 percent urban). That would suggest the need for more people in the cities. But even the small proportion of the population in the cities still yields an urban Chinese population of some 400 million people. The growth in the urban Chinese population is perhaps even more striking: China's cities experienced a

Mix of old and new architecture in Hong Kong, now again part of China. (*Chris Stowers © Dorling Kindersley*)

growth in their urban population of about 240 million people from 1975 to 2000—roughly equivalent to moving into Chinese cities the entire population of the United States.[3]

Too many people in the cities yields a surplus population that is willing to work more cheaply but strains urban resources: not enough water, electricity, sewers, schools, housing, transportation. Thus the Chinese have much the same dilemma with "illegal immigrants" from the countryside to the cities as the United States does with undocumented border crossing and visa violations. Millions of Chinese have moved from the countryside to the cities looking for work. Since the Chinese have had a strict system of residence permits that are either rural or urban, these migrants have often been in violation of their residence permits. Until recently, that was an actual crime. But punishment aside, the lack of proper residence permits affects access to all kinds of social services. These migrants—invaluable though they are to the Chinese economy—thus live a kind of floating shadow life in the cities. They are easy targets for very low wages and other kinds of discrimination. They may live in housing that is subject to demolition as entire city blocks are slated for renovation by the government. Their children may even be denied access to regular schools.

---

[3]The figures on urban populations are drawn from *World Urbanization Prospects: The 1999 Revision*, prepared by the United Nations Population Division.

These members of the floating population are not alone in their difficulties in adjusting to a rapidly changing Chinese economy. They are also joined in their pursuit of work by those who have lost their jobs in industries that were once prosperous but are now restructuring. As in the old North American industrial heartland, those who worked in what were once progressive, relatively well-paying industries, such as steel, now find themselves back on the streets living in marginal circumstances. The slogan of "Study Dazhai" from the days of Mao Zedong, when it meant to ever increase production through effort, now has a different meaning as the Dazhai plants produce, not steel, but unemployed workers.

Case Study
Computerization: Machines, Productivity, and People

Fresh from six months in Europe looking at refugee resettlement programs, I found myself back home faced with a collapse in plans for a research project on the role of the ethnic press in the United States. The funding hadn't come through. It was time for a "real" job. A newspaper ad led me to a job as a management consultant (yes, anthropologists do consulting); that job led in turn to a senior management position (yes, anthropologists do management too). That latter position was in state government in the area of workers' compensation. One part of that job included oversight over the computerization of the agency's work. It was time to see what an anthropologist could understand of these new tools, what they could accomplish, and how people related to them.

The good news was that the machines worked fairly well. They could crunch numbers, store vast amounts of information, and, once networked, could pass information around very effectively. All of a sudden, 500,000 case files didn't seem like very many. Much of the time you didn't actually even have to see the file. You could just look up the case on the computer and find out—more or less—what was going on with it. Everybody was pleased with that. Furthermore, if you needed to send somebody a letter, you could often automate that process as well. Finally, you didn't even need to go to the library to look up the case law; that now came on a CD with a variety of search options. So there were many good improvements and most people came to like what the computers did—especially when they could have a new computer with a color monitor, an engaging graphic interface, and a game or two.

There was bad news, though. One troubling problem was how individualistic the computers were. Even within a single set of computers ordered with exactly the same specifications at the same time, there were idiosyncrasies. The individuality of the machines could be entertaining at times. Thus when the electricity went out—and it often did because we had some bad wiring—you didn't really know which computers would survive. As the lights came back on, there would be the sound of dozens of computers rebooting throughout the building. Which ones wouldn't come back up? If they didn't come back up were they even worth fixing? I remember a distinct sense of comradeship as we all waited in the semi-dark to know which of the computers would return from the dead to work with us another day. The unpredictability, however, wasn't always so entertaining. The loss of a single work station was one thing, but the main databases were something else. I remember the agonies of system upgrades when I wasn't really sure that the data would survive. I finally came up with a system that backed up the data in three different ways so that I was pretty sure it could be reconstructed no matter what, but I was never fully easy in my mind.[4]

These new tools also had some interesting effects on social organization. Some people, for example, turned out to have a knack for computers. That meant there was a new kind of skill that was relevant to the work—and was a particularly good mechanism for getting a raise. There was something, then, a little revolutionary about these tools. They gave at least some people new and better work options. The computerization of information also provided some interesting protection against arbitrary authority. One day, an agency head was missing a file and claimed, in a rather nasty memorandum, that this was caused by the file clerks—the lowest paid of the organization's staff. Normally, the file clerks would have had to accept the accusation. Who were they to argue with the agency head? But now they had an option. A quick inquiry to the data processing department provided a computer-generated history of who had been doing what with the file. And, guess what, the file clerks hadn't even had the file at the time in question. An apology from the agency head! Score one point for the dignity of labor, thanks to the local computers—and computer staff.

Technology can make a positive difference. It can improve the efficiency and quality of work. It can also provide new and improved opportunities for people—including those who are relatively underprivileged. But there can be negative consequences as well. That agency head who was constrained to make an apology, for example, was also quite interested in whether he could monitor the computer e-mail of those same staff. Computerization, as everybody now knows, provides the basis for vastly increased surveillance in the workplace and highly effective intrusions into personal privacy at home as well. Therein lies the fundamental question for technological innovation: Are the benefits worth the dangers? Those dangers are heightened when a few can control that innovation for their own purposes.

---

[4]Any reasonable database will now do a variety of replications automatically. In the old days, however, the creation of a de facto replication was a little more difficult. I actually had to program a matching computer to think it was the primary data base machine since that was the only way I could get it to test a full reload of the backup tapes. That's a rather practical example of false consciousness and its virtues in the workplace.

SOURCES

Industrialism covers a vast territory as an academic subject. Unlike many other issues in which anthropologists have an interest, it crosscuts the territory of virtually every other social science. What distinguishes the anthropological approach to industrialism is its interest in industrialism compared to other human social systems and its tendency to look at some of the back roads and ill-lit corners of the industrial world. Thus anthropologists have been strongly interested in the fate of ethnic minorities; the growth of cities (thus urban anthropology); what happens to nonindustrial countries when industrial countries want something they have (thus colonial and postcolonial studies); what happens when humans and human relations are subject to large economic forces (thus interest in commodification, globalization, and migration); and how people view the world when there is rapid social and economic change (thus arguments about modernism and postmodernism). Much of how anthropologists sort these issues out can be traced through the main anthropology journals in terms of theory (especially the *American Anthropologist* and the *Journal of Anthropological Theory*) or in the things that anthropologists do (especially *Human Organization* and *Practicing Anthropology*). Bruno Latour's *We Have Never Been Modern* (Harvard University Press, 1993) remains a good statement of why anthropologists should *not* entangle themselves in the debates about modernity and postmodernity.

For the case study on China, two recent edited volumes will give something of the flavor of the enormous changes as China industrializes and urbanizes: *Chinese Society: Change, Conflict, and Resistance* (Routledge, 2000; Elizabeth J. Perry and Mark Selden, editors) and *The New Chinese City: Globalization and Market Reform* (Blackwell, 2002; John R. Logan, editor). Li Zhang's *Strangers in the City* (Stanford University Press, 2001) provides an invaluable interpretation of China's floating population. For a more rural perspective on economic development, see Gregory Ruf's *Cadres and Kin* (Stanford University Press, 1998). The computerization example derives from my own experience (see "The Promise and Perils of Computerization," *Journal of Applied Behavioral Science*, 1999 and "Better Tools, Better Workers," *American Journal of Public Administration*, 2003), but there are many anthropologists who are concerned with similar issues. Two books that give a sense of anthropological approaches to new technology include David Hakken's *Cyborgs@cyberspace? An Ethnographer Looks to the Future* (Routledge, 1999) and Julian Orr's *Talking about Machines* (Cornell University Press, 1996). See also the *Anthropology of Work Review* (published by the Society for the Anthropology of Work).

PART II

(*David Young-Wolff/PhotoEdit, Inc.*)

STRUCTURES

CHAPTER 8

INTRODUCTION TO PART II, STRUCTURES

The way human beings relate to different environments illustrates both the basic logic of human society and the extent of its variation. Another way to look at human societies is to focus less on environmental adaptation and more directly on the way people are linked together in society. That is the subject of this second part of the book. As the material in Part I indicates, kinship is very often the major basis for social interaction, and the anthropological record is very clear on the importance, variability, complexity, and pervasiveness of kinship in human society. There are, however, other bases for linking people together, conventionally assigned to the categories of politics, economics, and religion.

This chapter introduces Part II and its emphasis on the structures in which people jointly live. The chapter begins with a brief review of lessons from Part I, then turns to some common distinctions used in describing the structure of social relations. It concludes with a brief introduction to the five chapters in Part II and how they are organized.

SOME LESSONS ABOUT ADAPTATIONS

Many of the discussions and examples in Part II rest on insights from Part I. Several of these are worth reiterating.

CONTROL, DENSITY, COMPLEXITY, MOBILITY

Throughout the discussion of foragers, horticulturalists, agriculturalists, pastoralists, and industrialists, there have been four common themes. The extent of *control* over the environment varies greatly and is reflected in the degree of control over the society itself. In turn, increased control over the environment usually yields increased *density* of settlement. The greater the degree of density, the more often people will be organized into larger groups and the more frequently people will be dealing with people that they do not know well. They may even be dealing with total strangers. That control over nature and over society, combined with increased density, results in greater *complexity* of most social institutions. This does not mean, however, that all aspects of life will necessarily be more complex. Kinship, for example, becomes *less* complex in industrial societies than in most agricultural and pastoralist societies, as many of its functions are taken over by formal economic, political, and religious institutions. Yet, overall, industrial societies are indeed more complex in their social arrangements. *Mobility* is the unpredictable factor. Here societies end up in unusual combinations. Thus industrialists find themselves more aligned with foragers and pastoralists than with the agriculturalists, to whom they are otherwise rather similar.

CORE SOCIAL BUILDING BLOCKS

The examination of different adaptations also provides insight into the basic building blocks of human society. *Age* and *sex* are the most important. They are, however, joined by the great organizing principles of *kinship* and *location*. It is crucial to remember the range of possibilities in how these building blocks can be organized in particular societies. Differences by sex, for example, may be sharp or blurred: Men and women may work together or apart, property may be held by, or passed through, men or women or both. People's relationship to location is also highly variable. The resulting differences in the mobility of people have wide-ranging effects on social relations. Finally, consider the variation in how kinship is structured in different societies. Industrialists and foragers are at the opposite ends of the continuum in terms of control over nature, but their kinship patterns are closer to each other than to horticulturalists, agriculturalists, and pastoralists. Yet in terms of the need for individual mobility, that similarity makes sense. Both foragers and those in industrial societies often have to move and, when they do so, the portability of the nuclear family has great advantages.

SOME BASIC IDEAS ABOUT SOCIAL ORGANIZATION

Part II builds on these lessons from Part I by emphasizing the links among people rather than between people and the environment. In many cases, the discussions in Part II follow very closely from Part I. It will come as no surprise, for example, that agricultural and pastoralist societies have particularly extended kinship systems. Nor will it come as a surprise that agricultural societies have more elaborate political systems than horticulturalists. On the other hand, some of the discussions in Part II may provide some unexpected insights. The complexity of economic relations in technologically simple societies, for example, may come as a surprise, as may some of the similarities in religion among societies that seem so different in how they adapt to their environment.

STRUCTURES AND INSTITUTIONS

Central to the consideration of social relations in Part II is the notion of *structure*. The use of that term follows directly from the insights of the early structural-functionalists. Both Radcliffe-Brown and Malinowski viewed societies as what we normally call systems: They are composed of parts arranged in structured (rather than random) ways and different parts of the system provide useful functions for the system as a whole. This doesn't mean that everything in a society always works well. It only means that it is better to start off asking how things do work rather than assuming that they don't work or that they are simply leftovers from days gone by.

This notion of structure in society is also sometimes discussed in terms of the word *institution*. That word has two general meanings. The first, and the more relevant one here, has to do with a well-established pattern of behavior or relationships. Thus "marriage is an institution" means that marriage is a well-established pattern of behavior (people get married) and of relationships (people are related to each other directly or indirectly through marriage). The second meaning, and less relevant here, involves what are called *formal institutions.* Here things become a little murkier since marriage itself might be seen as a formal institution (it is a legal matter, after all) to some people while to others a formal institution ought to be something more concrete—like the church in which the marriage takes place. For either situation, however, something that is simply customary becomes formally established in a direct physical sense—either an actual building or some formal legal document.

What both structure and institutions provide, above all, is a reliable framework within which people can live. So if you are talking about the structures or institutions of a society, you are talking about all those things that do not have to be decided anew each day. They are there for you, and you can to a very large degree organize your life according to them. That does not mean that things won't change, but it does mean that—unless you are spirited off to a new world entirely—change will take place incrementally and in terms of that framework. Thus our institution of marriage involves a union of a man and a woman. While there is a debate in the United States about whether a same-sex union should have legal standing, there is no debate (except in very limited circles) about moving beyond pair-bonding in legal marriage—even though having multiple spouses is extremely common in the anthropological record. Clearly the institution of marriage in North America is indeed a relationship of couples.

SOME KEY DISTINCTIONS

In talking about the structures and institutions of a society, various distinctions are often used to help sort issues out. These typically come in pairs. One of the most common is the distinction between *status* and *role*. Status refers to a person's position in the social structure whereas role refers to the things they are expected to do. The two are, however, generally tied together. Thus if someone has a particular status (child, spouse, senator, student), they should act in ways appropriate to that. The point of the distinction is that the actual slots in the system and the behavior expected of people in those slots are not automatically the same thing. A related distinction is that between *individuals* and *persons*. An individual is a single human being. A person, in a technical sense, is that individual in relationship to others. It is the social face of the individual as part of a set of people. The Christian trinity is not, after all, about three individuals but about three persons. The point of the distinction is that in many (perhaps most) situations, people are not acting as autonomous detached individuals but are instead acting out expected social roles as persons.

Another important distinction is between *social relations* and *societal relations*. In complex societies, people have many of the same kinds of personal social relationships that they have in smaller-scale societies. But there are also relationships that have more to do with the society as a whole. Conventionally, social relations are about the specific personal relationships that people have, whereas societal relations are about broader relationships in the society as a whole. For example, kinship in industrial societies is extremely important in the personal social relationships of people, but it is not very important in overall societal relationships. The point of the distinction is that—especially in complex, large-scale societies—there are two stories: that of the individual people in their daily lives and that of the society overall.

A final distinction worth noting is between the *solidarity of sameness* and the *solidarity of difference*. One of the key questions for all human societies is what keeps people together. One option is that they are together because of their similarities. They see each other as the same and thus belong together. The other option is that they are together because of their differences. They see each other as complementary and thus belong together. Most societies will have relationships of both kinds. One of the most interesting examples in contemporary North American society is that of gender and the extent to which men and women are the same (as human beings) or different (based on their different reproductive roles). The main point of the distinction is to remember that what binds people together can be one or the other—or both.

Dealing with Diversity

CATEGORIES OF DIFFERENCE

In even the smallest scale society, there is a great degree of diversity. People must find a way to organize this diversity, to develop a clear way of distinguishing who other people are and how they should be treated. Perhaps they are family, friends, or neighbors. If not, there may still be some way to establish a connection. There may be, for example, a common ancestor, a common clan membership, or a common past experience (religious service, military service). On the other hand, some people may be truly unrelated and need to be either brought into the existing web of social relations or treated in some new or different way. If they are different, they may be highly educated and thus worthy of respect, rich and worthy of cultivation, or unreliable and perhaps dangerous, thus requiring careful watching. Whether people are the same or different does not necessarily determine whether there will be a relationship—whether weak or strong—but it is crucial to determining the nature of that relationship.

On an individual level, then, people need a way of categorizing other people that makes sense to them, is relatively easy to use, and also relatively practical. Each of these points is crucial. This system of categorization must *make sense*. If it doesn't make sense, people will object to it and the system will lose its value. Furthermore, the system must be relatively *easy to use*. If it is complex to apply, then the effort needed may be too great. This is one of the reasons why race, gender, and age are so often used in categorizing people. These categories seem to be fairly easily determined based on quick physical observation. Finally, the system has to be *practical*. If the system persistently yields wrong conclusions or wrong results it is counterproductive. Thus if white people don't act as expected—or women, or the elderly, or parents, or Asians, or Chinese, or Hispanics—the system becomes counterproductive.

SORTING DIVERSITY, MAINTAINING CONTROL

Dealing with difference thus requires some categories into which people can be placed. Almost any system of categorization, however, has problems. Sometimes the problems have to do with whether the basic criteria do or do not make sense. We could, as the phrenologists used to do, categorize people by the bumps on their heads. But it is not going to be much help since we now know that bumps on the head don't reveal much about people. That, of course, is a useful warning about how ways of categorizing people fade in and out of fashion. Another frequent problem is that people are not always easily classifiable even in the simplest systems. A system that relies on clear physical markers would seem to be the easiest to use. Yet categorization systems that rely on physical markers, such as race, are notorious for having very large numbers of people who cannot be accurately classified. They are somehow in between, a little of this and a little of that. It thus frequently turns out that some seemingly sensible way of categorizing people according to obvious physical features doesn't work very well. It then becomes necessary either to abandon the system or do some maintenance work to make sure that people fit cleanly into the categories. That means making sure people look the way they're supposed to look and behave the way they are supposed to behave. A system for sorting out human diversity thus often becomes a system of control. For example, if races or ethnic groups really are supposed to be different, then it will be absolutely essential that they not intermarry.

There are many bases on which systems of categorizing people can be developed. Age, class, religion, disability, and political opinion, for example, are all extremely important in how people think, act, experience life, and are evaluated by others. But perhaps the four ways that currently receive the greatest attention in the contemporary North American scene are race, ethnicity, gender, and sexual orientation. All seem to refer to some dimension of human diversity that is significant, all are seemingly open to relatively objective verification of what people do if not always exactly how they look, and all would seemingly provide some reasonable prediction of what people are like and how you might best deal with them. If nothing else, these categories help determine your similarity to, or difference from, other people. That is an issue, in the terms given above, of social relations. These categories of difference may also, however, be crucial to societal relations. Thus many kinds of social difference are built into the economic and political structures of a society. That suggests that understanding these categories of difference may be difficult, since the categories are operating on two levels: a personal one of sorting out difference and a societal one.

RACE AND ETHNICITY

Race purportedly refers to physical differences among people, but its accuracy to any significant human physical variation has been strongly contested by anthropologists for over a century. Certainly there is nothing like any clear breakdown of the human population into a defined number of races. But that has not kept people from believing that racial distinctions are real and from doing the maintenance work necessary to impose those distinctions in situations in which people do not conform to the stereotypes. The vigor in that maintenance work depends on the social, economic, and political issues at stake. In the colonial United States, for example, the constant search for cheap labor brought a wide range of migrants to the United States in various degrees of servitude. Some were temporarily indentured servants. Others were slaves. Even though an independent United States soon banned the "import" of additional slaves, there were very strong incentives to make sure slavery itself was not abolished. The economic system required the labor of slaves and the political system was perpetually threatened by the number of slaves—often the majority in particular areas. Thus it was vital to maintain racial distinctions to justify slavery and to make sure slaves could be easily identified and controlled. Even after emancipation, the racial distinctions remained. The result was a system of social differentiation and control almost as rigid as slavery itself. While supporters of the system might argue that the races lived "separate but equal" lives, the economic and political reality was of racial *stratification*—a system in which diversity is not of groups side by side, but of groups that are assigned to higher and lower strata in a social hierarchy.

Compared to race, ethnicity seems a relatively benign way to categorize people. Yet it usually invokes biology as well. Ethnicity is generally considered to be carried in the blood—you are what your parents were. Ethnicity, however, also acknowledges the experiential and cultural heritage of a people—you are what you grew up to be. Ethnicity as a system of categorizing people thus has its strength in being based in both biology and culture but not precisely limited to either. That combination makes it appear sensible. It is also eminently practical, since knowing people's ethnic background is a useful—even necessary—step toward knowing how to deal with them. Ethnicity also has clear markers that let you know how somebody fits into the system. Part of that is quite explicitly biological. Koreans, or Japanese, or Haitians, many people maintain, look a certain way. Not simply skin color, but height and heft, noses and ears. That physical differentiation is amplified by cultural markers: kind of clothing, hair style, bearing, gestures. Ethnicity is also usually announced with sound cues: a different language with a different pace, sound, and intonation, all of which often result in a distinctive accent in English. The blending of who somebody is by biological parentage and who that person is by cultural heritage is a powerful one. That power helps explain the broad use of ethnic categories in contemporary North American society.

Despite its virtues, ethnicity shares with race some fundamental problems. One is that ethnicity can also be turned to purposes of social exclusion and control. Indeed, ethnicity is in many ways a stronger statement than race. To say that somebody is ethnically different is to say that they are both biologically and culturally different. In many countries, there is not much distinction between racial and ethnic classification. For Japanese and Koreans, for example, being Japanese or Korean is something that is absolutely distinctive in cultural terms but also carried in the blood. North Americans are rather more flexible. For example, interracial and international adoption are common. Yet even in those cases, the adoptive parents may be unsure how much of ethnicity is carried in the blood, and thus how much their children have a separate heritage. The adoptive children, in turn, may seek out the "original" part of their identity. They may be American or Canadian by upbringing but something else by heritage.

Another difficulty with ethnic categories is that, as with race, many people do not fit neatly into the system. Identifying somebody as Korean American, for example, would seem to make general sense. But the range of that term is enormous. Was this person American-born? Does he or she actually speak Korean? Has he or she even been to Korea? Studies of immigrants consistently show the unpredictability of ethnicity depending on the personal situation of the person and the specific environment. Many people do not fit neatly into the categories because of mixed parentage. If one of your parents is native-born Korean and the other white American or perhaps American-born Filipino-American, what are you? Once again, a system of categorization chosen precisely because it seems to make sense, is easy to apply, and will help in dealing with other people, turns out not to be terribly reliable in any of those regards. Yet as with race, ethnic categories are often important for social, economic, or political reasons. It may thus be necessary to do some "maintenance work" to ensure that people do fit into the proper categories. Ethnicity will then be more carefully defined and regulated: People will have to belong to one group or another; intermarriage will be discouraged and perhaps outlawed; and behavior that is "improper" will be punished. Those lines may be drawn through free choices of those within the ethnic group, but they may also be imposed by the wider society.

GENDER AND SEXUAL ORIENTATION

Biological sex, like age, is an important kind of physical human diversity. Thus it is quite predictable that people will distinguish men from women, girls from boys. There are, after all, important biological distinctions between men and women. Women bear the children and are likely—for reasons of breast-feeding if nothing else—to be the primary caretakers during a child's very early years. Yet the actual way that men and women live and act varies by individual personality and by social and cultural context. If women do not bear children, for example, much of the logic of the division of labor by sex disappears. Thus differences between men and women are now conventionally discussed under the term *gender*, rather than sex. The term gender acknowledges the social and cultural ways in which "sex" is constructed. Gender, like race and ethnicity, thus encompasses both biological and social factors. As a way to categorize people, gender would seem to make good sense. Whatever the exact mix of biology and culture in the construction of gender, the combined impact is high, and people readily explain their own and other people's behavior based on gender. Since there is a great deal at stake in the relations between men and women—control of property, access to resources, reproductive rights, and thus the entire future of the social group—it is hardly surprising that differences between the genders are often sharply drawn and sharply enforced on both men and women.

The issues of gender take on added complexity when sexual orientation is added to the discussion. The anthropological record is very clear on the wide range of sexual activities and relationships in which humans engage. Sexual relations among men and among women are common in many cultures. In some cases, those sexual activities go against gender stereotypes. Thus the *berdache* in Plains Indian society was a man who generally acted as a female (thus *transgendered* in current terminology), even to the point of marrying a man. That was acceptable, but it did involve a de facto shift in gender. For many other societies, however, engaging in sexual relations with someone of the same sex is a quite customary form of sexual activity that accords with stereotypic gender status. Thus, as for the Etoro, men may have sexual relations with women for the purposes of producing children, but sexual relations with men are a normal, even preferred, form of sexual activity. As for the *mati* relationships among Surinamese women, Mati women may engage in sexual relations with women without being seen as unwomanly and without precluding sexual relations with men.[1]

These interrelated issues of gender and sexual orientation are now undergoing change and considerable debate in North American society. In the United States, the legalization of same-sex unions (Vermont) and then same-sex marriages (Massachusetts) has helped crystallize the combined issues into a broader social debate. The question is no longer about the range of human sexual activity, but rather about the specific sexual relationship with a single person that will be formally sanctioned as a legitimate marriage in the eyes of society, church, and state.

STRUCTURE OF THE CHAPTERS IN PART II

Part II has five chapters. The first two deal with kinship. Anthropologists have spent a great deal of time studying kinship. They have done so because they have found that human beings use kinship in far more extensive and interesting ways than we would know from the Euro-American tradition. As will be seen, the issue of kinship is, in fact, a set of several related issues: how people reckon their relations with others, whom they live with and interact with on a daily basis, what broader sets of kin they interact with on at least some occasions, and whom they marry. The next three chapters then address sequentially economics, politics, and religion. These are somewhat arbitrary categories since the anthropological record suggests that these domains often overlap. Nevertheless, these are the conventional categories and work reasonably well in sorting out different facets of society that then—as always with anthropologists—must somehow be put back together again to understand the society as a whole.

The structure of the chapters is more variable than in Part I since it is not possible to analyze kinship, politics, economics, and religion in exactly parallel fashion. Nevertheless, each chapter has roughly the same framework

---

[1]The respective sources are Raymond C. Kelly's *Etoro Social Structure* (University of Michigan Press, 1980) and Gloria Wekker's "Mati-ism and Black Lesbianism," *Journal of Homosexuality/Lesbianism* 24, 3–4 (1993): 145–158.

and begins with two or three major issues to provide a general orientation to the topic. Each chapter then moves to more detailed considerations and more technical material—often including the specific terminology that has been developed to give some precision to anthropological analysis. As with Part I, each chapter concludes with two case studies. Several of those case studies are continuations from Part I. The Nuer, for example, reappear in the chapter on politics and the Vietnamese in the first of the kinship chapters.

CHAPTER 9

KINSHIP: TERMINOLOGY AND HOUSEHOLDS

Trying to understand kinship has probably been anthropology's biggest challenge. What is in some ways very simple turns out to be complex and highly variable across different societies. Some societies recognize relatively few relatives; others recognize a far greater number. Some societies remember only a few generations of ancestors; others maintain lists of ancestors that cover hundreds of years. Some societies are content to acknowledge a large number of relatives under such a general category as "uncles and aunts" or "cousins"; others demand that the exact relationship be specified. Even the basic notions of motherhood and fatherhood vary: For some societies, the blood relationships through the father determine who the most important kin are; for other societies, the crucial blood connection is through the mother.

This chapter is the first of a two-chapter sequence dealing with kinship. This first chapter introduces four key questions about kinship and then addresses in more detail the first two of those questions: what terms are used to describe kin in different societies, and what kin live together on a daily basis, usually in what we call a household. The first of the case studies at the end of the chapter returns to Vietnam for a discussion of kin terms. The second provides a discussion of households among the Western Apache, a matrilineal society. The succeeding chapter will then address the issues of how larger kin groups are formed and how marriage is organized.

FOUR QUESTIONS

The discussion of kinship in this and the next chapter is organized in terms of four key questions. A brief preview of these four questions may be of assistance.

First, how do people reckon who their kin are? After all, there are numerous people with whom one is related to some degree by blood—or by marriage. Sometimes the relative importance of the kin seems clear. Your brothers and sisters, for example, are biologically closer than your cousins, and your parents are closer than your uncles and aunts. However, trying to prioritize—at least for us—different kinds of cousins, aunts, and uncles is more difficult. It thus makes sense as an initial foray into kinship simply to ask people who their kin are and how they categorize those kin. This identifies the specific terms that people use for kin in particular societies and thus permits some comparison among different societies. This is the question of *kinship terminology.*

Second, with which particular kin do people actually live? Some people may live in large three-generational family groups; others in smaller nuclear families of only father, mother, and children. Those kinds of household group reflect the history of who is added to the group and who moves away. Many of those comings and goings are relatively predictable. When children are born, for example, they will usually live with their parents until adulthood. However, there is one crucial decision point in almost all societies: getting the parents together in the first place. After all, the mother-to-be and father-to-be usually (although not always) grow up in separate households. If they are to live together—as they usually do—somebody has to move. This is the question of *postmarital residence.*

Third, how are large kin groups constructed? In many societies, and certainly most horticultural, agricultural, and pastoralist societies, kin groups can extend far beyond the immediate household. Those kin groups can include hundreds, even thousands, of people. That requires a different level of organization of kinship and usually some very clear rules about who belongs to these larger groups. The variations are extensive, but the largest groups and the most versatile kin structures usually involve a clear rule about whether people belong to their mother's (and her mother's) group or to their father's (and his father's) group. Those are, respectively, the *matrilineal* and *patrilineal* options. This is the question of *descent.*

Fourth, how do men and women come together in marriage and what implications does that marriage have for their relatives? Marriage is highly variable. In some societies, people may marry only one person at a time; in others they have multiple spouses—having multiple wives is rather common but having multiple husbands also occurs. The exact choice of spouse is crucial for the couple, for the families in which they grew up, and for the children they will have. For example, if a society has two large kin groups and those kin groups always marry people from the other group (Lees marry Smiths and Smiths marry Lees), those groups will be strongly allied to each other. They will share grandchildren—which is a strong bond indeed.

Discussion of kinship terminology and postmarital residence follow below; larger kin groups and marriage are discussed in the next chapter.

KINSHIP TERMINOLOGY

The first question, then, is what people call their kin. This is a very simple question and a typically anthropological one. Why make assumptions about a society's kinship system when you can just ask the people themselves? From

A three-generation Mexican family. (*N. Frank/The Viesti Collection, Inc.*)

this simple question about kin has come some interesting material that does not usually match the Euro-American experience. Anthropologists have thus had to find a more specific, descriptive way of talking about kinship than using such words as "aunt" and "uncle," which reflect our own cultural categories about who our kin are. A brief introduction to this more technical way of talking about kin is needed.

Figure 9.1 provides a simple chart with four generations. Several points need to be made about this diagram. First, this is a very simple diagram. There could easily be multiple brothers and sisters, and multiple marriages as well. There are often missing people and replacements for them: For example, a father dies and the mother remarries a man who already has children of his own. Kinship can become very complex. This kind of diagram inevitably understates that complexity.

Second, some kind of reference point is needed to anchor any discussion since, lacking such a reference point, a particular person might be a mother, a sister, or a daughter. That is the purpose of having a shaded figure. That person is called *ego*. In this case, the box (meaning a person of either gender) is shaded. Therefore, the triangle directly above the shaded box would be identified as "*f*" for father or, more technically as *ego's father*.

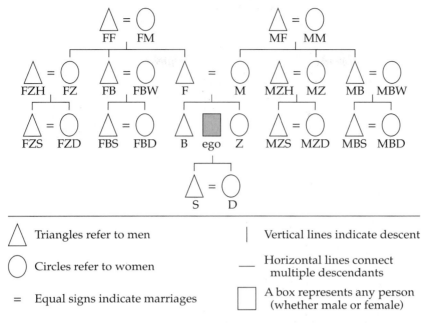

FIGURE 9.1 ANTHROPOLOGICAL CONVENTIONS FOR REFERRING TO KIN

Finally, the diagram helps in tracing relationships *a step at a time.* This avoids ambiguity. For North Americans, for example, the person labeled *"fb"* (father's brother) would be an "uncle." But "uncle" is ambiguous since it also refers to *"mb"* (mother's brother) and even to the husbands of *"fz"* (father's sister) and *"mz"* (mother's sister). It is the same with people we would call cousins. In the chart they are indicated by their exact relationship: for example *"fbd"* (father's brother's daughter) or *"mzs"* (mother's sister's son).

When we look at kinship, our own terms like "uncle," "aunt," and "cousin" are ambiguous. This is an early warning that different societies may have very different ways of organizing kin relations. There are four general ways in which kin are reckoned in different societies. Although these systems vary, there is very good logic in all of them. Much of that logic reflects the basics of age and sex, generation and gender, that were discussed in Part I of this book. Gender is universally recognized in kin terminology (fathers differ from mothers, sisters from brothers) as is age (one's own generation is distinguished from the parental generation). Kin terminology is thus always based partially on the elements of generation and gender that affect so much of social life. Indeed, the first of the four major kinds of kinship terminology can be explained entirely on that basis.

GENDER AND GENERATION

The simplest kind of kinship terminology (see Figure 9.2) is based solely on the two issues of gender and generation. There are separate terms for "mother" and "father." Those terms mean "female and male one generation up." Your sisters and brothers are *not* one generation up, so they have separate terms. "Sister" and "brother" mean female and male of your own generation. Likewise (not shown in the chart), "daughter" and "son" mean female and male one generation "down." Thus one's father is called "father," one's mother "mother," and so on. And that's it. Your father's brother (*fb*) is thus also a "father" since he too is a male one generation up. So also is your mother's brother (*mb*), and even your mother's sister's husband (*mzh*). All the women one generation up are "mothers," all the males of one's own generation are "brothers," and all of the females are "sisters." This is called, eponymously, *Hawaiian kinship terminology*—even though many other societies have a similar system. This does not mean that Hawaiians don't know who their immediate parents are and can't describe them if they want to. But the core terminology is elegantly simple in its invocation of the elementary principles of gender and generation. It has the nice implication that there is a general parental quality to all people one generation up (the *ascending* generation), a general child quality to those one generation down (the *descending* generation), and a general brotherly or sisterly quality to those of one's own generation.

GENDER, GENERATION, AND NUCLEARITY

From a Euro-American perspective, what is oddest about Hawaiian kinship terminology is precisely this reference to "aunts" and "uncles" as "mothers" and "fathers." The terminology seems to ignore the fundamental importance of one's actual mother, one's actual father, and one's actual brothers and sisters. The terms ignore what we take to be the boundaries of the nuclear family. The solution would be to add a third principle that should be recognized in the terminology: whether or not a relative is part of the immediate, nuclear family. The addition of nuclearity to gender and generation produces the

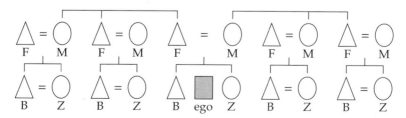

FIGURE 9.2   HAWAIIAN KINSHIP TERMINOLOGY

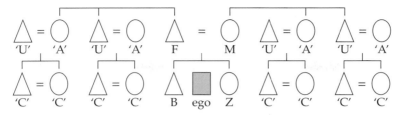

FIGURE 9.3 ESKIMO KINSHIP TERMINOLOGY

terminology shown in Figure 9.3. Here "brother" and "sister" are reserved for the actual brother (*b*) and actual sister (*z*). "Mother" and "father" are likewise reserved. All the other relatives one generation up are thus "not fathers" and "not mothers" and all the other relatives of one's own generation are "not sisters" and "not brothers." This is, again eponymously, *Eskimo kinship terminology*. It is, of course, standard North American terminology as well. In our terms, the "not mothers" are "aunts" and the "not fathers" are "uncles." For "not brothers" and "not sisters," English speakers don't even distinguish by gender; they are simply "cousins."

GENDER, GENERATION, AND LINEALITY

Although the Eskimo system has its merits, one result is that terms like "aunt," "uncle," and "cousin" cover a very wide range of people, including people to whom you are related through your mother and through your father. The terms also include people who are spouses of your blood relatives rather than being themselves your blood relatives. The Eskimo terminology is thus extraordinarily vague about all your relatives except the ones in your immediate nuclear family. One alternative is to discard the principle of nuclearity and instead consider the principle of lineality—whether relatives are related to you through your mother or through your father. This alternative terminology would indicate gender and generation, of course, and in addition to that, the *side* of the family for each relative. The result (see Figure 9.4)

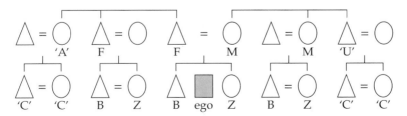

FIGURE 9.4 IROQUOIS KINSHIP TERMINOLOGY

has some interesting implications. "Mother" is again no longer restricted to your actual mother, but includes your mother and her sister (*mz*). This makes some sense even in Euro-American terms because insofar as you have a "backup" mother, the most likely relative would be your mother's sister. Likewise, your father and his brother (*fb*) would both be "father." The children of the brothers and sisters of your parents now fall into two groups. Those who are the children of your "father" (*f* and *fb*) or of your mother (*m* and *mz*) are necessarily your "brothers" and "sisters." The others (*mbd, mbs, fzd, fzs*) are not. This is called *Iroquois kinship terminology*[1] and it is a very common kind of terminology.

GENDER, GENERATION, NUCLEARITY, AND LINEALITY

Iroquois is a good general-purpose terminology. It separates out your relatives based on whether they are linked through the mother or through the father. That is helpful if the society uses patrilineality or matrilineality as the basis for some kind of larger kin groups (as will be discussed in the next chapter). However, the result still fails to distinguish your "real" father from your father's brother and your "real" mother from your mother's sister. The system also lumps together a variety of people as brothers and sisters, including not only nuclear and non-nuclear relatives but also relatives from both sides of the family. In that sense, it seems to defeat its own purpose of distinguishing the two sides of the family. Given such problems, one might argue that it would be more precise to distinguish *both* nuclearity and lineality rather than choosing between them. The result is what is usually called, again eponymously, *Sudanese kinship terminology*. It is also sometimes simply called *descriptive kinship terminology* precisely because it does what the anthropologists try to do: Describe each kin relationship exactly. Sudanese kinship terminology is diagrammed in Figure 9.5. Here, your father, your father's brother,

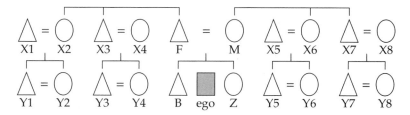

FIGURE 9.5   SUDANESE KINSHIP TERMINOLOGY

---

[1]There are variants of Iroquois that are tailored to match the specific needs of patrilineal and matrilineal societies. These are called, respectively, Omaha and Crow. With reluctance, I am not including a discussion here for purposes of brevity.

and your mother's brother are all clearly distinguished; likewise, your mother, your mother's sister, and your father's sister.

Perhaps the most general implication of this discussion of terminology is the variation. Different human societies conceptually organize their world of kin in different ways. That variation in kinship terminology reflects the human basics of gender and generation, with the addition of distinctions about whether kin are inside or outside the nuclear family and whether they are on the mother's or father's side of the family. Terminology thus provides a useful guide to kinship in particular societies and to the common human basics seen in all societies. Yet the terms are, after all, just terms. A different starting point in looking at kinship provides a contrast—one that emphasizes not kin terms but the actual people with whom one lives.

POSTMARITAL RESIDENCE

FAMILIES AND HOUSEHOLDS

In most societies, most of the time, people live together in households of some sort. Those households are generally composed of kin, either by blood or marriage. Most people, most of the time, are thus living in something we might call family households. Those family households provide the framework for much of daily life: for eating, sleeping, social relations, and much of economic life as well. These households nevertheless vary greatly in their composition. They may be big or small. Some may include only relatives and some may include nonrelatives. They may have the same membership throughout the year and for many years, or they may shift in composition over the seasons (as with nomadic groups) or change every few years. These households also live in varying physical structures: from temporary huts and camps to imposing high-rises; from small structures (in which the whole family may sleep in the same room) to very large ones. Finally, the boundaries of households may be firmly fixed or be relatively porous. Individual households, in some societies, tend to be part of larger compounds—and that compound may be the arena for much of the daily interaction. On the other hand, what seems like a single, large household may, in fact, include groups of people whose daily lives are largely separate from each other. They may, for example, have a separate hearth where they cook and around which they eat their own meals.

All these various kinds of family household share one fundamental dilemma. In their midst are children who are (usually) the offspring of a married couple within that household. When those children grow up, they will then usually marry and have children themselves. That means that somehow those two people from different households are going to have to get together. If they are to live together, at least one of them (and possibly both) will have to move. That decision about who will move is a fateful one, for it shapes what the future household will be. This is why the issue of *postmarital residence* is so crucial.

There are various types of postmarital residence. The major ones are as follows:

Neolocal: One resolution to the dilemma is for the new couple to set up their own household, separate from either of the households in which they were raised. This is the common pattern in North America. This is thus a new (*~neo* means new) household rather than the continuation or extension of an existing one.

Uxorilocal: Here the couple resides with the wife (*~uxor*). This assumes that the wife has already established her own household to which the husband comes. This occurs but is relatively rare because women tend not to live alone—rather, they remain with their original family until marriage.

Matrilocal: Here the couple resides with the wife's family. Technically, this is sometimes called *uxorimatrilocal*—specifying that the residence is with the wife's mother (rather than with the husband's mother). This common form of postmarital residence has some significant advantages that will be discussed below.

Virilocal: Here the couple resides at the husband's (*~vir*) household. This assumes that the husband has already established his own household. That is more often the case than with the wife, so virilocal residence is more common than uxorilocal residence.

Patrilocal: Here the couple resides with the husband's family. Technically, this is sometimes referred to as *viripatrilocal*—specifying that the residence is with the husband's father (rather than the wife's father). This is also a very common form of postmarital residence with some significant advantages—and disadvantages—for both men and women.

Avunculocal: It is also possible that the couple will reside with a different relative. Sometimes this is simply a matter of chance: Perhaps a husband's father has died but the husband's father's brother is managing his property and the couple goes to live with him. However, it is sometimes also the case that the preferred residence is with an uncle (*~avunculus*). This is common in matrilineal societies where—as you may remember from the discussion of Malinowski and Radcliffe-Brown—a man inherits from his mother's brother and not from his own father.

None or Intermittent: It is, of course, possible that husbands and wives will never live together at all. This is rare but it does occur. Usually the men continue to live in a men's house for their entire lives, sleeping only occasionally with their wives. It is also possible that the co-residence of husbands and wives is very intermittent. This can happen when men take jobs that are far away or when a person with multiple spouses lives only with one of those, thus effectively *not* living with the others.

NEOLOCAL, MATRILOCAL, AND PATRILOCAL: ADVANTAGES AND DISADVANTAGES

Of the previously listed options, three deserve additional discussion because they occur very frequently and because they demonstrate some of the trade-offs for the different people involved. These are neolocal, matrilocal (technically uxorimatrilocal), and patrilocal (technically viripatrilocal).

For the couple themselves, there are some obvious merits to *neolocal* residence. The couple starts off fresh on relatively neutral ground. They need not be far from their parents and may interact with them on a daily or perhaps weekly basis. While the couple is thus spared interference in much of their daily lives, there are some offsetting disadvantages. There will be greater social distance between the couple and their parents even if they live close by and, perhaps even more importantly, between the couple's children and their parents—that is between grandchildren and their grandparents.

Both *matrilocal* and *patrilocal* residence have the inverse advantages and disadvantages. Here, the couple's parents and children will inevitably be closer together and there will be closer grandparent/grandchild relations as well. The parents are likely to have some significant assistance in their daily lives from their own parents (the grandparents to their children). If one agrees with Margaret Mead that cultural transmission really requires three—not two—generations, then building three generations into a single household has great merit. On the other hand, with two adult generations in a single household, there are likely to be questions about who is in charge of what. The grandparents may have the major authority role in the household since it is probably their house in which all are living. The parents of the children thus may lose some of their own authority as parents.

Although there are some similar advantages to matrilocal and patrilocal postmarital residence, there are also some differences between the two. Consider the advantages of matrilocal residence. If men are gone for long periods of time, divorce their wives, or die relatively early in life (in war, for example), children who are already living with their mother in her mother's house are not subject to any great dislocation. Consider also the dangers of patrilocal residence. If a women leaves for any reason, she is probably more likely than the father to take the children with her, especially if they are very young. Thus the grandparents (the father's parents) could lose the very grandchildren that patrilocal residence has provided to them. In such situations, there are often strong efforts to control the daughter-in-law and make sure she does not have the option of leaving—no matter how bad or even abusive the marriage is. If she leaves, she may take the children. For the husband and his family that is intolerable, for in the world of kinship, no children means no future.

The choice of postmarital residence not only sets the tone of the marriage but the structure of households. With neolocal residence, households are inevitably of nuclear families. Although other relatives may occasionally co-reside, the basic structure is parents and children. Once those children get married, they move into their own households. On the other hand, if there is continued residence with one set of parents, then households inevitably grow to include three generations at least some of the time. In such cases, household dynamics will be more complex since they involve more people, and there may be struggles between the parents and the younger couple, between the younger couple about the parents, or between the parents and their child combined against the child's spouse who is the outsider. On the other hand, the broader resources of these households may yield both an emotionally richer family life and a more profitable economic one. The decision about postmarital residence is indeed a fateful one.

Case Study
Vietnamese Kin Terms

The complaint that might be lodged against Hawaiian, Eskimo, and Iroquois kinship terminologies is that they lump too many relatives together in too few categories. On the other hand, a fully descriptive system, like the Sudanese, has the reverse problem: too much detail. There are, however, options in between. Vietnamese kinship terminology provides an example of one such option. It is very detailed in certain areas that are essential to the kinship system, yet, in other areas, it lumps large numbers of different kinds of relatives together.

Vietnamese kinship is patrilineal. That is, it emphasizes a line of relatives linked through males. That line goes back in time to distant ancestors and goes forward in time through one's male descendants. *Lineality* is thus essential to the system and to the terminology: It is absolutely essential to distinguish the father's side of the family from the mother's side. Vietnamese terminology also distinguishes between one's actual parents and their siblings. *Nuclearity* is thus also a principle of the system. Furthermore, Vietnamese kinship terminology distinguishes—as do all kinship terminologies—*gender* and *generation*. Thus Vietnamese kinship terminology provides all of the distinctions that are

Vietnamese parents reading to their children. (*Bob Daemmrich/The Image Works*)

provided separately in Hawaiian, Eskimo, and Iroquois terminology. Finally, since patrilineal kinship needs some ordering among the males, *seniority* is also important. The result is the terminology shown in Figure 9.6. The terminology for one's parent's generation has distinct terms for a variety of males: your actual father (*ba*), your mother's brother (*cau*), your father's older brother (*bac*), and your father's younger brother (*chu*). Note particularly that the two "uncles" on the father's side of the family have separate terms. Father's elder brother (*bac*) is in a highly respected position, whereas father's younger brother (*chu*) can be treated with more informality. Although Ho Chi Minh, the late communist leader of Vietnam, was indeed often photographed in happy interaction with children, the English translation "Uncle Ho" fails to convey the deep respect and authority accorded to him as *bac* Ho (father's older brother Ho).

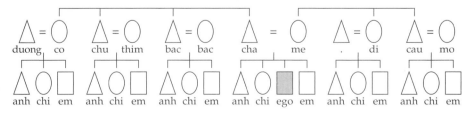

FIGURE 9.6   VIETNAMESE KINSHIP TERMINOLOGY

A few other points of the terminology deserve note. For the parents' sisters, as would be expected, "mother" (*ma*) is not the same as either mother's sister (*di*) or father's sister (*co*). Furthermore, those women are also distinguished from women marrying into the family: Thus there are additional terms for "mother's brother's wife" (*mo*) and the wives of the father's brothers (*bac* [*dau*] and *thim*). For one's own generation, seniority is also seen in the terms for brother and sister. There is one term for older brother (*anh*), one for older sister (*chi*), and a separate gender-neutral term for younger sibling (*em*). This is a terminological system with considerable detail about gender, generation, lineality, nuclearity, and seniority.

Yet, despite the specificity about relatives in the ascending generation, Vietnamese terminology in other regards seems extraordinarily simple. The sibling/cousin terminology is virtually Hawaiian. All children of any of the parent's brothers and sisters are "older brother," "older sister," or "younger sibling." Both sets of grandparents are called *ong* (grandfather) and *ba* (grandmother).This doesn't mean that Vietnamese can't add additional words to distinguish their immediate brothers and sisters (they call them "intestinal" siblings) or to distinguish the two sets of grandparents (the father's parents are the "inside" grandparents). But it does suggest that in the core kin terms, the Vietnamese have struck a balance between being very specific in areas that are crucial to patrilineal organization and rather general in other areas. The focus of the system is on the first ascending generation and there the terms are extraordinarily precise.

Case Study
Matrilocal Residence among the Cibecue Apache

The Cibecue Apache are among the westernmost-dwelling of the Apache in Arizona. Although their lifeways changed greatly during the course of the nineteenth and twentieth centuries, they retained many (although not all) of the features of their traditional life. The Cibecue Apache, being relatively more isolated from the surrounding society than other Apache, have tended to maintain relatively large portions of that traditional culture. That includes a very strong attachment to the land and also a strong commitment to the spiritual world. Many Apache have individual connections with spirits that help guide them through their lives. Sometimes those spirits come to them and sometimes the Apache seek them out.

The Apache are matrilineal. That means that the relations among women as mothers, daughters, and sisters govern most of the organization of social life. Clan membership, for example, is based on who your mother is. The relations among women are also crucial to decisions about postmarital residence. Since Apache households (*gowa*) tend to exist as clusters of households (*gota*), both kinds of grouping require discussion.

The household (*gowa*) consists of a married couple and their unmarried children. At this level, then, the Apache have nuclear family households. Since the couple set up their own household when they get married, this is technically *neolocal postmarital residence*. The *gowa* may even actually include multiple buildings, with the couple sleeping in a small one-bedroom house while the children are out in a *wickiup* (a brushwood hut covered with mats) or sleeping in an open air shelter. The *gowa*, however, is usually part of a cluster of households called *gota*. These *gota* are matrilineal in structure. When a man marries, he does indeed set up a new household with his wife. However, that household is located among the households of his wife's kin, including her parents, her sisters, and the husbands and children of her sisters. At the level of the family cluster—the *gota*—this is thus *matrilocal postmarital residence*.

After marriage, men go to live with their wives and among their wives' relatives. This is not always an easy process. The man needs to be on his best behavior, since his wife's parents will be carefully watching him. He would be wise to be sober, work hard, and be respectful. He would also be wise not to spend too much of his time away from his wife and her family or spend too much time with, or money on, his own family and friends. If he is too generous with his own family or friends, that may well be considered a betrayal of his wife and her family. The young son-in-law is thus in a somewhat awkward position, and possibly an unpleasant one. After all, the women are the framework of the system, the trunk of the kinship tree. The husbands are merely the leaves and, as the Apache put it: "The leaves drop off but the branches and the trunk never break."

There are, however, benefits for the man. He will have the satisfaction of rearing his own family and having them close to at least one set of grandparents. Furthermore—as is common in matrilineal societies—his status in his wife's family is likely to increase over time and eventually he may well become head of the *gota*—the cluster of households. For, when all is said and done, it is still the men who are the heads of the households clusters. A man can not inherit such a leadership role but instead will have to earn it under the watchful eyes of his wife's family.

SOURCES

Kinship has received a great deal of attention from anthropologists—far more than can be conveyed here. Robin Fox's *Kinship and Marriage: An Anthropological Perspective* (Penguin, 1967) remains a very good guide for basic discussions of kinship and descent and is useful both for the material here and the next chapter. Almost all anthropology texts provide a good overview of kinship and most will include a discussion of Crow and Omaha—excluded here in pursuit of brevity. The film in the *Strangers Abroad* series on W. H. R. Rivers may be worth watching. Its subtitle, *Everything Is Relatives,* is apt and the case of the Toda remains interesting.

For the case studies, Hy Van Luong's work on Vietnamese kinship terminology is essential. The fullest version is in his *Discursive Practices and Linguistic Meanings: The Vietnamese System of Person Reference* (John Benjamins Publishing Company, 1990). There is also some excellent recent work on Vietnamese kinship more generally, especially regarding household structure: For example, see Danièle Bélanger's "Regional Differences in Household Composition and Family Formation Patterns in Vietnam," *Journal of Comparative Family Studies* 31 (2000): 171–189, and Minh Huu Nguyen's *Tradition and Change in Vietnamese Marriage Patterns in the Red River Delta* (Ph.D. dissertation, University of Washington, 1998). Vietnamese social scientists are rethinking the nature and implications of Vietnamese kinship in the light of very sharp economic and demographic changes that accelerated during the 1990s. That makes for interesting reading. The discussion of the Apache is taken from the work of Keith Basso—the details coming from his early book *The Cibecue Apache* (Waveland, 1986; orig. 1970) although his more recent *Wisdom Sits in Places* (University of New Mexico Press, 1996) provides much of the impetus for including them here. As with the Vietnamese example, I have elided the historical changes and regional variability in the society in order to provide reasonably lucid discussions of how kinship works.

CHAPTER 10

KINSHIP: DESCENT AND MARRIAGE

The previous chapter introduced the topic of kinship and this chapter continues that discussion. While in the previous chapter the emphasis was on how individuals classify their kin and the kinds of immediate kin among whom they live, this chapter emphasizes the larger groups that can be constructed based on kinship (largely through principles of descent) and the way that different groups can be linked to each other (largely through marriage). It is through this creation of larger groups and more extensive links among groups that kinship can serve as the basic framework even for relatively large societies. There are advantages to having such larger social groups based on kinship. As noted for pastoralists and some horticulturalists, kinship is a relatively portable framework for social relations. Another advantage is that kinship can extend intimacy across distance even for settled groups. If a neighboring town or village contains kin—perhaps the family of one's mother or even a sibling—that town is effectively and affectively far "closer" to you than its geographical distance would suggest.

The discussion in this chapter begins with the ways kin relations can be used to create groups and then focuses more specifically on the options of patrilineality and matrilineality. Both options are effective in organizing people into descent groups—although their implications for men and women are rather different. The chapter then turns to marriage: who gets married to whom and how that marriage links kin groups together. After that discussion, even the terms *hypergamy* and *hypogamy* will begin to make sense. Of the two case studies at the end of the chapter, one concerns son preference in China and Vietnam and the other considers the issue of same-sex marriage in the United States.

BEYOND THE HOUSEHOLD

Although much of the story of kinship is about the immediate relations of people living together within what are usually family-based households, kinship often extends far beyond the household. As the discussion of terminology suggested, those people related by blood (often called *cognates*) and those related by marriage (usually called *affines*) can be categorized in various ways. Distinctions by generation and gender are nearly universal, distinctions by nuclearity (e.g., immediate brothers versus what we call "cousins"), by lineality (e.g., father's brother versus mother's brother), by seniority (e.g., father's older brother versus father's younger brother), or by cognatic versus affinal tie (e.g., father's blood brother versus his brother-in-law) are common in many societies.

KINDREDS

One way to create larger kin groups will be familiar from the kinds of kinship chart presented in the last chapter. Consider the kin identified in the chart on Eskimo terminology (Figure 10.1). From your point of view (i.e., from the shaded box that we technically call *ego*), there are two sets of grandparents and the people descended from them, including siblings of your parents, their spouses, and a variety of people termed "cousins" in Eskimo terminology. Here is a set of people that makes good sense for you as a larger group of relatives. All the people of your own generation (your brothers, sisters, and cousins), for example, have at least two of the same grandparents as you do. They are the children of a brother or sister of one of your parents. That's a pretty close connection. If you need to assemble a fair number of people for a specific purpose—a wedding, for example—then this set of kin will work well. When those people show up at the wedding, many will know each other, you will know most of them, and most of them will be inclined to be generous toward you. Such a set of people will work well for other purposes. In early Anglo-Saxon common law, for example, this was the set of people who would pass judgment on you if you were accused of committing some crime.

Such groups are called *kindreds*. They are *ego-oriented*, which means that the kin group is figured from the point of view of the individual. That is the strength of the kindred: It is the set of relatives who are closest to you. Since kindreds are ego-oriented, different people have different kindreds. Your own brothers and sisters will have the same kindred as you, but nobody else will.

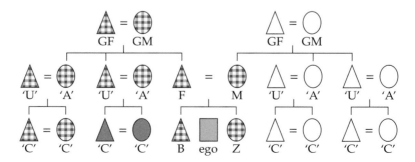

FIGURE 10.1   KINDREDS

When you go to your cousin's wedding, you will see many people you know, but probably many that you do not. If the cousin is on your father's side (say your *fbd* or *fbs*), you will see your relatives from that side of the family, including one set of grandparents (the checkered men and women in Figure 10.1). But your mother's relatives (and your other set of grandparents) probably won't be there.

If the purpose is to assemble an occasional group in support of a particular individual, kindreds are a very effective kind of kin group. However, kindreds have three serious limitations. First, they do not last over time. The kindred of a particular person disappears when that person and that person's siblings die. Once you and your siblings pass on, your kindred disappears. The people who were part of your kindred may still be alive, but their connection to each other, which was through you, is lost. Second, since no people (other than siblings) have the same kindred, kindreds have limitations as structured social groups since people belong to many kindreds. Sometimes it is important that people know which single group is their most important connection. With kindreds, people will always have overlapping membership. Third, kindreds pose increasing problems as they become larger. Constructing a kindred through relations with those with the same grandparents may not be too difficult. Trying to trace a kindred through four sets of great-grandparents is likely to be extremely difficult. Kindreds are thus transient, have overlapping membership, and are inherently difficult to expand beyond a fairly modest size—such as those who share at least one set of grandparents.

COGNATIC DESCENT

One alternative to kindreds is to create groups not from your perspective (that of *ego*) but from the perspective of an ancestor. This is called *cognatic descent* (~ *cognatic* meaning related by origin). All the people descended from a particular ancestor are thus members of the kinship group. This has some significant advantages compared to kindreds. Above all, the anchor point of the group does not change over time or according to the individual involved. The question of membership is always the same and a very simple one: Are you descended from a particular person or not? If that person is a famous person, Thomas Jefferson for example, the task is easy. Even people who may not know the names of their great grandparents may well know that they are descended in some fashion from this famous person.

Cognatic descent groups thus have the advantage of an anchor point that endures over time. For someone to know whether or not they belong to the group requires only that their parents have told them that they have a certain ancestor—and a relatively famous ancestor is an advantage. Because they can reach so far back in time, cognatic descent groups can also become very large. Thus if you want to bring together a very large set of people—an Independence Day picnic, for example—then cognatic descent groups will work well.

The people may not know each other intimately but they will share at least the memory of one person: the original ancestor. Yet cognatic descent groups also have one of the same limitations that kindreds do. Individuals can easily belong to multiple groups. You might be both a Smith and a Lee. That overlap in group membership may seem fine in general, but what happens when you have to make a choice—when both the Smiths and Lees are having picnics on the same day? Or what happens when the Smiths and Lees go to war against each other on the battlefield or in the courtroom or boardroom. Which side are you on?

UNILINEAL DESCENT

The final major option is also based on descent but avoids this problem of overlap. This is done by specifying only one line of descent, called *unilineal descent*. Although you have two parents, you are considered to be formally descended from only one. This works exactly the same as the more limited "inheritance" of family names that is common in most parts of North America. Thus if your father is a Lee and your mother is a Smith, you are a Lee. The North American convention is thus *patrinomial*, meaning that the name (~ *nom* for name) comes from the father. The alternative of using both family names recreates exactly the problem of cognatic descent. Names from both parents may work for one generation, but one can't accumulate them forever. Some have to be dropped and, furthermore, you have to choose which name comes first. A joint surname like Lee-Smith or Smith-Lee is plausible (but who comes first?). However, if in the succeeding generation a Lee-Smith (or was it Smith-Lee?) marries a Kim-Jefferson . . .

Inheriting names is a fairly minor issue—although it is one about which people often have very strong opinions. Yet it illustrates well the central problem of descent. If all descent is to be reckoned, then people will belong to multiple overlapping groups. That may have some advantages. But it will not be very helpful if there are more specific tasks to be done, property to be inherited, or even people to marry. For such purposes, unilineal descent has distinct advantages. At birth one becomes a member of *either* the Smith or the Lee group. That doesn't mean you are unrelated to the other group, but only that when the occasion calls for it you know where you belong as your primary membership. When the call goes out for "Smiths over here and Lees over there" it's not very helpful to have a large number of people milling around in the middle, neither here nor there, mumbling how they are related to both groups and just don't know which group to join or what to do.

In order to get people into one group or the other, a decision thus has to be made about what the basic rule will be to establish this single line (thus *unilineal*) by which you will be attached to a specific kinship group. The basic options are to establish that line through the mother (*matrilineal*) or through the father (*patrilineal*). If a child is born into a society and is considered to belong to the mother's group, then that is a matrilineal society since the line of attachment runs through the mother to her mother, to the mother's mother, and so on. If a child is born into a society and is considered to belong to the father's group, then that is a patrilineal society since the line of attachment runs through the father. Anthropological research has shown a great variation in how unilineal descent groups are structured and has also shown that this distinction between matrilineal and patrilineal oversimplifies the options that people actually use. However, the matrilineal and patrilineal options are the predominant and certainly the simplest forms of unilineal descent. Since they are so frequent in human society, and since they provide interesting alternatives to each other, the next section focuses on them in more detail. How do matrilineal and patrilineal kinship systems work and what are their implications for men and women, adults and children?

MATRILINEALITY AND PATRILINEALITY

Matrilineality and patrilineality are in some ways similar options for developing unilineal descent groups. Both provide a basic rule for deciding who belongs to what group and that rule is automatically applied at birth. Thus in a matrilineal society, when a child is born she or he will be not only a part of an immediate family group, but also part of the mother's line. Similarly, in a patrilineal society, when a child is born, he or she will be a part of the father's line. In both cases those "lines" can be used as the basis for forming a variety of kinship groups that can endure over time. Those groups of people are called *lineages* or, more specifically *matrilineages* in matrilineal society and *patrilineages* in patrilineal society. A lineage is generally defined as a set of people related through a known line of ancestors. That is, you are a member of a particular lineage because you can trace yourself to a particular ancestor and thus know you are related to anybody else who can trace their descent from that same ancestor. Those lineages can be relatively small if descent is only traced for a few generations or very large if descent is traced for many, many generations. In some societies, there are lineages within lineages. Thus there may be a set of small lineages contained within a larger lineage. There can be several such nestings. Among the Nuer, who appeared in the chapter on pastoralism and will reappear in the chapter on politics, there are four distinct layers of lineages ranging from a minimal lineage (tracing back four or five generations), a minor lineage (tracing back another generation or two), a major lineage (with yet another generation or two), and a maximal lineage (tracing back something like nine or ten generations).

When ancestors are not far removed (your grandparents, for example), it is easy to trace the links. In a society that writes down full genealogies, you can trace exact lines of descent for hundreds of years. However, unilineal systems still work well even if all the connecting links aren't known. Thus you can be a Lee or a Smith without being able to exactly trace your ancestry back to the original Lee or Smith. All you have to know is what your parents are. The system thus works *whether or not the actual links are remembered*. There is thus often a leap in matrilineal and patrilineal societies from known ancestors to something more like presumed or even mythical ancestors. Anthropologists often use the word *clan* to describe such a group, and sometimes the more specific words *patriclan* and *matriclan*. Exactly as with a lineage, you are born into a clan based on who your mother (matrilineal societies) or father (patrilineal societies) is.[1] A clan, then, might consist of a number of lineages with some presumed historical relationship. In turn, clans may themselves have relationships with other clans—perhaps a legendary connection among the clan founders. Such sets of clans are usually called *phratries*. Finally, lineages or clans may be organized into a system that has two overall groups whose members marry each other. Such binary divisions are called *moieties*.[2]

This simple decision at birth about whether a person belongs to the mother's or father's line thus permits the development of a wide range of groups with clearly defined membership. If you are a Lee, you *are* a Lee and you are therefore *not* a Smith. The problem of overlap in membership that occurs both with kindreds and cognatic descent groups is thus avoided. "Lees here and Smiths there" yields two distinct sets of people with no one wandering around in the middle. That clarity of organization has many advantages, especially in identifying particular rules for social action. For example, if you are a Smith you would probably pass your property along to a Smith (not a Lee), provide hospitality and assistance to any other Smith (but not to a Lee). Yet you would probably have to marry a Lee (*not* a Smith).

This does not mean that women are ignored in patrilineal societies or that men are ignored in matrilineal societies. In fact, in matrilineal societies, men often inherit property and titles from men. It's just that they must inherit from a man who is related to them through women. Thus it is that the mother's brother holds such an important position in matrilineal societies. But the importance of the line *does* mean that it is absolutely essential for people to have sons in patrilineal societies and daughters in matrilineal societies. Without that, there can be no future for the group: A patrilineage that produces no sons is at an end; so too a matrilineage without daughters.

There is, however, one fundamental problem in both matrilineal and patrilineal descent systems. It is easy to specify that a child shall belong to either the mother's or father's line. But what happens when they marry? Consider

---

[1]A warning is in order here. This particular distinction between clan and lineage is far from universal. Indeed in the Nuer case, Evans-Pritchard was clear that many of the units he called lineages were based on precisely this kind of presumption of relationship. Alternately, in the Chinese case, many "clans" are based on actual known relationships. I maintain the lineage/clan distinction here simply because the issue of known versus presumed ancestry is an important one.

[2]Moieties can also exist on their own without clans.

the patrilineal case with a marriage between a Smith man and a Lee woman. It is likely in a patrilineal society that the couple would live with, or near, the husband's family. The woman will, after all, be bearing children who carry on the male Smith line. If she decides she is unhappy with the marriage and wants to return to her family, that will be bad enough. If she has had children already and wants to take them with her, that would be a disaster. She would thus be taking with her the very future of her husband's patrilineage. It is hardly surprising, then, that in patrilineal societies there is much effort taken to ensure that this doesn't happen. Thus her husband and his family will do their best to make sure that she is fully and irrevocably absorbed into their family. She will likely have to forsake her birth identification as a Lee and become a Smith. The lot of the daughter-in-law in patrilineal societies is not usually an easy one.

The situation in matrilineal societies is in certain respects simply the reverse. When the Smith man marries a Lee woman they are likely to reside with or near her parents. It is, after all, from her parents that they and their children (both male and female) will inherit property. If, after marriage, the man decides he is unhappy with the arrangement and wants to go home, however, the problem is far less severe. He is less likely to want to take the children with him. If the children remain with their mother and she with her family, far less long-term damage is done. There is no threat at all to the matrilineage since the children are staying where they belong: with their mother and her kin. This does not mean that in matrilineal societies marriage isn't valued or that a woman's family doesn't appreciate their son-in-law. It does mean, however, that there can be greater flexibility about marriage and about sexual relations in general. Even the notion of "illegitimate" children changes sharply. A child that is with its mother is automatically "legitimate"—the child is in the right place whoever and wherever the father might be.

MARRIAGE

MARRIAGE AS A SOCIAL CREATION

The discussion of matrilineality and patrilineality suggests how variable the implications of marriage can be for the people involved. Indeed, marriage is important not only to the individuals involved but to the families and larger kin groups within which they belong. Whether a person marries, when they marry, and whom they marry are all vitally important to these larger kin groups. It is no wonder, then, that in many societies parents and other relatives do their best to control the outcome of the marriage. And marriage is controllable. Much of what happens to people in life is not so easily controlled. People are born and people die. Societies may pay great attention to those events, clothe them in elaborate ceremony, and try to influence them, but there are limits to what they can do. Marriage, on the

Musicians lead a band of guests in a traditional Iranian wedding. (*Omnia/Getty Images, Inc./Hulton Archive Photos*)

other hand, is a social creation. Neither whether people marry, nor the timing of marriage, nor the extent of its celebration, nor the particular person married happens automatically.

Since marriage is a social creation, there is predictably a great deal of variation in how it is carried out. Sometimes there are rules or specific preferences about whom one should marry. Sometimes that involves a specific relative. For example, in matrilineal societies a man might be encouraged to marry his mother's brother's daughter. Such a marriage helps tie together two people in whom the mother's brother has a direct interest: his own blood daughter (who is a member of his wife's matrilineal group) and his sister's son (who is a member of his own matrilineal group). In some patrilineal societies, on the other hand, there is a preference for a man to marry his father's brother's daughter. Here the couple are both within the same group and thus the new wife does not have to move to a different patrilineal group.

In contrast to these cases in which the ideal spouse is easily identified, in many other societies there is a more general requirement (e.g., that Smiths marry Lees) or, alternately, certain kinds of people who should *not* be married. Certainly people within your nuclear family are inappropriate spouses and often some kinds of cousins as well. Sometimes what we call "cousins" consist of good marriage partners *and* bad marriage partners: Thus "cross-cousins" (father's sister's children or mother's brother's children) might be fine while "parallel cousins" (father's brother's children or mother's sister's children) would not be.[3]

---

[3]It may be helpful to remember that in Iroquois kinship terminology, those parallel cousins would actually be called "brother" and "sister."

MARRIAGE TYPES AND VARIATIONS

In order to talk about prescriptions, proscriptions, and simple preferences about marriage, a variety of terms are used. These are largely "-gamy" words (~*gamos* for marriage) just as those used for postmarital residence were largely "-local" words. The major of these are given below. These terms provide a conclusion to the discussion of kinship in these past two chapters. Even hypergamy and hypogamy should now make sense.

> *Monogamy and Polygamy:* *Monogamy* indicates there is only one (~*mono* for one) marriage partner. This does not mean that people can't have more than one spouse during their lives, just that they can't have more than one at the same time. (Having multiple sequential spouses is sometimes called serial monogamy.) Some societies do, however, frown on remarriage—especially for widows in patrilineal systems. *Polygamy* indicates having multiple (~*poly* for many) spouses at the same time. When a man has multiple *wives* that is *polygyny* (~*gyne* for female). Polygyny is very common although it has largely disappeared in industrial societies. When a women has multiple husbands, that is *polyandry* (~*andro* for male). Polyandry occurs but is far less frequent than polygyny.

> *Fraternal Polyandry and Sororal Polygyny:* Polygamy and polyandry involve some complexity in managing multiple marital relationships. One solution for this is for a man to marry sisters or for a woman to marry brothers. These are, respectively, sororal polygyny and fraternal polyandry. One reason for such marriages is that as co-spouses brothers or sisters might be better at managing their potential conflicts than would strangers. The other reason is that by marrying a second person from the same kin group, you are relying on (and strengthening) what you have already found to be a good relationship with that group.

> *Sororate and Levirate:* It is also possible that when a woman dies, a sister may replace her as a wife (called the sororate) or, when a man dies, his brother may replace him as a husband (called the levirate). Both practices reflect the fundamental social fact that a man and his brother, or a women and her sister, are the only people who are exactly identical in kin terms. It is they alone, for example, who have the same kindreds. The argument is partially that one kin group may "owe" another a replacement for a lost spouse and partially that the linkage between the two kin groups is a good one and worth maintaining.

> *Endogamy and Exogamy:* *Endogamy* (~*endo* for within) refers to marrying within a particular group while *exogamy* (~*exo* for outside) refers to marrying outside a particular group. The terms are applied to local territorial units (e.g., *village exogamy* means people do not

marry within their own village) and to kin units (e.g., *clan exogamy* means people do not marry within their own clan). The terms can also be used more broadly to describe issues of religion, class, ethnicity and so on. Endogamy and exogamy can involve formal rules or general preferences. The effect of rules of endogamy and exogamy is to narrow the choice for marriage to those who are neither too close nor too far away.

Hypergamy and Hypogamy: Hypergamy and hypogamy refer to whether people are marrying "up" or marrying "down." If one person is marrying up, the other is marrying down so, in order to avoid confusion, the terms are always used from the perspective of the woman. Thus *hypergamy* (*~hyper* for over or above) means a women marries up and *hypogamy* (*~hypo* for under) means she marries down. Although marrying up or down can happen for a variety of reasons, it intuitively makes most sense when comparing matrilineality and patrilineality. If a women in a patrilineal society is marrying down, there can be problems. After all, she is probably expected to give up most—perhaps all—of her connections to her own family for that of her husband's. If she comes from a higher status or richer family, she is less likely to subject herself to the new family and might even feel free to go back to where things were better. Thus hypergamy makes sense—and is very common—in patrilineal societies. In matrilineal societies, the argument is exactly the reverse. If the woman is marrying up, then her husband who comes to live with her and her family will be all the less likely to devote himself to his marital life. Instead he will tend to return as he wishes to visit with, or work for, the family in which he was raised. Thus hypogamy makes good sense in matrilineal societies.

DEATH AND DIVORCE, REMARRIAGE AND BLENDED FAMILIES

Discussions of rules for descent and marriage must be supplemented by a recognition that sometimes things go wrong. A family in a patrilineal society may lack sons; a family in a matrilineal society may lack daughters. It is rare for families simply to give up in such circumstances. Instead they are often flexible and rather creative. A son-less family in a patrilineal society, for example, may well decide to find a good husband for their daughter and then formally adopt him as their "real" son. In more extreme situations they may even decide to consider their daughter as a "son," find her a "wife" who then has children. If they have a son, but that son dies before being married, they may also provide a wife after the fact in what is sometimes called a ghost marriage. The physical details of impregnation are easily handled (perhaps by an especially discrete kinsman) although the public explanation may involve a nighttime sighting of the dead man's spirit near the sleeping place of his new wife.

In contemporary North American society, death is a relatively rare occurrence among the young. However, divorce is extremely common. North American families are built largely on the ties of couples (whether heterosexual, gay, or lesbian) but those ties are far from durable or reliable. Divorce is not only practically difficult but is a sharp challenge to the very meaning of families since it retroactively undoes the history on which the family is based. In that way, it is more damaging than death itself. Death takes away a spouse but does not make the marriage retroactively "wrong" or meaningless; divorce often does. Although some divorced couples retain friendly or at least cooperative relations, many remain hostile—perhaps especially if divorce was based on the violation of marital vows of fidelity.

One solution to the statistical danger of marriage is to avoid it altogether. Couples may decide to simply live together, perhaps have children, and consider marriage later—if ever. Another solution is to go ahead anyway, taking your statistical chances, and muddling through as best you can if things don't work out. Many people do just that. The result is that when divorce does occur, families fracture into pieces. Single parents struggle with the enormous practical and emotional problems of raising their children and noncustodial parents (whether voluntary or forced) struggle with *not* raising their children. Children, in turn, may struggle with split allegiances between hostile parents or try to manage split residence with parents who have chosen some form of joint custody. Grandparents may find themselves cut off from the grandchildren they have grown to love, but may also find themselves once again de facto "parents" to their grandchildren while their own child (the actual parent) tries to balance a career and single parenthood.

Just like son-less patrilineages and daughter-less matrilineages, North American families are flexible. The childless adopt. Those who have been divorced remarry. Children who have moved away from their parents move back in with them—or the parents with the children. More distant relatives take on roles usually associated with parents and grandparents. As these people move in together, or come to live nearby in active daily and weekly interaction, they bring relatives of their own. Biologically unrelated children, for example, come to be brothers and sisters. This blending of people into new families is not without stress and confusion for the children. Is your father your biological father? Or is he the man who married your mother and adopted you when you were little? Or is your father the man who is currently married to your mother? There is also stress and confusion for parents. Who has full authority over the child? Is it the original biological parent? Or the parent who is most frequently at home? Despite such problems, these new blended families serve as a reminder of how flexible human beings can be in constructing and reconstructing their family relationships. Indeed, the best measure of a society's kinship system may be how well it functions when things are *not* going quite according to plan.

Case Study
Son Preference in China and Vietnam

If a society is patrilineal, then it needs sons to carry on that line. It might be presumed, then, that patrilineal societies will value sons more than daughters. If families have many children—that is, if there is high fertility—then the odds are rather good that they will have sons. However, if families begin to have smaller families, then their odds of having sons are greatly reduced. If—as has happened in China—families are only allowed to have one child, then their odds drop to about fifty-fifty.[4] This puts families in a difficult position if they have a daughter, since they then have no additional opportunity to have a son. This problem has received much attention in China, where there are frequent claims that tens of millions of women are "missing" from the population. Some may have truly disappeared; others are likely simply "off the books." The availability of sonograms during pregnancy is thus a volatile issue since that would even increase the disparity in births of girls and boys. That disparity in boys and girls, of course, later becomes a disparity between men and women, which causes another set of problems. Either some men will remain bachelors or women will have to be found somewhere else. That problem underlies the fact that some of the trafficking in women—especially out of Southeast Asia—is not simply for commercial sex workers but for wives for these Chinese men.

The situation in Vietnam is somewhat different. Here, as well, the society is patrilineal and here, as well, the government has supported reduced fertility. However, Vietnam's "two-child" policy is more expansive than China's "one-child" policy and it seems to be the case that it has been implemented far less stringently. Nevertheless, the combination of patrilineality and pressure toward reduced fertility led a range of researchers to look at what could be found out about "son preference" in Vietnam. That research has been a blend of ethnographic work, which is particularly good at determining how people look at the situation, and demographic analysis, which is particularly good at determining if those social views actually correlate with broader data that represents the population as a whole.

The ethnographic research produced a very strong indication of son preference. Indeed many of the women interviewed (largely by Scandinavian social scientists) had rather harrowing tales of how much their own worth as women hinged on producing sons rather than daughters. Another set of researchers began looking at contraception. They hypothesized that if son preference was strong, then it was more likely that couples who had a daughter but no son would "forget" to use contraception or that the contraceptive would

---

[4]Actually the odds are slightly above fifty-fifty. The chance of the birth of a son is statistically higher, all other things being equal.

somehow "fail." That also turned out to be the case, suggesting again the importance of "son preference" and the use of a convenient excuse.[5]

There thus seemed good evidence of son preference. But was it sufficient, as in China, to produce an imbalance in the proportion of male and female children? Here the demographers became involved, looking at several sets of data on actual births and at least partial information on the parents and their prior children. The results were interesting. The data did suggest that there was sufficient imbalance in male and female births to suggest a preference for sons among those who didn't yet have sons. On the other hand, the imbalance was very modest, suggesting that the strength of the attitudes about the importance of sons was *not* reflected in anything other than a modest imbalance in actual births. Furthermore, there was also some evidence of a *daughter preference* among those people who already had a son. That would suggest that emphasis on son preference was obscuring some other very important values of parents. Those values could be seen either as an actual daughter preference in addition to a son preference, or perhaps more accurately a preference for having both a son and a daughter.

This combination of data suggests two general points. First, general notions of kinship—such as unilineal descent groups—have very broad and profound effects on the ways people organize their social lives. They can become even more, rather than less, important during the processes of industrialization. Second, these general notions of kinship often turn out to be rather complex and unpredictable. Thus, the Vietnamese data suggest that a preference for sons does not rule out a separate preference for daughters. Just because a patrilineally oriented society is likely to value sons, it doesn't follow that they necessarily won't value daughters as well. The reverse is certainly true for matrilineal societies, in which men often fare very well indeed.

Case Study
Same-Sex Marriage in the United States

The creation of legalized same-sex unions in Vermont in 2000 was soon followed by even broader actions in other places: with questionable legality at the city level (especially San Francisco) and then formally at the state level in Massachusetts in 2004. The response to all these actions has been positive among many people, but fiercely negative among others. President Bush

---

[5]Contraception in Vietnam involves a variety of means, the major of which are condoms and IUDs. Both are subject to failure.

A lesbian couple is married in San Francisco. (*Sam Morris/AP Wide World Photos*)

hailed heterosexual marriage as a fundamental "institution of civilization" and proposed a constitutional amendment to ban same-sex marriages. The American Anthropological Association weighed in with its own statement opposing such a ban, based on the broad experience of anthropologists with marriage throughout the globe. The anthropological record is indeed extremely clear that human beings have a wide range of sexual practices that frequently include people of the same sex. The anthropological record is also clear that human beings have a wide range of more or less formal relationships that we would generally call marriage. These also may include people of the same sex.

Simple opposition or support, however, often fails to convey the complexity of the positions people take on the issue of same-sex marriage. Some people accept the general right of people to live together, but have hesitations about a gay or lesbian couple assuming custody of children from prior heterosexual relations, and balk entirely at any right to adopt children into a same-sex relationship. Gay and lesbian couples themselves hold a variety of views. Some object to the basic structure of marriage in the United States since they maintain it is inherently based on a heterosexist model. Nevertheless they maintain their right to enter into such a marriage on the same basis as other people. With new reproductive technologies, others argue that the very basis for heterosexual marriage has ceased to exist—or will do so at some point in this century.

But what is the view of the couples themselves? Ellen Lewin has both conducted research on same-sex marriages and herself been in one. Her comments on what is at stake from the couple's point of view thus carry considerable weight. She suggests two main points. First, the marriage ceremony itself provides an important *ritual* acknowledgment of the union for the couple and for their friends and relatives, gay and straight. Commitment is a highly valued quality in personal relationships and its public acknowledgment, based inevitably on invocations of love, often brings tears to those participating—even those not entirely supportive of same-sex unions. One argument for same-sex marriage is thus simply that without such a ceremony people lose the right to make a public commitment that is emotionally and socially fulfilling to them and to those around them.

Second, she notes how important is the formal *legal* acknowledgment of the union. There are important practical rights at stake. Legal spouses have access to many employment, health, retirement, and death benefits that do not apply to nonlegal partners. But more than the practicalities, Lewin stresses the emotional impact of having official legal status granted by the state. She recounts her own experience going across the border into Canada to be married there. In Canada, the processing was routine. Yet even from a routine civil ceremony in a foreign country, with no family or friends present, came a strong emotional sense of being truly "married." Even after returning to the United States, where that Canadian marriage did not affect any of their legal rights, that sense of being truly married persisted.

Lewin thus suggests from her own experience and that of the couples she studied that the approval both of religious and secular authority was important for same-sex couples. That approval attests to the authenticity of their relationship and permits them to emerge from concealment not only about sexual orientation per se but about the importance to them of a specific life partner—someone with whom they may already have been involved for years, even decades. That official certificate of authenticity may be especially important for same-sex couples who have children—or desire to have them. As always with kinship, the implications of state rules, religious practices, and social responses designed for the adult generation tend to play themselves out on the succeeding generations.

SOURCES

To expand the information on descent and marriage, some of the sources noted in the last chapter are also valuable, particularly Robin Fox's *Kinship and Marriage* (Penguin, 1967). The early social anthropological volume on *African Systems of Kinship and Marriage* (Oxford University Press, 1950; A. R. Radcliffe-Brown and Daryll Forde, editors) remains a useful indicator of the sheer range of possibilities in descent systems as well as being a who's who of classic British social anthropology. Because these issues of marriage and descent can take some time to absorb, I do recommend two commercial films. One is the Chinese film *Red Firecracker, Green Firecracker,* which concerns the potential tension in patrilineal systems when there aren't sons. In the film, that problem is "resolved" by designating the daughter as a son. The other is the Dutch film *Antonia's Line,* which suggests how something like a loose matrilineage might develop in European society.

For the case studies, a few sources that will help track the issue of son preference in China and Vietnam are Tine Gammeltoft's *Women's Bodies, Women's Worries* (Curzon Press, 1999); Dominique and Jonathan Haughton's "Son Preference in Vietnam," *Studies in Family Planning* 26 (1995): 325–337; Susan Short and others' "China's One-Child Policy and the Care of Children," *Social Forces* 79 (2001): 913–943; and Dudley Poston and others' "Son Preference and the Sex Ratio at Birth in China" *Social Biology* 44 (1997): 55–76. The material on same-sex marriages is drawn from Ellen Lewin's comments in a special issue of the *Anthropology Newsletter* 45 (May 2004): 11–12. That special issue also includes other useful articles exploring family ties in the wake of President Bush's call for a constitutional amendment on heterosexual marriage. See Lewin's *Recognizing Ourselves* (Columbia University Press, 1998) for more detail on her research and Linda Stone and Nancy P. McKee's *Gender and Culture in America* (Prentice Hall, 2002) for a broader review of contemporary gender issues.

CHAPTER 11

ECONOMICS

Although kinship may be the area of human relationships toward which anthropologists have devoted the most attention, other ways in which human beings are linked together are also the focus of anthropological research. The next three chapters present three of those other ways: economics, politics, and religion. It is somewhat arbitrary to present these as separate topics since, in the reality of people's lives, they often intermingle. Things or relationships that we think of as "economic" are often also political; those we call "political" are often also economic. Religion, in turn, is a complex subject that permeates all aspects of people's lives—whether involving kinship, politics, or economics—and is, in turn, influenced by those other aspects of human life.

Despite such concerns, these conventional categories of economics, politics, and religion help sort out some different aspects of social and societal structure. This chapter focuses on economics. It begins with an overview of the crucial issues in looking at economics from an anthropological perspective, and then continues with separate discussions of production, circulation, and work. The first of the case studies concerns gift-giving in Japan and the complex web of social relations created through those gifts. The second case study concerns Anglo and Hispanic working women in the American Southwest and how they attempt to balance the worlds of work and home.

THE NATURE OF ECONOMICS

Economics is a vast field in its own right. There are many potential ways to approach the subject. Often people are most interested in the particular kinds of economic system found in industrial societies, or in how the economic systems of industrial societies have affected nonindustrial societies. Often people are interested in specific aspects of economic systems. The nature of money, for example, is itself a fascinating topic. One can study economics as a large-scale system in which individual people are almost invisible or as a general background against which to look at individual people and how they relate to that broader economic system. Overall, one might look at economics as a specific, narrowly defined academic field or as the very basis on which all human life rests. In that broader sense, for example, most of the discussion of adaptations in Part I of this book might itself be viewed as about economics.

In this chapter, the focus on economics is narrower and concerns three issues that are particularly important in anthropological analysis: first, the *production* of goods and services; second, the *circulation* of those goods and services; and, third, the nature of *work*. These issues are not unique to anthropology, but there is a distinctive flavor to anthropological work on these issues that reflects the discipline's broad cross-cultural approach. Thus the consideration of production is not limited to our own industrial society but includes the full range of how things are produced—and have been produced—in all human societies. The anthropological consideration of circulation requires attention to a far broader range of goods and services exchanged than would occur in a more formal study of economics. Finally, the examination of the world of work requires consideration of how people's work fits with other aspects of their lives. The anthropological approach to economic issues thus reflects anthropology's emphasis on the diversity of the human experience and the need to study all aspects of people's lives.

PRODUCTION

RESOURCES, TECHNOLOGY, AND LABOR

In the earlier chapter on industrialism, a simple graphic model for production was presented (and is repeated in modified form in Figure 11.1). The figure suggests that combinations of resources, technology, and labor go into "products." In the case of agriculture, the product is a particular crop: rice, for example. The production of rice usually includes a surplus and that surplus can be used in a variety of ways: consumed, saved for later consumption, traded, converted into a more durable commodity (such as money), stolen, taxed, and so on. In the case of industrialism, a variety of products might be produced: fertilizer and tractors, for example. Here almost the entire production is, from the point of view of the producer, a "surplus" that needs to be traded, converted into money, or used for other purposes. One implication of the model is the likelihood that in industrial societies—but not generally in agricultural societies—considerable mobility of labor is needed. Another implication is a sharp shift in the components going into that product model, away from labor and toward technology.

In using that basic model, three points must be stressed. First, the model is a general one, but it can also be applied to specific cases. For those specific cases, it is necessary to look at the particular resources, technology, and labor that are used in production. If resources are scarce, technology complicated, or the particular labor needed expensive, that will affect the relative investment in the three areas. Second, there are crucial control issues that

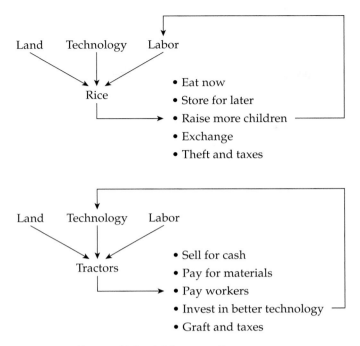

FIGURE 11.1 A MODEL OF PRODUCTION

arise in production. All the elements (resources, technology, and labor) are subject to some kind of "ownership." Differential access to resources affects the degree of social equality. Third, the model's emphasis on the product as a "surplus" is a reminder that production is tied into circulating the product to where it is wanted or needed. Production amounts to very little indeed if the products cannot be moved.

AN EXAMPLE: GRAPE PRODUCTION IN THE UNITED STATES

Overall, then, the model suggests the need to (1) look at the specific resources, technology, and labor going into particular products, (2) consider who owns or controls those resources, technology, and labor, and (3) assess the places to which, and means by which, the products will be circulated. As an example, consider grape production in the United States.[1] The United States is the

---

[1]For a good, comparative introduction to the implications of grape production, see Philip L. Martin's "Unauthorized Workers in U.S. Agriculture," in *Illegal Immigration in America,* edited by David W. Haines and Karen E. Rosenblum (Westport, CT: Greenwood Press, 1999). Excellent updates on such agricultural issues and their labor implications appear in *Rural Migration News* (see Web site at U. C. Davis: http://migration.ucdavis.edu).

world's third largest producer of grapes (after France and Italy) and nine-tenths of that production is in California.[2] What makes the example interesting is that producing "grapes" ends up involving several very different grape products. Specifically, over half of the grapes (54 percent) are used for wine, about a quarter (24 percent) are used for raisins, and about a seventh (15 percent) are used for fresh table grapes—with the remaining small percentage used for grape juice.

Consider first the difference between producing table grapes and wine. For *table grapes*, it is absolutely essential that the grapes be ripe yet not too ripe, that the bunches be evenly ripe, and that there be no damage to any of the grapes. The product needs to taste good but it also needs to look good. Although the actual growing of the grapes can be technologically complex—especially with good irrigation systems—the harvesting will clearly have to be done by hand. This harvesting is thus labor intensive and, predictably, the price that is charged for table grapes ($.36 per pound) is higher than for other kinds of grapes. On the other hand, the harvesting of *wine grapes* is very different. Although the grapes will also need to taste good, they don't have to look good since consumers will never see the grapes in their unprocessed form. Here, then, considerable automation in harvesting is possible. Machines go down the rows of vines shaking the ripe grapes loose. Those grapes fall onto conveyor belts that carry the grapes down to the ends of the rows. At the end of the rows, the conveyor belts drop the grapes onto large gondolas that are then hauled off for processing. Good wine grapes command a lower price than table grapes, but at $.21 per pound there is adequate reward for a rather expensive automation process. Some of the machines cost upwards of $100,000, but they are far more productive than human labor and, without complaint, will work all night.

Wine grapes and table grapes thus represent two very different production processes: one highly automated and one highly manual. The differences between the two make sense in terms of what technology is available and whether that technology is appropriate to the specific "product"—in this case wine versus table grapes. The situation of *raisin grapes*, however, is less clear cut. On the one hand, raisin grapes do need to be relatively complete and treated with some care. People don't want raisin paste; they want something that is recognizable as individual raisins. That argues for a manual harvesting of the grapes. On the other hand, much of the surface of the raisins is so transformed by drying that it would seem less attention would be needed to the grapes' original appearance. That would be an argument for automated harvesting. People have developed such an automated system that is called,

---

[2]Canada has also increased its vineyards in recent years (particularly in Ontario) but the value of the wine produced is more than matched by imports of table grapes and grapes for home wine-making.

appropriately enough, DOV (dried-on-the-vine) processing. The system requires growing grapes on pergolas. The pergolas support the vines. The vines
can then be cut when the grapes are, on average, ripe. The grapes then dry on
the cut vines, which are held up because they are attached to the pergolas.
When they are dried—and thus much more resistant to damage in handling—
they can be shaken loose by a machine, run on conveyor belts down the rows
and into the gondolas and hauled off for cleaning and packaging.

Despite that option for automation, raisin harvesting has tended to remain a manual process, partly because the DOV method requires significant costs up front. The machinery is expensive and the fields need to be
reworked to provide the pergolas. Furthermore, the average age of the landowners is relatively high—about sixty-three years according to one survey—
and the size of their holdings is not very large. Thus the long-term arguments
for automation tend to be minimized—especially since raisin grapes command only about $.12 per pound. The high cost of technology is less easily
recoverable and the owners of the fields—because of their age—may be
looking at shorter time frames in which to recover those costs. Finally, the
cost of manual harvesting is not all that high, since the work is largely done
by recent immigrants, many of whom are undocumented ("illegal"). They
are willing to work for lower wages and in kinds of work that are largely unacceptable to the native-born population. Thus, even in a highly industrialized country, the "old-fashioned" way of manual labor wins out over
advanced technology. This also explains why agricultural producers—who
might be assumed to be relatively "conservative"—are always a major force
in efforts to protect undocumented migrants and even to provide legalization for them.

This single example of grape production illustrates the broader need for
detailed attention to specific production processes. Though it is argued that
North America is entering a post-industrial period, much of the production
continues to be manual and, at best, like the early industrial assembly-line
work of a century ago. Much of grape production today still looks a great deal
like simple, manual harvesting; thus, assumptions about advanced industrial (or post-industrial) economies may get in the way of understanding how
things are produced. The example also provides useful reminders of the social aspects of economic production (as with the age of the raisin-grape owners) and even its political aspects (as with shifting immigration polices).

CIRCULATION

Although anthropologists have always been interested in how things are produced, it is probably fair to say that it is the way goods move among people
that has been their stronger interest. Indeed, many anthropologists would
argue that the circulation of goods among people is the very framework of a

society. When you watch goods moving from person to person you are watching the society's internal movements and witnessing the very processes that make and remake its social structure.

Anthropologists distinguish three general ways in which goods circulate in a society: reciprocity, redistribution, and exchange. Although these will be discussed in more detail below, the specific implications of the words can be easily noted. *Reciprocity* invokes a give and take between people that is more than simply economic. It is often phrased in terms of gift-giving rather than economics per se. *Redistribution* invokes a more centralized and ordered circulation of items from places where they are produced to where they will be used. Finally, *exchange* invokes a kind of circulation that is based more strictly and narrowly on our customary notions of "economic" factors. One kind of thing is given in exchange for another or, more conveniently, one item is sold for a certain sum of currency, and another is bought with that currency. For each of these kinds of circulation of goods, anthropologists are concerned not only with the circulation itself but also with the relationships among the people involved.

RECIPROCITY

One way to circulate goods is simply to give them away. Gifts are important in all human societies and in almost all cases a gift given implies that there will also be a return gift. This give and take of gifts, the anthropological record tells us, is sometimes quite simple and at other times very complex. At its simplest, gift-giving occurs between individual people. Thus, as during the end-of-year Christmas period in North America, people give gifts to family and friends. There is a general expectation that if you give people such gifts, they will also give gifts to you. There is also an expectation that the value of the gifts will be roughly equivalent. An expensive gift is not to be reciprocated with a cheap one—nor a thoughtful gift with a perfunctory one. Balance is needed. Thus this kind of reciprocity between individuals is called *balanced reciprocity*.

Yet even a simple, simultaneous exchange—as at Christmas—can be complex. Some people (like parents) are much richer than others (like children), so the equivalency can't just be cash value. If the issue is not cash value, then what is the measure of equivalency? Attempts to assess the equivalent thoughtfulness of, for example, gifts between lovers can be excruciating. Achieving balance in reciprocal gift-giving becomes even more complex when the return gift comes later or when the value of the gifts in either financial or emotional terms is high. To give somebody a very valuable gift that has no possible immediate return gift thus requires a considerable amount of *trust*.

There is another kind of reciprocity that is not so much between individuals as among groups. Consider a North American wedding. The bride's family is likely to pay much of the cost of the event, for which they will themselves get little return. Various members of the family may also make contributions for specific things: for food or drink at the reception, for example. Those attending will give gifts to the new couple and receive only token gifts in return. In some cases a gift may be returned at a subsequent wedding, but in many cases there will be no direct return at all. The older generation, after all, is generally already married, so this cannot be a system of exact balance among all those involved. Anthropologists call this *generalized reciprocity.* In the long run, there will be return gifts to other people and these generalized distributions may eventually even out: Those who receive more at one wedding may, over time, contribute roughly equivalent gifts in return at other weddings.

With balanced and generalized reciprocity, goods are circulated but in a way that is not precisely "economic" in our usual sense of the term. Instead, the circulation is based on personal, social relationships that require some measure of trust between and among the people involved, one implication of which is that the relative value of these gifts must be determined by the parties themselves. If people see the return gift as not balancing the original gift, then social relationships are likely to be damaged. That's one reason why return gifts are often somewhat more valuable than the original gift. If the return gift is "cheaper" in any way than the original gift, the return gift may well be seen as insulting. Better to err on the high side.

REDISTRIBUTION

A different kind of circulation occurs when someone has the authority—or simply the raw power—to determine that certain goods should be moved from one place to another and from one person to another. This often occurs on a small scale in households. Sometimes it is the father, sometimes the mother, sometimes a grandparent, who collects money or other goods from the family members and then redistributes them to meet the household's needs. Redistribution also occurs on a large scale when governments tax people and use those taxes to support public activities. Those activities may not even benefit the people who paid the taxes—both nonparents and parents, after all, pay the taxes that support public schools. Redistribution may also occur at intermediate levels of society. Thus in societies with strong lineages, lineage organizations may have taxes or dues that move wealth from the more affluent members toward those with fewer resources. Some property may even be held in common by such groups. That saves a step in the redistribution process: The goods to be distributed don't need to be gathered first.

What is crucial to understanding redistribution is, as with reciprocity, that goods are circulated in a way that is not exactly "economic" in the usual sense of the word. Instead, there is some person or set of people who have the authority to direct how the goods will be circulated. Redistribution thus often looks more political than economic. Those overseeing the redistribution may do so on behalf of the people or do so through their own raw power. One important implication is that the parties themselves do not decide if the re-distribution is fair—that is the role of whoever is in charge. Thus an unequal relationship is implied by redistribution. Another implication is that the re-distribution may become rather impersonal compared to the direct, highly personal nature of reciprocity.

EXCHANGE

Finally, goods may be exchanged based on more utilitarian principles. Some-times this is simply bartering one commodity for another. If a wide variety of goods needs to be circulated, an actual physical market place has much to recommend it. Instead of going to different people in different places for dif-ferent commodities, all goods can be brought together at one time. Weekly or monthly markets may suffice—and are very common in agricultural societies. With sufficient volume, as in cities, a continuing market may develop. That continuing market may have its own physical structures or simply be a set of stalls set up in an open area or along the sides of a road. The more formal and institutionalized these markets are, the greater the likelihood that they be-come impersonal. "On-line" buying is an extreme version of that. There is ef-fectively no personal contact at all. On the other hand, some elements of personal interaction tend to creep back into even such explicitly economic transactions. After all, doing business with people on a regular basis requires something of the same trust seen in balanced reciprocity.

The most important thing to note about exchange is that it is indeed pri-marily economic. In particular, it benefits from the use of a standard curren-cy so that all goods are automatically priced in terms of a single standard. The presence of money, in turn, often changes social relationships. Money, unlike perishable products and single-use items, can be accrued indefinitely. That tends to undermine the logic of giving things away rather than hoard-ing them. These more mercenary exchanges also usually require some legal structure, since people are no longer dealing with each other on the basis of personal connections and reputations. Yet despite the formal, impersonal na-ture of economic exchange, it remains difficult to completely remove the per-sonal, social aspects from even the strictest economic transactions. As will be seen in the Japanese case study later in the chapter, people often want to take strictly economic transactions and recreate them as personal and reciprocal arrangements.

THE WORLD OF WORK

People spend much of their time in activities that we generally describe as "work," whether collecting nuts and berries, hunting game, clearing a gar-den, sowing fields, building factories, or writing computer programs. We

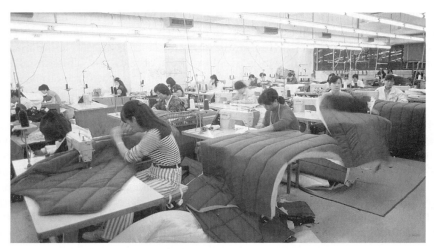

Women at work in an apparel plant in Macau, China. (*Macduff Everton/The Image Works*)

generally contrast work activities with such nonwork activities as being with family and friends, relaxing, playing, and even learning. The balance between work and nonwork parts of life is often used to assess the overall quality of life. One argument about the relative value of foraging and horticulture in Part I, for example, was precisely the relatively low number of work hours each week that were required to meet basic economic needs.

Although the issue of balance between work and nonwork time is important, it is also useful to look more specifically at the work component of life. Consider, for example, how pigs are used as a food source in foraging societies compared to how they are used in industrial societies. In foraging societies, pigs would be hunted in the wild. If multiple people were in on the hunt, those people would likely be kin or close friends. Those people would usually be using tools (bows and arrows, spears) that they themselves had made. When the pig is killed, it would be shared among the hunters who would, in turn, share it with their kin and friends. It's nice to share and, besides, hoarding isn't going to work very well without refrigeration. That's the practical logic of reciprocity. In industrial societies, by contrast, pigs are, for the most part, commercially grown. Those who kill the pigs do so in a specific work area using tools that are provided to them. They do so when and how they are told to by people who are their "bosses." Those bosses are generally trying to maximize the money they are making, rather than proving their social status by giving away the profits to the workers. On the work floor, people are often strangers to each other and may not even have time to talk. Finally, from this job, the workers take home not the pig but money, which they then share with a different set of people than those with whom they work.

The world of work has become something very different in industrial so-cieties from what it is in other kinds of societies. One could even argue that work in modern societies is inherently unnatural and inhuman compared to what we know of human beings in other kinds of societies. This unnatural and inhuman world of work has been a focus of much anthropological re-search on contemporary societies. Some anthropologists have looked at how to make the work itself more productive—especially with new technology. Others have been more concerned with the social aspects of work and what helps people integrate their work with the rest of their lives. Yet others have sought to integrate all these issues into a comprehensive approach to the world of work. For such a comprehensive approach, it is helpful to note the four dis-tinct problems that arise with work: First, the *actual work* may pose problems by being difficult, complex, or changing; second, *managers* often introduce ad-ditional problems, including unresolvable tensions about what the ideal work-er is; third, *coworkers* are usually necessary to the job but have their own conflicts, which may undermine the work; and, fourth, workers also have *home lives* and usually people at home (family, neighbors, friends) who are potentially in conflict with what is required by the world of work itself.

THE WORK ITSELF

In terms of the actual work being done, people do not generally set the guide-lines and control the setting for the work. Their work takes place in structured settings, by set time schedules, and according to set procedures. It is a rare job indeed where people can work where they want, when they want, and according to their own ideas of how the work can best be done. The work may be performed by the worker, but it is neither of the worker nor for the worker. In the contemporary world of work, these problems are compound-ed since the work itself is changing, and often changing very rapidly. That usually means that the set procedures are either not yet set or were set to yes-terday's requirements.

MANAGERS

As they do this work, employees must usually deal with managers ("boss-es") who are supervising the work, even though they may have had little input themselves in the design of that work. Managers are also usually em-ployees themselves, who thus have the same problems of responding to ex-ternal requirements about where, when, and how to do their work. Perhaps most importantly, managers are subject to inherent conflicts about what they want in the people who report to them. They want employees who are com-petent, respond well to supervision, and are also relatively inexpensive. That is a tall order. If people are competent, they are likely to want higher wages. Furthermore, if they are competent they are likely to contest a manager who tells them to do the work in a way they don't think is effective. That problem becomes more severe if the nature of the work is very technical or is rapidly changing. The employee is then likely to know the work far better than the manager and to be increasingly resistant to management's interference in the work. These already problematic relations between employees and management become even more complicated when the employee and manager are different from each other in terms of gender, age, ethnicity, religion, or even native language. "Dealing with the boss"—understandably enough—becomes a job in itself. Yet every minute spent on that job of dealing with the boss is time not spent on the real job.

COWORKERS

Relations with coworkers also provide potential problems. Those coworkers may, on occasion, be kin or friends, or may, over time, become kin or friends. Yet they are often strangers. Furthermore, coworkers are potentially in conflict. If one employee, for example, starts producing a great deal more than other employees, that puts pressure on the others to also produce more. Thus highly productive workers ("rate-busters") are often resented by their coworkers. That resentment can turn to outright hostility if there is a lack of job security or limited promotion opportunities. Coworkers then become competitors. Worse yet, management may very well use coworkers against each other: singling some out for special favors, enlisting others as informers on their colleagues, or punishing yet others to set an example. Getting along with your coworkers—understandably enough—can also become a job in itself.

WORK AND HOME

As employees are struggling to do their work, appease management, and maintain peace with their coworkers, they are also at risk in their home environment. Their work provides the economic means to maintain their homes, but it also requires their absence from those homes for very long periods of time. Life is split between work and home. It doesn't take much expansion of work hours (and commuting time) to make time at home a rather small share of waking hours. Furthermore, if all household members are working (or going to school), much of the time at home will be devoted to simple maintenance. That means that the domestic group is functioning on very limited amounts of shared interactional time. As different household members go off to different work and different work environments, they drift apart. Yet once back at home, they have little time to do the kinds of social repair work needed to reestablish and strengthen their relationships. The fragmentation of families in contemporary society is one result. The more time people spend away from each other, the more time is needed for catching up with each other—but the less time there is for actually doing so.

There are thus seemingly unavoidable problems with the world of work in contemporary society. Such problems make the relatively seamless lives of foragers rather appealing—which helps explain why their lives are often romanticized. Wouldn't it be good to work with the people you know and know the people you work with? Wouldn't it be good to do your own work rather than somebody else's?

Case Study
Gift-Giving in Japan

In Japan, gift-giving is an elaborate, well-developed social art. Gifts are given for many reasons and return gifts for them are expected. Those return gifts then create an expectation of their own return gifts. The balancing of gift and return gift (and return gift for the return gift and so on) is a difficult one. A common warning to newcomers to Japan is that it is very easy for the process to get out of control. With a tendency for the return gift to be more elaborate than the initial gift, this "balanced" reciprocity may turn out to be unbalanced and lead into an escalating and financially ruinous relationship.

Honda's humanoid robot ASIMO celebrates a birthday with children of a nursery school in Tokyo. (*Tatsuyuki Tayama/Fujifotos/The Image Works*)

One particularly interesting aspect of Japanese gifts is their packaging. Even such token gifts as *omiyage*—gifts brought back from trips for friends, families, and coworkers—are elaborately wrapped. Indeed the wrapping and presentation are so extensive that it is sometimes hard for foreigners to tell what the object is and even whether it is something durable (a set of napkins) or something edible (a set of rolled sweets). More elaborate gifts are packaged in multiple layers. A black lacquer box with the imperial design that came to my family when I was young (and sits in my dining room today), for example, came inside a carefully wrought paulownia wooden box, which was wrapped in silk, and then placed within another well-crafted box. One result of this packaging is that it is very hard to forget that an object is indeed a gift. The packaging is itself so intricate that it is likely to be kept rather than discarded. The object itself can thus never be extracted from its social context. Indeed, such gifts are often kept in their original packaging and only brought out occasionally. That helps explain the clean interiors of Japanese houses. There's little clutter of objects since most things are only brought out when it is actually time to appreciate them. They are then unwrapped once again.

This packaging has some interesting implications for actual gifts, but perhaps even more interesting implications for things that we would not consider gifts at all. For example, if one purchases a service from somebody, it is not generally appropriate simply to pay for it by counting out currency. That would imply that this was an economic transaction devoid of any human respect. Thus money is invariably placed in an envelope and presented more as a gift than a payment. Actually, it would be better yet to wrap the money in some nice paper, place that in a very nice envelope, and perhaps also give a small token gift at the same time—which would, of course, also be wrapped. What would seem to be simple economic transactions are thus "packaged" as personal social relationships.

All this packaging does very well in underlining the social aspects of reciprocity in Japanese society. Even economic exchanges can be packaged as gifts and return gifts thus bringing the cold world of cold cash back into the warm glow of human reciprocity. There are, however, some potential negative implications as well. It can become difficult, for example, to distinguish a gift from a bribe. Was that very nice piece of Satsuma pottery that now sits on my bureau simply a gift to acknowledge a neighbor or was it intended (as my father feared when he received it many years ago) to "buy" favorable action on a property dispute. Is the "gift" of a rather large sum of money for a rather modest New Year's door decoration anything other than extortion when the people providing the decorations are from the local underworld (*yakuza*)?

Case Study
Sunbelt Working Mothers

Work is a world of its own. The way work is accomplished, the kinds of tools people use, the social organization of the workplace, the training and educational requirements for work, the very culture of the workplace, all these have occupied the attention of anthropologists. But work is also only a part-world and the workplace is only a part-culture.[3] Work is inextricably connected to the home. For the organization, the purpose of the work may be to produce something, but for the workers, the purpose of work is to support a life away from work. The two worlds of work and of home thus need to be studied together. Louise Lamphere, Patricia Zavella, and Felipe Gonzales attempted exactly that kind of integrated analysis with their study of women working in new industries in Albuquerque, New Mexico.

Albuquerque was an attractive place for many employers for a variety of reasons. Labor was available at relatively low wages and with relatively low levels of unionization. Thus employers could hope to have an inexpensive and tractable work force. Many of the new jobs that became available also had positive features for workers, especially for women. Sometimes there were flexible work hours that enabled women to balance their work and family lives. Sometimes wages were good. Even though women were systematically paid less than men for equivalent work, these jobs in emerging industries provided higher wages than their previous job options, and sometimes higher wages than men could make in other Albuquerque jobs. Women were thus simultaneously victimized by lower wages (as they have been since the early days of factory work) but also beneficiaries of better wages than they could earn from other sources.

This world of Albuquerque factory work raised a number of issues about the relative effects of gender, ethnicity, and marital status. Ethnicity among the working women (roughly split between Anglo and Hispanic) did not appear to make much difference in how the women approached their jobs. Instead, women varied in their approach to work depending on the relationships they had at home, particularly the relative importance of their salaries to the overall support of their families. There were distinctively different strategies for single mothers, women whose income was the major support for their families (i.e., their husbands earned less), women whose income contribution was only a supplement (i.e., their husbands earned more), and women whose income was roughly equal to that of their husbands. It was these different

---

[3]Michael Maccoby, "The Corporation as a Part Culture," in *Anthropological Perspectives on Organizational Culture,* edited by Tomoko Hamada and Willis E. Sibley (Lanham, MD: University Press of America, 1994), pp. 267–277.

household situations that explained how women approached their jobs. It also explained how they approached their families. When both wives and husbands contributed roughly equivalent amounts of money, for example, there was far more equal division of household responsibilities—although men were more likely to help out with childcare than with house-cleaning. In the world of the home, ethnicity appeared as somewhat more significant than at work. Hispanic women typically had a broader range of kin and friends upon whom to draw for assistance. Yet the basic dynamics of marital roles seemed to reflect very practical considerations about who in the family was providing what level of financial contribution to the household.

The implications of this combined analysis of work and home lie in several areas. For example, it is helpful to recognize that ethnic distinctions have limited use in understanding how women negotiate the world of work, the world of home, and the connection between the two. Instead, it is the practical work options and home constraints that seem most important. That very practical nature of women's decisions suggests how important it is that there actually be an array of work options. For Albuquerque at the time of the study, those options were fairly good: new, expanding industries with a range of jobs, relatively high wages, and significant flexibility in working conditions. However, those options can change, and in Albuquerque they did. Many jobs disappeared with layoffs and sometimes complete plant closings. Experiments with flexible working conditions lost out to managerial desires for greater control. There were other problems as well. Sometimes the short-term benefits of the new jobs were offset by long-term hazards. In one department of one of the companies they studied, exposure to chemicals and other materials caused serious physical problems for workers. Specifically, some forty-nine women lost their uteruses to cancer, tumors, or excessive bleeding. That is a useful reminder that when such jobs are sent overseas (as they often are), the benefits to the corporations lie not only in lower wages from overseas workers but also in lower accountability and costs for occupational accidents and disease.

SOURCES

Economics is so central to most anthropological work that it is especially difficult for this topic to provide merely a few citations. Nevertheless, three sets of work merit particular attention. One is the work on actual markets, for which Clifford Geertz's *Peddlers and Princes* (University of Chicago Press, 1968) still serves as a good example. Another is the early work in industrial anthropology that is covered well in the edited volume *Applied Anthropology in America* (Columbia University Press, 1987; Elizabeth M. Eddy and William L.

Partridge, editors). The third is the more recent analysis of contemporary work, for which a very good source is the *Anthropology of Work Review*, a publication of the Society for the Anthropology of Work (itself a section of the American Anthropological Association). Two relatively recent reviews of economic anthropology are *New Directions in Economic Anthropology* by Susana Narotzky (Pluto Press, 1997) and *The Anthropology of Economy: Community, Market, and Culture* by Stephen Gudeman (Blackwell, 2001).

For the topic of gift-giving in Japan, a good starting point is provided by Joy Hendry. She has written on the subject in various of her books, but the best introduction is probably her *An Anthropologist in Japan* (Routledge, 1999). Almost any book on Japanese culture—indeed almost any travel guide about Japan—will provide the basics not only of gift-giving but of some of the interpersonal styles that also make sense in terms of reciprocity. Bruce S. Feiler gives a nicely engaging account in his *Learning to Bow: An American Teacher in a Japanese School* (Ticknor and Fields, 1991). The case study on working women is drawn from *Sunbelt Working Mothers: Reconciling Family and Factory* (Cornell University Press, 1993) by Louise Lamphere, Patricia Zavella, Felipe Gonzales, and Peter B. Evans. Janet Benson has written some complementary material on immigrant and refugee families in the meat-packing industry: "Households, Migration, and Community Context," *Urban Anthropology* 19 (1990): 9–29 and "Undocumented Immigrants and the Meatpacking Industry in the Midwest" in *Illegal Immigration in America* (Greenwood Press, 1999; David Haines and Karen Rosenblum, editors).

CHAPTER 12

POLITICS

In the European tradition, politics is conventionally defined in terms of formal government or conveys an implication of shrewd maneuvering to gain desired ends. For anthropologists, however, the term is far more general in meaning. It covers a wide range of political forms, processes, and functions. Indeed, one of the main concerns of anthropologists is precisely this great variability in political activities from very small societies of a few hundred people to countries like India and China with populations of over a billion. For anthropologists, as well, politics is not only about personal maneuvering for power but also about the tasks that societies must accomplish in order to maintain themselves.

This chapter introduces the issue of politics from an anthropological perspective. A brief overall introduction is followed by discussion of three major concerns that anthropologists have in looking at politics: first, the different kinds of political system that have been found throughout the world; second, the basic functions of politics (external relations, internal control, and infrastructure); and, third, the way in which people function in political roles. The chapter's two case studies describe "headless" government among the pastoral Nuer in the Sudan and the situation of indigenous minorities (specifically the Yanomami of Brazil) within modern state systems.

THE NATURE OF POLITICS

Politics in its broadest sense is about social organization. The term assumes a social entity of some kind beyond the immediate family that has its own interests, options, obligations, and characteristics. In the contemporary world, politics is usually seen in terms of nation-states that are geographically based, have clear borders, and a formal political apparatus. This need not always be the case. Social groups can be based on factors other than fixed territory, can move across boundaries, and often have no formal political roles. Yet such groups still have political systems and functions. They also have a sense of a definable set of people, a "we," who are bound together in a common destiny. Much of politics is about exactly that definition of one's own group as compared to that of others. The nature of that common destiny depends on who the "we" are and who else—the "they"—is nearby. One set of people living in relative isolation may well have a very different political system than a similar set of people living in close contact with others.

The nature of the common political destiny also hinges on the sheer mass of the society. In discussing the different adaptations in Part I of this book, for example, the four themes were control over the environment, density of settlement, complexity of social organization, and mobility. Nowhere is this clearer than in politics. The more *control* there is over nature, the more essential will be common responsibilities to maintain and monitor that control. For example, the more extensive the irrigation, drainage, and flood control structures of an agricultural society, the more vital it will be to maintain that infrastructure over time. The greater the population and the *density* of settlement, the more likely that there will be disputes and that those disputes will often be among strangers. Simple dispute resolution thus becomes a broader and more difficult public task. The greater the *complexity* in social organization, the greater the need for oversight and harmonization of the different parts and subsystems of that complex social organization. Finally, *mobility* is crucial. The greater the mobility of the people, generally the more difficulty there will be in tracking them and ensuring that people are in the "right" place, especially that they are not moving at will across the borders of political systems.

These issues of control, density, complexity, and mobility explain the first two of the topics to be discussed below: the *different kinds of political system* and the *basic functions of political systems.* As political systems become more complex and more formal, however, a third issue arises. If there is to be a stable and effective political system that meets common needs, then there must be people to do the work. Those people must work to the public good rather than to their own personal interest. This problem of finding competent people who will work for the public good has been one of the most intractable problems of government. No sooner does someone gain political power, it seems, than corruption begins. Those in politics thus become all too "political." That issue, then, is the third of the topics addressed below: the distinction between *politics* and *governance.*

FOUR KINDS OF POLITICAL SYSTEM

The different political systems that anthropologists have found correlate closely with the different kinds of adaptation described in Part I of this book. The kind of political system found among foragers is called the *band.* Among horticulturalists are generally found *tribes,* which are in anthropological terms political systems based explicitly on kinship. Among some agriculturalists and pastoralists, there are more formal political systems that transcend kinship;

these are called *chiefdoms*. Finally, in larger agricultural and industrial societies are found *states*—the form of government with which we have the most experience. These four types of political system are outlined below in terms of (a) their essential characteristics, (b) the kinds of special political roles that exist, (c) the kinds of external and internal conflict to which the society must respond, and (d) the way in which effective social organization is achieved by that system.

BANDS

Bands are small, loosely organized groups with only informal leadership.

a. Band societies are found among foraging societies and are characterized by small, mobile, and flexible social groups. For most band societies it is difficult to even distinguish a separate political system. Politics, economics, and kinship seem seamless.

b. In band societies there is thus very little in the way of formal political roles. There may be leaders, but their roles are relatively informal and task-limited. They are "first among equals" (*primus inter pares*) rather than having a formal political role that distinguishes them from other people.

c. Band societies are subject to both internal and external conflict but usually have the option of resolving such conflict informally. Since ties to particular pieces of territory are not strong, external conflict can be avoided simply by moving away—and perhaps returning later. Internal conflict can be resolved through discussions among the relatively few members of the group.

d. The relatively small size of bands is crucial to how they work. The people have usually lived together and worked together for many years, and often for many generations. They know with whom they are dealing and they know from experience that they need to have good relations with everybody. The key to resolving these problems is thus *everybody knows everybody else*.

TRIBES

Tribes are well-defined groups structured along the lines of kinship, although with little formal leadership.

a. Tribal systems are common among larger groups—usually horticultural or pastoralist—that have more complicated organizational needs. There is a separate political system, but that system is grafted onto a kinship structure. In many cases that kinship structure is based on a very careful accounting of blood relations; more often it is a combination of careful accounting of some blood relations and the assumption of prior blood relationships with other people. That means, in the kinship terms already described, that tribes will include both lineages and clans, and probably some assumed relationship among clans.

b. There will be some formal political roles in tribal societies, but these will be largely based on status in kinship groups. A tribal council, for example, is likely to be a council of the heads of the constituent kin groups. A tribal leader may well be the head of the most important lineage or clan, although sometimes a particular person could be chosen by council consensus.

c. Tribes have both internal and external conflict. External conflict may be hard to avoid. For pastoralists, for example, reliance on resources even at one time of year—water in the dry season, for example—may require some defense of that area even though it is only needed during that one time of the year. For such reasons, greater coordination of larger numbers of people will be necessary. Internal conflict is likely to be more common and more complicated because of the greater value of property and the increased number of people.

d. Perhaps the most important characteristic of tribal societies is that everybody knows and is part of the kinship structure on which the political system is based. People may not necessarily know all the people with whom they deal, but they will certainly know the significance of the kinship groups to which they and others belong. The key is thus that *everybody knows everybody else's group.*

CHIEFDOMS

Chiefdoms are centralized political entities with inherited political offices that have both practical and ceremonial functions.

a. With chiefdoms, political systems emerge as separate and distinct systems. In agricultural or horticultural societies where there is some storable and transportable surplus, different groups of people become united under a chief who may be outside their immediate kinship group or their local territory. Thus chiefdoms can unite people from different groups—even groups that are antagonistic to each other.

b. In chiefdoms, there are political roles that are not simply the same as kinship or economic roles. The chief is a ruler to whom special obligations are owed and who performs special political duties. The chief frequently decides disputes and determines issues of external conflict and peace. Chiefs have their own resources and their own power.

c. Chiefdoms are likely to have more frequent internal and external conflict. For both, the simple presence of a surplus that has been conveniently gathered together for the chief will itself cause potential conflict. Those outside the chiefdom may well be interested in obtaining some of that surplus for themselves; those inside the chiefdom may envy the chief's position and riches. The more opulent the chief's lifestyle, the more clear it will be to those within and outside the chiefdom that there is indeed something here worth taking. Furthermore, the complexity of the society within the chiefdom, which may include multiple groups, increases the likelihood of friction and dispute.

d. In chiefdoms, then, there is increased potential for conflict of various kinds. Such conflict cannot be resolved on the same basis as in band societies, where the very small scale of the society permits a very personalized social interaction. Nor can it be resolved as in tribal societies where everybody knows the kin groups of everybody else, and exactly what obligations are mutually owed. What is held in common in a chiefdom is the chief. People may not know each other personally or understand how to interact according to rules of kinship. They do, however, know that they are all subject to the chief. The key is thus that *everybody knows the chief.*

STATES

States are complex, centralized political entities with defined borders and numerous full-time officials.

a. State societies are generally based on intensive agriculture or industrial adaptations. They are thus larger, far denser in population, and linked very strongly to territory. They are also likely to have large, varied surpluses and significant infrastructure. The combination of valuable resources, transportable commodities, and people who often don't know each other very well is a volatile one.

b. In state societies, the political system is highly developed and based largely on territorial, rather than personal or kinship, bases. The political system usually includes a wide range of formal organizations and specific tasks, whether these involve dispute resolution, irrigation systems, tax collection, or military action. Because many of these government jobs are crucial for the general public good and have significant technical requirements, one of the major tasks in state systems is to recruit dependable, competent, honest people.

c. Because state systems are comparatively rich both in their resources (such as well-developed agricultural fields) and in their surplus (often concentrated in a capital city), they are natural targets both for their citizens who may want a piece of the pie and for neighboring states and tribes who might like to claim the entire pie. There is thus great potential for internal and external conflict. Compounding that problem, most state societies are rather diverse in their population, so many ordinary day-to-day conflicts (over who inherits land, for example) are not easily resolved on a personal level since people may not share the same beliefs or customs—or even language.

d. State systems are thus run neither on the basis of individual personal interactions nor on the basis of kin groups. Nor can everyone possibly have direct access to the "chief." Although many local matters may be resolved informally, in state systems there will generally be recourse to a wide range of formal government agencies. Indeed, there are likely to be several layers of government, from the head of government (president, emperor, queen, commander) through a mid-level division (states, provinces) to the local level (appointed village head, district judge). What makes the system work is not that people know who is in each of these positions, but that they know the positions exist. The key is thus that *everybody knows the system*.

THE CORE POLITICAL FUNCTIONS

The different kinds of political system can be largely understood in terms of the variation in societal size, complexity, and density. But whatever the specific kind of political system, there are core political functions that have to be met. These functions may be performed informally by kin and neighbors or formally by designated bureaucrats. They may be decided at the whim of a chief or according to the formal written laws of a state. These three central functions are external relations, internal order, and infrastructure.

EXTERNAL RELATIONS

Few societies are so isolated that they don't have neighbors. Those neighbors may be very similar to them or very different in terms of their general adaptation to the environment, their customs, their language, their beliefs, or their economic practices. Yet it is a rare neighbor—no matter how similar and apparently peaceful—who does not pose at least some potential threat. That threat may be unintended or intended, small or great, immediate or long-term, but that potential threat cannot be ignored. It may be possible to form

Belmonte Castle, La Mancha, Spain. (*Jose Fuste Raga/AGE Fotostock America, Inc.*)

alliances, but alliances may dissolve and, in any case, they simply spread the responsibility for risk rather than resolving it. Furthermore, alliances may raise the stakes of any potential conflict, making it wider and more destructive than it would otherwise be.

External relations can be handled in a variety of ways. If neighbors are potential problems, why not engage them in mutually beneficial trade or give them occasional gifts? If they show tendencies to attack, why not put up a wall to keep them out? The problem is that such inherently defensive approaches generally also require some offensive capability. A wall itself, for example, will not solve problems. It can only slow down an attack. Even an impregnable citadel is not sufficient. While you wait out the enemy, they are likely to pillage the countryside on which you depend for food, so that the cost of victory might be famine. Given the likely need for some offensive capability, you might decide that an offense is itself the best defense. If your neighbors have resources you desire, why not simply take them? If they pose a threat, why not take them over or destroy their agricultural base so that they will pose a reduced risk?

The nature of external relations depends greatly on the type of political system and the basic adaptational strategy of the society. Band societies, for example, have some significant advantages on both offensive and defensive levels. They are relatively mobile and thus can move away from danger; likewise, if they have access to a fast means of movement, such as horses, they can be a very strong raiding force. Tribal societies, because they are based on very clear organizational principles of blood, are often very easily and quickly mobilized. If they are pastoralists rather than horticulturalists, they too will be able to move away from danger without losing their resources, since they can drive their animals with them. As with band societies, a fast means of transport will make them effective raiders and their larger political systems—based on kinship—will make their impact even greater. Thus did the Mongols under Genghis Khan sweep out of central Asia and take over much of both Asia and Europe.

Chiefdoms and states, because they are more thoroughly sedentary, face somewhat different problems. They cannot afford to let an enemy run loose on their territory since the destruction of their agricultural base would be the destruction of the very foundations of their society. Conflict must occur outside the society's agricultural land, clear borders must be established, and some kind of army must be created to defend the borders. Additional diplomatic strategies may help. A big state (like China) might then develop a set of client states beyond those borders that could absorb the brunt of any attack; a smaller state (like Vietnam) might decide to send tribute to a larger state (like China) in the hopes this might lessen the danger of an attack.

INTERNAL ORDER

The second central political function is maintaining internal order. Again, the nature of that function varies among the different kinds of political system, the nature of the basic adaptation, and the society's size and density. In band societies, with relatively little property to argue about and long-term personal relationships, order is maintained by informal means. In large state societies, with a great deal of property to argue about and relationships that are often between complete strangers, more formal means will be needed. Thus in band societies, the resolution of disputes is likely to be on a personal basis and assessed in terms of the relationships among the people in dispute. In state societies, on the other hand, the resolution is likely to be more impersonal, based on how any person should behave—whether friend or stranger.

This distinction between informal and formal mechanisms for maintaining order and resolving disputes is seen in a variety of contrasts between band societies and state societies, with tribal societies and chiefdoms ranged in between.

> *Negotiation, Mediation, and Adjudication:*   In band societies, resolution of disputes is through *negotiation* between the parties since there are no formal authorities. If that negotiation doesn't work, there will likely be *mediation* by friends and relatives who want the dispute resolved for their own reasons. In state societies, on the other hand, the dispute is likely to be *adjudicated* by such formal authorities as judges.

Custom and Law: In band societies, the resolution is likely to be based on *custom* that reflects the common experience of all those involved. In state societies, the resolution is likely to be in terms of formal written *law*. Those laws may have developed from customary practices but have superseded them.

Compensation and Punishment: In band societies, the goal is usually *compensation*. The purpose is to return relationships to their prior balance so that people can again cooperate with each other. In state societies, on the other hand, the goal is more often *punishment*.

Sanctions: In band societies, the *sanctions* used against people are usually social. *Gossip* and *ridicule* are often enough to bring somebody back in line. If those measures don't work, there is always the threat of *ostracism*. In state societies, on the other hand, the sanctions are more formal and physical: *Fines* can be levied, *seizures* of property can be ordered, and *incarceration* imposed.

Death: Death is a particular kind of sanction used in many societies but the way it is used as a sanction varies greatly. In band societies, although rarely used, it may occur as a kind of compensation extracted by the parties themselves. In state societies, however, it is a formal punishment that can only be imposed by the state itself. Many states, it should be noted, no longer use the death penalty on the grounds that it is inherently inhumane.

INFRASTRUCTURE

In addition to the responsibilities in external relations and internal order, most political systems—although particularly chiefdoms and states—have responsibilities for some aspects of the infrastructure of the society. The extent of this responsibility varies widely. Even among contemporary state societies, for example, some see a stronger government role than others. Communist governments, for example, have tended to see an absolutely central role for government in economic planning, while capitalist-oriented governments see a lesser role. Such variation aside, there are three major kinds of infrastructure in which most political systems take an active role.

The first is *economic development*. In early state societies, this responsibility is especially strong in terms of irrigation, drainage, and flood control. These are typically governmental responsibilities because of their scope and their centrality to the whole society. The interest of the government is not entirely selfless. A breakdown in the basic economic infrastructure, after all, would mean not only problems for the people but a decline in the tax base.

The second is *transportation*. Again this is partly a matter of the scope of the requirement but also of its centrality to the tax base. In agriculturally based societies, for example, it does little good to have an agricultural surplus at the local level if this cannot be transported to the cities and to the other places where it is needed: for example, to armies at the borders of the society. Roads and canals thus become essential.

The third is *communications*. The bigger the political system the more likely that there will be different languages, different currencies, and different standards of measurement. Yet if there is to be standardized dispute resolution, there will need to be written laws. If there is to be a standard tax levy, there will need to be standard currency or standard measurement of commodities. The larger the political system, then, the more likely governments will look to standardize communication whether that requires a standard language or common units of measurement.

POLITICS AND GOVERNANCE

Whatever the kind of political system and the basic function to be performed, some practical problems remain. These problems become increasingly difficult as the scale of the political system grows. Four of these problems deserve particular note: a high standard of rationality, mobilization of public effort, recruitment and training of government workers, and management of social diversity. These are discussed below, largely in terms of state societies for which these problems are most acute.

RATIONALITY

Although general functions of the political system may be clear—flood control, for example—the way to accomplish specific tasks in support of those functions is not always clear. Especially if the effects of error or miscalculation are high, there must be a very careful, very rational assessment of how to get the work done. Furthermore, since most core functions of political system are continuing, rather than one-time efforts, there must be very careful followthrough on the work. After all, the public good is at stake, and very possibly the survival of the entire society. For that reason, many of the functions of government must be separated from ongoing political debates and contests. *Governance*, the system of getting things done, must thus be separated from *politics*, the system of determining allocation of resources, specific tasks to be done, and who is to do those tasks.

MOBILIZATION

Another challenge is how to *mobilize* people to get the work done. Why do people follow their government and leaders? At one extreme, they may do so because of governmental *power*. Those governing the society may simply have the raw means to force people to do things. At the other extreme, the political system may rely on its *authority*. Here people follow leaders because those leaders are believed to have the right to provide direction. A related contrast is between the need to *persuade* people to do something and the ability to *coerce* them to do so. Most political systems have some measure of each of these. Governments based solely on power are subject to rebellion or less formal resistance such as sabotage. Yet even governments acknowledged to have the right to govern will require occasional use of force—against recalcitrant taxpayers, for example.

A CIVIL SERVICE

Although the government as a whole may take on common tasks and responsibilities, the will of the government must be accomplished through people who work for the government but nevertheless have their own personal interests. The situation is very much like that described for the world of work in the previous chapter. As workers, those in government from the very top to the very bottom must balance the demands of their work as they understand it, the nature of the work as those around them understand it, their own personal self-interest, and the calls on them of their family and friends. The *recruitment* of people for public service thus becomes very difficult. Even if recruitment is effective, the demands of the world of government work may result in people straying from their official responsibilities into issues of personal gain. Most large-scale governments face periodic problems of *corruption*. One solution—as the Chinese decided very early—is to have officials whose job it is to monitor other officials. The early Chinese version of this is usually translated as the *censorate*. In the contemporary United States, that function is partially met at the federal level by such government agencies as the General Accounting Office or various internal audit agencies. It is also met increasingly by nonprofit "watch-dog" groups. Indeed the very existence of an independent *civil society* is considered one of the best ways to maintain government accountability.

MANAGING DIVERSITY

A final problem is one of diversity. Although band and tribal societies may be composed of similar people with similar characteristics, chiefdoms and states inevitably consist of different kinds of people. Those people may be different in language, religion, marriage patterns, or other fundamental issues that make them who they are as a people. Such differences are often described in terms of *ethnicity*. Ethnic groups are sets of people we recognize as having their own internal solidarity of sameness that is different from that of other people. Although issues of ethnicity are important in all areas of life, it is especially in the political arena that the problem of how to establish solidarity despite such differences must be confronted. The contemporary world is filled with examples of political states that have fractured because of such ethnic differences, and often fractured into bloodshed and even genocide. Balancing different ethnic groups is perhaps most politically complex when language differences are also involved. Even Canada's much admired bridging of the Anglo-Francophone divide, for example, has not gone unchallenged, and it is only a rare province (New Brunswick) or state (New Mexico) that has been willing to take on the practical requirements of bilingualism. Coping with the vast range of languages and cultural traditions of recent immigrants to North America has placed these issues of ethnicity at the very center of the political agenda.

The people within a political system may also be diverse in more strictly economic terms. They may, for example, have different kinds of jobs. If those jobs are very different, and particularly if those jobs pay very differently (the multimillion dollar salaries of CEOs, for example), such differences can also create social divisions. People are not just different, but richer or poorer, higher or lower. This is what is meant by *stratification* (a system that organizes people hierarchically) or *class* (a particular level in such a stratification system). Class can sometimes be very sharply defined. In many premodern complex political systems (such as India), differences in occupation were inherited and thus class divisions hardened into what are called *castes*. You inherited your identity from your parents, were restricted to marrying people within your own caste, and were subject to serious punishment if you acted in ways inappropriate for that group. In many other societies, class differences are inherited only in a general sense. In premodern China, for example, if you came from a wealthy family you would have far better access to education and thus a far better opportunity for social advancement. Yet it was also possible for the less wealthy to improve their position and that of their families. There was the possibility of *class mobility*. Finally, as in contemporary North America, there are people who have more wealth than others, yet there are opportunities for the less wealthy to carve out new wealth for themselves. We may argue about the extent of equal opportunity in North America, but we agree that it should exist.

Finally, there are other kinds of diversity that exist in all societies but take on a different meaning within complex political systems. *Age* differences are one example. In a modern industrial democracy, the "old" are no longer simply somebody's gramps and grannies, but an extremely potent bloc of voters. Turning eighteen and twenty-one are no longer just regular birthdays, but convey the rights to vote and to drink. The changes in the implications of *sex* are also significant. In contemporary North American society, men and women are less frequently defined in terms of their personal relationships to each other (as fathers, mothers, sisters, uncles, and so on) and more often as individual human beings with—on paper at least—equal political and economic rights. In modern industrial democracies, men and women function in a wide range of situations in which their sex has become irrelevant (voting rights) or should be (equal pay for equal work).

Case Study
"Headless Government" among the Nuer

The Nuer are pastoralists who live along the upper reaches of the Nile River in the Sudan. Cattle are central not only to their livelihood, but to their very conception of life. Cattle are valuable as images of beauty and as the "currency" through which social interactions are conducted. Exchanges of cattle, for example, are essential to marriage negotiations. Yet, again like most other pastoralists, the Nuer also grow crops, particularly maize. Nuer life in the Sudan is governed by the seasons. As the rains begin, the Nuer move to higher ground, planting fields and moving their cattle into corrals. After the rains end and the waters start to subside, the Nuer begin moving into the lower land, letting their cattle graze over the new vegetation. As conditions become dryer, there are increasingly large concentrations of Nuer among the increasingly limited available sources of water for the cattle.

In political terms, the Nuer face several problems. First of all, since the Nuer move during the course of the year, the political system must itself be *mobile*. It cannot be based on territory. The alternative is to base the political system on kinship since kinship is inherently mobile. One's neighbors may change when one moves, but one's relatives don't. The Nuer political system, like that of most other pastoral groups, is thus based on kinship. Furthermore, as again with most other pastoral groups, it is based on kinship largely structured through the male line. This is thus a *tribal* political system in the technical anthropological sense.

Second, since the size of groups varies during the course of the year, the political system must be relatively *flexible*. Although one's relatives don't change, during the course of movement some relatives who lived close by may be physically separated and some who were far apart may be reunited. Kinship needs to be an extensive framework to which all people can be assigned so that everybody fits into the system somewhere. This, then, is not a situation only for nuclear families or only for extended lineal groups. It is a situation that may require both.

Third, the Nuer are not a small group; they number in the hundreds of thousands. This increases the requirements on the system to be *inclusive* and *detailed*. It must be sufficiently large to include everybody and sufficiently detailed so that all people know how to relate to a very large number of other people. Thus not only must the lineages go back very far in time but there must be a way to account for the relationships among lineages. For the Nuer, this means that people know both the details of their own lineages and the relationships among the lineages. For the Nuer, lineages are grouped into clans and the clans themselves are known to have some original connection of some kind with each other. Thus *all* Nuer can be placed within a single kinship system.

The result is a political structure that accounts for several hundreds of thousands of people, is mobile and flexible, is without any formal political authorities (i.e., "headless"), and is sufficiently detailed to provide an indication of how one should relate even to strangers. In meeting a stranger, one has merely to list one's ancestors to provide a basis for a relationship. A shared grandfather would yield a close *lineage* relationship; a shared *clan* membership a more distant one. A quick assessment of the current situation then yields the significance of that relationship. If a dispute arises with somebody within one's own clan, one can probably count on the assistance of someone from the same lineage. In an outbreak of raiding between clans, shared clan membership is adequate to knowing which side one is on. Finally, if there is a threat from the outside—from non-Nuer—clan hostilities can be put aside to face a common enemy. That is precisely what the Nuer have done both against the British in the colonial period and against the largely Muslim northern part of the current state of Sudan in a civil war that has lasted the past quarter-century.

Case Study
Indigenous Minorities and State Systems: The Yanomami

State systems are rarely homogenous in their composition. Indeed, they are often extremely diverse. A state may include different kinds of territory with very different ecological adaptations and ways of life: horticulturalists and foragers in the hills; agriculturalists in the valleys and on the plains. A state may include different languages that limit communication or merely regional dialects that fuel mutual suspicion. There may be different religions, some coexisting relatively harmoniously and others subject to violent outbreaks of mutual hostility. Sometimes different groups within the state will have relatively similar resources and power; sometimes they will differ greatly in numbers and resources, perhaps with a single majority and several minority groups. Among those minorities are many indigenous groups who were originally on the land but subsequently overwhelmed by newer arrivals. Indigenous minorities exist in most parts of the world—the United Nations estimate is 300 million worldwide. With the growth of agricultural systems, industrialism, and the strength of central state power, they are usually pushed to the margins, either up further into the hills or back into wilderness areas that have limited agricultural or industrial use. The increasing reach of global economic systems (anxious to use any possible natural resource) and border-conscious political states (anxious to assert their control over even the most remote parts of their territory) make such refuges increasingly scarce.

A group of Yanomami in the remote Roraima area of northern Brazil. (*Richard House/AP Wide World Photos*)

Brazil's Amazon basis provides an example. Among the many peoples living along the Amazon basin are the Yanomami. Their territory stretches north from the Amazon and across the border into Venezuela. They number some 10,000 and represent the largest of the Amazon indigenous groups that maintained their lives in relative isolation. That isolation disappeared in the 1970s. A road project that began in 1974 headed north of the Amazon through Yanomami territory. Although it was not finished, it still brought destruction to the southern part of Yanomami territory and, perhaps worse, the workers on the road brought diseases, particularly influenza and measles, that were often deadly to the Yanomami.

At the same time a survey of the Amazon's mineral wealth was published. That survey indicated the presence of significant amounts of uranium, tin, diamonds, and gold on Yanomami territory. The regional government itself pursued the mining of tin and titanium, but it was the invasion of small-time miners searching for gold (the *garimpeiros*) who created the gravest problems. It was a gold rush. Miners invaded by the thousands, bringing further disease and destruction. They killed Yanomami, several times in massacres, and even took over a Brazilian military outpost when it appeared the military would enforce the laws that limited mining operations. The miners were far better armed than the Yanomami and their supporters—and far better connected to the government. At one point when protests from anthropologists, missionaries, and others concerned about the situation escalated, the Brazilian government responded by requiring all those people to leave the region. When they were finally allowed to return some two years later, they found a population reduced by perhaps a fourth, with the remainder sick and often starving.

Ultimately a Yanomami reserve was set up by the Brazilian government in 1992. It was far smaller than the one originally envisioned by
Yanomami advocates, but still far better than the series of small, separated
reserves originally suggested by the Brazilian government. Yet even this
formal reserve remains vulnerable. It has been subject to periodic reinva-
sion by the *garimpeiros*. It is also now home to Brazilian army bases from
which emanate further diseases and accusations of sexual abuse of Yanomami women. The mining industry has continued to press for opening up the
reserve for mining and the Brazilian military has continued to stress that,
since the reserve is within 60 kilometers of the border, it is necessarily subject to national security oversight. The Yanomami are thus confronting perhaps the two strongest forces in the contemporary world: the desire for
economic expansion on the one hand and for absolute control over borders
on the other.

SOURCES

For overviews of the development of political systems see Cohen and Service's *Origins of the State* (Institute for the Study of Human Issues, 1978) and,
for a review of the anthropological engagement with political issues, see Joan
Vincent's *Anthropology and Politics* (University of Arizona Press, 1990). *Ongka's
Big Moka* about the Kawelka in New Guinea provides an engaging glimpse
into the difficulties faced by a Big Man as he attempts to solidify his authority through a feast for an allied village. Jack Weatherford's *Tribes on the Hill*
(Greenwood Press, 1985) provides an anthropological view of the operations
of the U.S. Congress.

Regarding the case studies, see E. E. Evans-Pritchard's *The Nuer* (Ox-
ford University Press, 1969) for this classic discussion, which is rather dan-
gerously abridged here. As noted in the prior discussion of the Nuer in Part
I of this book, Sharon Hutchinson's *Nuer Dilemmas* (University of California
Press, 1996) provides a more recent view of the Nuer and Jon Holtzman's
Nuer Journeys, Nuer Lives (Allyn & Bacon, 2000) provides an astute discussion of the trials and tribulations of Nuer coming to Minnesota as refugees.
The Yanomami still living in relative isolation are well known through the
writing and film of Napoleon Chagnon. For a more recent account of the
Yanomami, see Alcida Rita Ramos's *Sanuma Memories: Yanomami Ethnogra-
phy in Times of Crisis* (University of Wisconsin Press, 1995). A short discus-
sion of the Yanomami (from which I have drawn here) is included in David
Maybury-Lewis's *Indigenous Peoples, Ethnic Groups, and the State* (Allyn &
Bacon, 2002).

CHAPTER 13

RELIGION

This final chapter in Part II addresses religion. Religion is a difficult subject both because it is complex and because people often have difficulty talking about it in an educational context. Nevertheless, religion is essential to people's lives and provides one of the most important structures within which they operate. Religion not only provides a general framework for behavior, relationships, and institutions, but also a framework of beliefs through which people find and create meaning in their lives. It is thus an appropriate bridge to the more extended discussion of meaning that is provided in Part III.

This chapter begins by introducing the complexities of religion and the many different vantage points that people take on it. After those introductory concerns, the chapter then turns to three central dimensions of religion: general understanding of what the world is about, specific explanations of why particular things happen at particular times, and the search for assistance and guidance. A short discussion of ritual rounds out the discussion. The first case study at the end of the chapter concerns the acquisition of "power" among the Cibecue Apache; the second describes the politics of Islam in Indonesia in the context of 9/11 and the subsequent U.S. invasions of Afghanistan and Iraq.

The Nature of Religion

Religion is a complex and contentious subject. One indication of that complexity and contentiousness is the range of descriptions and explanations of religious beliefs, activities, and institutions. Consider some common issues raised about religion from psychological, sociological, political, and economic perspectives:

> *Psychological:* There are several varieties of psychological explanations of religion. Many people, for example, note how representations of the Judeo-Christian god look all too much like a typical,

bearded male head of household. The implication is that people portray a god who matches their childhood images of authority figures. Another common strand of psychologizing about religion involves noting how religious beliefs and activities serve to ease people's tensions and uncertainties about their lives. Some people even argue that religion is an "opiate" that masks the true realities of their lives—a sort of back-handed compliment about how effective religion can be.

Sociological: Many sociological discussions of religion stress the very positive functions that shared religious beliefs and activities have on people. It is valuable for people to have a shared framework of meaning, and activities that honor that framework of meaning. It is not uncommon for fellow believers to see themselves as kin, people who have become bound to one another not by their shared blood or their shared territory, but by their shared beliefs. Religion is an admirably effective social glue, producing a strong solidarity based on sameness. In fact, it is so good at gluing some sets of people together that it increases their hostility to people who don't share the same beliefs.

Political: The effectiveness of religion as a social glue underlies its frequent political importance. If people share the same general beliefs and belong to the same organizations that follow those beliefs, then religion can become the basis for social action and for political action. Religion can also be an effective form of social control within a society. If a political leader or political system can claim a religious mantle, then political authority may be increased. On the other hand, if those without power find a religious mandate for their action, their efforts are greatly strengthened. Religion is thus a potent political force whether for alliance or conflict, oppression or resistance.

Economic: The effectiveness of religion as a social glue also has analogous utility in economic areas. Most economic transactions, ranging from very personal forms of reciprocity to relatively impersonal forms of market exchange, require some measure of trust. Who better to trust—aside from kin, perhaps—than people who are bound to you by ties of shared belief? Another economic aspect of religion is that some religions are simply more supportive of particular kinds of economic activity—whether that activity involves tilling fields, hunting game, or engaging in trade. Finally, ritual activities can bring people together in ways that permit or even encourage economic exchanges (whether of ritual objects or more mundane ones).

These psychological, sociological, political, and economic considerations suggest the extent to which religion cuts across other areas of human life. To understand these pervasive implications of religion, however, it is essential to understand religion on its own terms. On its own terms, religion addresses three quite distinct issues: first, a *general framework* through which to understand how different aspects of the world and human life fit together; second, *specific explanations* of why particular things happen at particular times; and, third, assistance and guidance in both the practical and spiritual aspects of life—let's just say *help!* These are discussed in order in the following sections.

A GENERAL FRAMEWORK

Religion provides a general understanding of the nature of the world—or, perhaps more accurately—of the universe. That framework of understanding helps situate the individual and the society.

BINDING PLACE AND TIME

The first thing that religion does as a framework of meaning is to bind together the different physical places in the world. An example from Colin Turnbull's *The Forest People* illustrates this point. When Turnbull's assistant, Kenge, first comes out onto the plains east of the forest in which he lives, he has great difficulty in recognizing distances and animals in this visually new environment of open vistas rather than the foreclosed world of the forest. For him, it is "the forest" that is alive and good. It doesn't take him long, however, to expand that notion to this new place and to realize that "this God must be the same as our God in the forest. It must be one God."[1] As Kenge's epiphany suggests, it's not much of a religion that doesn't include all the places in your world. Religion as a framework of meaning thus binds together *place*.

The second thing that religion does as a framework of meaning is bind together *time*. It would be a poor religion indeed that didn't somehow tie together events that have already happened, those that are in process now, and those that will come to be in the future. The ways in which past, present, and future are bound together vary. For societies in which ancestors are very important, the line that runs through the present from the past to the future is the line of blood. In that sense, you don't really die since you live on in your descendants. Alternately, many people have a notion of rebirth similar to the

---

[1]Colin M. Turnbull, *The Forest People* (Simon & Schuster, 1961), p. 258.

Hindu devotions in Bali, Indonesia. (*Otto Stadler/Das Fotoarchive/Peter Arnold, Inc.*)

Hindu and Buddhist notion of *karma*. Your current life is a result of your actions in your past lives and your future lives will be the result of this one. For yet other people, the future lies not in death or rebirth in this world but a passage to a much better place—some kind of "heaven" that will be an eternal reward for a life well spent. What all these beliefs provide is a mechanism to link one's current life back to the past and forward to the future.

BINDING THE ANIMATE AND INANIMATE

Religion also binds together all the animate and inanimate things in those different times and places. Since religion includes all places (whether seen or unseen, known or unknown) at all times (places that now exist, may once have existed, or may someday exist), the inventory of those animate and inanimate entities is likely to be long and complex. Many, many people believe in a variety of "spirits." Some may be the "ghosts" of people who once lived; others are spirits of animals, of natural forces, or of natural objects. Some of those spirits are sufficiently developed that they are called "gods." Spirits and gods may be good or bad; helpful or indifferent. Those spirits and gods, in turn, may be seen as subordinate to a higher, more inclusive "God" or as the manifestation of a more impersonal, pervasive force underlying the material world—such as the *mana* of Polynesia—roughly equivalent to "the force" of the Star Wars saga.

In order to come to terms with this complexity, there is likely to be some effort among the people themselves (and the anthropologists) to impose some order on these beliefs. Thus from both a believer's perspective and an anthropological one, Christianity is usually called "monotheistic" because there is a single God. However, it is also the case that Christians acknowledge a wide range of spiritual forces (for example, saints and angels) and the emphasis on a triune God (Father, Son, and Holy Spirit) is an acknowledgment not only of unity but of diversity. Tylor's original notion of a "Supreme Being" thus turns out to be a rather better label than the "monotheistic" one.[2] These arguments about how to label religious beliefs may seem quibbling but they often have serious consequences. If religion is to be a framework for how people understand their world, then there are likely to be efforts to control that framework: to decide what exactly are the proper beliefs and the proper behavior. The religious quest for a framework of meaning may have important social consequences that are divisive (expelling the unbeliever and wrong believer) while uniting the true believers.[3]

AN EXPLANATION FOR EVENTS

Understanding the general nature of the world (and universe) provides a useful framework. However, it does not always answer the more specific question of why particular things happen to particular people at particular times. In everyday life, for example, people know that death occurs from a variety of causes such as traffic accidents, cancer, homicide, and, now, terrorist attacks. The statistical probabilities for many of these kinds of death are also well-known. The probabilities can be adjusted for your specific age, gender, and perhaps even occupation. Yet that does not explain why particular people die at particular times. After all, many of the people who die

---

[2]The conventional categories may be worth noting, although, as I have indicated in the text, attempting to stuff people's complex religious views into these conventional boxes is dangerous—an orthodoxy of analysis rather than an orthodoxy of the believers. In any case, *monotheism* is used to note a religion in which there is one god or at least one who has overriding authority and power; *polytheism* refers to the presence of multiple gods (who are not simply different versions of each other); *animism* refers to belief in spirits; and *animatism* refers to more general beliefs that what we would call supernatural power is an animate force underlying and pervading the natural world. By these definitions, "ancestor worship" is a kind of animism.

[3]Sometimes this effort may be *ecumenical,* meaning that it seeks the common ground among different beliefs and practices. On the other hand, the effort may be to define *orthodoxy* ("straight" or correct beliefs) and *orthopraxy* ("straight" or correct practices). In such cases, *heterodoxy* ("other" beliefs) and *heteropraxy* ("other" practices) may then be the grounds for persecution—even unto death.

from different causes are not even in high risk groups. There is still a mystery, then, as to why a particular person dies at a particular time. Statistical probabilities are not a great comfort. In times of catastrophic loss, the reverse question also arises. Why was this person spared when so many others perished? People escaping danger often find their personal relief turned into guilt by the nagging question of why someone else did not survive when they did. Thus, although people have a general framework for understanding why events take place—whether "scientific" or "religious"—the specifics of loss or survival still require attention.

AN EXAMPLE: THE AZANDE

One classic example of this problem of specific explanations was provided by E. E. Evans-Pritchard. His discussion of the Nuer was noted earlier, but this case derives from his work among the Azande, who live somewhat to the west of the Nuer in northern Africa. The Azande believe in witchcraft. As a good social anthropologist, Evans-Pritchard was not content to simply note the Azande belief in witchcraft as part of their traditions; he wanted to understand the logic of their belief in witchcraft, and his explanation is as follows.

The Azande construct huts to provide protection from the elements. The huts are built from long poles, and pyramidal roofs are constructed on top of the huts. These huts are simple structures. The Azande know very well that termites eat wood and that, with the number of termites they have, the pillars that support the roofs will eventually be eaten away and the huts will collapse. The Azande therefore, like us, have a very clear and "scientific" explanation of why huts collapse. When a hut collapses, they are not surprised and have no need for "supernatural" explanations. The termites did it.

However, if someone is under the roof when it collapses, especially if that person is injured, the situation becomes very different for them. They have an empirical explanation of why huts collapse in general but react to a hut collapsing on a person with more suspicion. They are not satisfied simply with a probable explanation. They—like us in many ways—are inclined to believe there might have been foul play. They—like us again—are likely to investigate. However, their suspicions run deep and their explanation of how the foul play occurred extends beyond our customary explanations. We might suspect that somebody caused the collapse by hollowing out the wood to make it weaker. They suspect that someone used sorcery to make the hut collapse at the specific time the victim was under it. How else, they would argue, could this particular hut have collapsed at this particular time when this particular person was under it? That this is just a coincidence is, from their point of view, a rather dubious assumption. The Azande are thus likely to conclude that sorcery is involved if a hut collapses when a person is under it. That conclusion, of course, is drawn from their more general framework for understanding how the world works, which includes the notion of witches. Yet the example suggests they have two distinct ways of explaining things: One is a general framework that is largely "scientific" in our terms and the other is a more specific explanation that invokes witchcraft.[4]

This tension between general explanations and specific ones is not uncommon. Cambodians, for example, have a general Buddhist framework for understanding the world, which includes notions of *karma*. They may also acknowledge Buddhist scriptures, which suggest an apocalypse that is to come. Yet on the personal level, these frameworks do not do very well in explaining the holocaust that occurred in Cambodia in the late 1970s. It does not explain why they survived and so many others, including the other members of their families, died. The general framework of Buddhism is for many not adequate to the weight of the specific case. The general framework can explain why there is suffering in the world but cannot explain why so much suffering was visited on Cambodia in such a short period of time.

SEEKING HELP

Both the general framework and the specific explanation provide some help in understanding how and why things happen. It is useful to have an understanding of the general structure of the world and explanations for why specific things happen to specific people—like you. However, such understanding does not resolve problems. Diagnosis is not a cure and much of religion is about the cure: how to change the way things are. To change things, you will probably need assistance of some kind. Obtaining such assistance hinges on what resources are available, whether you yourself can obtain or connect with those resources, and, if not, whether there is someone else who can connect to those resources for you. These issues of "what's available" and "how to connect" each deserve comment.

KNOWING WHAT HELP IS AVAILABLE

In most societies, there is a belief in a broad range of what we would call spiritual forces. There may be a general force or power that resides within, below, or above the world of everyday life. Sometimes that power has

---

[4]They would, however, probably argue that sorcery is as empirically "real" as the physical laws that govern hut collapse in general.

concrete manifestations—for example, great serpents may twine beneath the surface of the world. Sometimes it is less concrete: an energy that you absorb with your very breathing. There may also be more specific forces within particular objects, associated with particular animals, or freely moving on their own. There may be spirits of particular parts of the land (sacred mountains, for example) or of particular animals (reflecting the strength of eagle, whale, or bear). If one's ancestors remain nearby as spirits, they may be a particularly useful source of assistance. Finally there is a wide range of gods sometimes visualized as a vast pantheon, sometimes as a single entity with many manifestations. There are thus in almost all societies multiple spiritual resources from which to seek assistance. Some may be more effective than others and some may be more inclined to help than others.

KNOWING HOW TO CONNECT

But how do you connect to these sources of assistance? The anthropological record is particularly rich regarding the different ways in which human beings make such connections. Those connections fall into two general categories: direct connection or connection through an intermediary. A *direct connection* with a particular spiritual force or being may be the result of a planned attempt at contact (a vision quest, for example) or may be the result of an illness that brings you close to death and thus, inevitably, closer to the spirit world. Sometimes the connection is made through your own control over the spirits, sometimes it is made through supplication to the spirits, and sometimes it is made through the spirits' control over you. A sorcerer might thus "command" a spirit to work for good or ill, while a penitent might beseech a god to mercifully grant some benefit. On the other hand, if you yourself do not have the ability (or opportunity) for such direct contact, an *intermediary* is needed. Thus some people (mediums in American society, for example) have greater familiarity with the spirit world and can help others make contact with it. Anthropologists usually make a general distinction between *shamans* (individuals who have established some direct personal contact with the spirit world and thus can more easily do so again) and *priests* (individuals who represent an established religious organization). There are, however, many options in between shamans and priests. Even objects can become intermediaries to the spirit world. Bones cracking in a fire or tea leaves in a bowl may bring a message from the spirit world. Spiritual forces themselves can also be intermediaries: Your personal guardian spirit may intercede with other spirits, the Virgin Mary may intercede with God, or the Buddhist Goddess of Mercy (*Guanyin/Quan Am*) may be a more approachable figure than Buddha himself.

RITUAL

In making a connection to the forces and beings that lie beyond the limits of everyday life, people are dealing with a domain that is special, difficult to reach, and sometimes very dangerous. Connecting to that domain will likely require considerable effort. That suggests it might be useful to be organized about it. For example, if you do achieve some kind of connection, you would want a way to continue or at least periodically recreate that connection. Such connection and reconnection are often conducted through *ritual*. Think of ritual as a kind of package deal for connecting to the spiritual domain.

The word "ritual" in North American usage has two contrasting meanings: One is that of a particularly *meaningful* set of repeated activities ("the ritual of first communion was very important in our church") and of a repetitive and *meaningless* set of activities ("what a ritual!"). There are three distinctive features of ritual, whether meaningful or meaningless. First, ritual is indeed *structured and repetitive*. It wouldn't be much of a ritual that was not generally the same each time; in most cases the attempt is to do exactly the same things each time. Second, ritual involves separation from the everyday world in terms of *location*. A sacred mountain, a mosque, a grove of ancient trees, a sylvan glade . . . all those will do very well. If the more poetic options aren't available, at least some marking of space is needed. An altar on a family's living room wall might provide a space for the ancestors; lighting incense will help transform that space into something special and more appropriate for prayer. Third, ritual is also separated from the everyday world in terms of *time*. That issue of time has to do with the actual time of the ritual (dawn, the equinox, the new moon, a death anniversary) as well as marking off the ritual with beginning and ending events. Just as taking off one's shoes entering a Buddhist temple helps mark the edge of a special space, a call to worship marks the beginning of a special time. Putting one's shoes back on marks the return to the regular world and a benediction or final prayer marks a return to normal time.

Given the nature of ritual with its repetitive activities and marking off of space and time, it is hardly surprising that the word "ritual" has these two meanings. Clearly if all this works and somehow people are brought closer to the spiritual world, then ritual is a positive thing indeed. If the effort yields only the smell of one's own dirty socks in a "temple" that worships an unknown ghost, the effort may seem wasted and the ritual becomes "just a ritual." Even under the best conditions, things may go awry as the spirit fails to move into this opening created at the heart of the ritual. Yet whether successful or not, elaborate or minimalist, heavily spiritual or merely social among close family, rituals provide a very useful guide to what people consider worthy of the effort needed to prepare a special time and place for some greater communion.

Case Study
The Practice of Religion: Finding and Living with Power

The Cibecue Apache—the matrilineal Arizona people discussed earlier—live lives in which things can go wrong. Some of those things are relatively minor (losing your truck keys) and some are major (serious disease); some are short-term and some long-term. There are also things that can go right: getting some money, finding a good spouse, or just finding those keys. In all these aspects of life, it is good to have some help. It is good to have help from your friends and family and also good to have help from the spirit world. For the Apache, that means it is good to have *diyi*, which can be loosely translated as a "power."

There are many different kinds of *diyi*. Some match basic elements of nature. Thus there are powers of wind, rain, lightning, thunder, water, moon, and sun. Some match animals (such as the powers of bear, eagle, snake, wolf, coyote) and at least one matches a plant (the root of the manzanita). Some are more like deities: the *gan* (male deities who appear in masked dances) and Changing Woman (who appears during the girls' puberty ceremony). The Apache thus have—as most people do—a broad range of spiritual forces that they recognize. Furthermore, the Apache believe that there are vast supplies of each of these powers and that some portion of that power can be gained by human beings. That raises two questions: First, how do you get a power, and second, what can you do with it?

The Apache distinguish two ways of getting a power. One way is for *you to find it*. For the Apache, that means choosing a particular power and then learning the chants that are associated with that power. Learning the chants is likely to be time-consuming and also expensive. You have to find somebody who knows the proper chants and get that person to teach the chants to you, including what they are and how they should be performed. You then have to memorize them—perhaps fifty or sixty chants, some of which require a half hour to complete. That will get you a connection to the spirit and, probably, the spirit will then act on your behalf—although it may take some time for the spirit to accept you as worthy of its help. The other way is for *it to find you*. Sometimes a power may find you to be so worthy that it will manifest itself to you. That may be in a dream or it may be in waking life. A dream of lightning, or a lightning bolt striking close to you during waking hours, might mean that lightning power is making itself available to you. After that initial contact, however, you will also need to learn the chants associated with that power in order to continue the connection.

Getting a power is not an easy process; but, then again, it's not prohibitively difficult considering the potential advantages. Sometimes, the advantages are relatively clear and predictable. Thus when Changing

Woman temporarily enters a girl during the puberty ceremony, the implication is of health and long life—for Changing Woman is herself forever
living. For most powers, however, the specific advantages are not always
immediately clear. Rain power might help with rain but might help with
something else instead. Deer power might help one man in gambling but
help another man in hunting. For an Apache, living with a power is a trial
and error process. Over time you find out what the power is capable of
and what it is willing to do for you. Power may also leave you, especially
if you become old and weak (without enough power for the power), if you
treat it with disrespect, or if you become unworthy of it. While you have
it, however, you will have some good practical assistance (finding those
keys perhaps) and some general protection as well. You are also likely to
be respected by other people—unless they come to believe you are using
your power to their disadvantage.

Case Study
The Politics of Religion: Islam, Indonesia, and 9/11

Religion is a very powerful force in human life. That is true on the personal
level and on the political one. When people share the same religious beliefs
and expressions, they are often brought very close together socially and politically. When they do not share those beliefs, the potential for conflict is
high. That conflict may be muted and managed in a spirit of ecumenism.
On the other hand it may erupt very quickly into violence. In Nigeria, a
country split largely between a Christian South and an Islamic North, a
peaceful demonstration in October 2001 against a Miss World pageant de-
generated into rioting. The roots of that conflict were partially tribal (Hausa
in the North, Yoruba and Ibo in the South), partially economic (most resources go to the South), and partially colonial (it was the British who pieced
together these two very divergent regions). Still it is the images of Christianity versus Islam that have become predominant in Nigeria. Christian
and Muslim militias now attack each other with frequency and force. Christian militia descended on the Muslim (Hausa and Fulani) village of Yelwa
in May 2004, killing probably several hundred people. That was in response
to an incident in Yelwa earlier that year in which dozens of Christians who
had taken refuge in a church were killed by Muslims.

   The images of Islam and Christianity in violent conflict have become
commonplace in recent years. In those images, however, is often lost the

Men at prayer in an Islamic mosque in Jakarta, Indonesia. (*Thomas Renaut/Getty Images, Inc./Stone Allstock*)

extent to which religions—whether Islam or Christianity—are themselves internally divided. Thus the apparent conflicts between Islam and Christianity are often as much about internal conflicts within each of those religions. In Indonesia, for example, comments about the United States after 9/11 were often harsh. There was talk of "sweeping" all Americans out of Indonesia hotels, of assassinating the U.S. ambassador, of burning down the embassy. Even generally conciliatory comments by the Indonesian president had an edge: Perhaps the United States ought to learn from these events and cleanse itself of its sins.

As a long-time observer of Indonesian politics, Robert Hefner notes that the events of 9/11—and the subsequent U.S. military actions in Afghanistan and Iraq—came in the midst of discussions among Indonesian Muslims about the proper political role of Islam. The confrontation in Indonesia between Christianity and Islam must, he argues, be understood in the context of this internal debate with Indonesian society. For Indonesia, the world's largest predominantly Muslim country, the three years before 9/11 had been traumatic ones. The three-decade rule of President Suharto came to an end in 1998, but only after Suharto had been instrumental in supporting a neo-fundamentalist turn in Indonesian Islam and in its relationship to Indonesian politics. New alliances with conservative Islamic organizations were intended to save his regime. Those alliances did not save him, but were valuable to his supporters and allies as they tried to unseat the moderate Islamic president who succeeded him.

One mechanism that was used to undermine the new regime was to fuel existing antagonisms. Some of these antagonisms were ethnic. The Chinese, who had been among the hardest hit in the massacres that had led to Suharto's initial rise to power some thirty years earlier, were again singled out. One government official described them as "rats." The most effective tactic, however, was to fuel existing Muslim-Christian antagonism. The ideal place for that was Maluku (the Moluccas). There, on a set of smallish islands, the numbers of Christians and Muslims were roughly equal and the tensions were high. The Islamic neofundamentalists seized the opportunity to inflame the situation. They called for volunteers to go and fight on the Islamic side. Although the government officially opposed this, many individuals in the government, often holdovers from the Suharto years, were themselves supportive. Thus the volunteers crossed the sea to Maluku on government ships and were often accompanied by military personnel.

The resulting strife helped end the presidency of the Muslim moderate who had succeeded Suharto as president. A combination of anti-Americanism and anti-Christianity proved to be a very effective political tool. The world became clearer in this neofundamentalist vision: Economic problems and political instability must surely be the result of the United States and its allies, of Christendom, of the Vatican, of Jews, and of disloyal elements within the society—Christians, of course, but also Chinese, other minorities, and even moderate Muslims. Democracy itself could be added to the list of enemies since it permitted the freedom and diversity that undermined the quest for a conservative Islamic society and government. Those favoring a conservative Islam against a moderate Islam were thus able to use the United States and Christianity as foils in their own pursuit of political power.

SOURCES

The debt to Evans-Pritchard on appreciating the "logic" of religion in a philosophical kind of way will be clear; see his *Witchcraft, Oracles and Magic among the Azande* (Clarendon Press, 1992, abridged). For general discussions of religion from an anthropological perspective see *Religions in Practice: An Approach to the Anthropology of Religion* by John Richard Bowen (Allyn & Bacon, 2001) and *Conceptualizing Religion: Immanent Anthropologists, Transcendent Natives, and Unbounded Categories* by Benson Saler (Bergahn Books, 1999).

The first case study is drawn—as was the previous discussion of the Apache—from the work of Keith Basso, specifically his early general monograph *The Cibecue Apache* (Waveland, 1986). For a contrasting view of a situation in which it is the women who are shamans, see Laurel Kendall's *Shamans, Housewives, and Other Restless Spirits* (University of Hawaii Press, 1985). The Indonesia example is drawn from Robert Hefner's discussion in the *American Anthropologist* a year after 9/11: *American Anthropologist* 104, 3 (2002): 754–765.

PART III

(*Philip and Karen Smith/Getty Images, Inc./Stone Allstock*)

MEANINGS

CHAPTER 14

INTRODUCTION TO
PART III, MEANINGS

As Parts I and II have indicated, anthropologists are interested in understanding people in the specific environments in which they live and through the structures that organize their lives. These are, in many ways, relatively objective concerns. Although anthropologists may be close to the people and involved in their lives, much of what they describe is how life might look from the outside: People have actual characteristics, perform real actions, and relate to each other in particular ways. Yet anthropologists are also keenly interested in the meaning of human life. To attain that more subjective understanding of life, they must grapple with the same issues that confront others in both the humanities and social sciences: How do people experience life and how do they themselves make sense of it? Since anthropologists themselves are also trying to make sense of life, this quest for meaning is a two-channeled story that involves both the anthropologists and the people they study.

This quest to understand the meaning of human life is the focus of Part III. This introductory chapter addresses the basic question of what we mean when we talk about meaning. At the risk of simplification, I will suggest three ways to look at meaning: as a *set of core values,* as an *arena of negotiation* (and sometimes conflict), and as an *act of creation.* As a specific example of these three, *identity* will then be discussed. The chapter concludes with a brief introduction to the structure of Part III and some key themes that will emerge in it.

THREE APPROACHES TO MEANING

In looking at the issue of meaning, anthropologists have taken a wide range of approaches. Such an inquiry ultimately requires a kind of cross-cultural philosophy, incorporating issues of ontology, epistemology, and phenomenology as constructed not only in the European tradition but in those of other areas of the world as well. However, for introductory purposes, three general approaches can be singled out to provide a general road map to the anthropological consideration of meaning.

A SET OF CORE VALUES

The first way of looking at meaning is as a set of core values. Thus—as in the previous discussions of religion—we might say that people have a general framework for understanding their lives and that the framework is based on a core set of values. Those values provide a guide for action. The meaning of life and the things one should do are thus related. This approach to meaning implies a set of values and beliefs that is reasonably coherent, reasonably durable, and shared among at least some people. This approach—whatever its philosophical merits—has some practical advantages. Perhaps most importantly, it forces an inquiry into what values are most important in people's lives, most likely to endure, and most widely shared. Events in Afghanistan, for example, raise again the standard discussions of the *Puktunwali*—the central code of the Pashtun (the majority ethnic group in Afghanistan). Much of the history of the country and of current events can be understood in terms of the two central elements of that code: hospitality and revenge. This emphasis on meaning as a set of core values yields a relatively simple framework of two key values (hospitality and revenge), which, in turn, are very powerful tools in understanding (and simplifying) much of the complexity of Afghan social and political life. This reduction of meaning to core values is very effective as a means to describe how a people and their culture are maintained over time.

There are dangers, however, in this emphasis on a core set of values. One such danger is oversimplification. The neater and more satisfying explanations— both for the outsider and the insider—are likely to be the ones that boil it all down to a single nugget or two. That will tend to eliminate other issues that are minor or perhaps contradictory to the core principles. Furthermore, a consideration of meaning as a core set of values runs the danger of ignoring the diversity in values that exists even among well-integrated communities. Values among men and women, among old and young, for example, are likely to be rather different. One might well ask, for example, whether the Puktunwali is a Pashtun code or simply a code for a certain set of Pashtun adult males.[1] Despite such problems, an emphasis on meaning as a core set of values is common in anthropology since it matches so well the anthropological impulse to find out who other people really are, how they live their lives, how their traditions endure, and how understanding their lives can enrich our own.

AN ARENA OF NEGOTIATION

It is also possible to look at meaning in other ways. One problem with the core set-of-values approach is that values are neither universally shared nor necessarily enduring over time. Instead, one might see meaning as an arena

---

[1] A useful film portrayal is included in *The Pathan* (David Ash and Andre Singer) from the *Disappearing World* series.

of negotiation. Meaning is thus not set but is, to a greater or lesser extent, in flux. Values need not be internally consistent and may even be in conflict: for example, mercy versus vengeance. Nor are values necessarily equally shared by all people in a society. This suggests the need to look at the change, diversity, and inconsistency in meaning rather than its durability, commonality, and consistency. If meaning is variable and in flux, then there must be some dynamic by which one interpretation of things is accepted rather than another. Rather than looking at core values, then, one looks at the different values that exist in a particular society and how those different values are applied, not applied, or modified to suit the occasion. If inconsistent values come to the surface, one very interesting question is how those inconsistencies are resolved. Sometimes one value may win over the other. Sometimes there may be an attempt to seek a broader framework that can incorporate a variety of diverging values. Much of the recent North American interest in multiculturalism has precisely this purpose: to create a new overarching value of diversity within which a broad range of different cultural values can coexist.

This emphasis on meaning as an arena of interaction may be seen in terms of a negotiation among different options or, more baldly, as a power conflict about who can impose their views on other people. Since anthropologists often work with societies that have borne the brunt of colonialism (or other external control), they are particularly sensitive to situations in which there are differences in relative power. Such differences in power greatly affect the outcome of any conflict about meaning. The dominating society may even take action to completely eradicate "old" ways and beliefs. One mechanism used for that purpose with indigenous peoples in both North America and Australia was to put the children in boarding schools, thus ensuring there would be limited opportunity for the transmission of core values from the older to younger generations. While it is possible to look at this contest between different values as a relatively sportive event with teams that are equally matched, anthropologists are likely see the darker side of a contest between strong and weak where there are no rules of fair play and no incorporation of diversity. Instead, there may be an attempted obliteration of the smaller group's values—a sort of cultural genocide.

AN ACT OF CREATION

A third option is to see meaning as an act of creation. After all, even a well-established set of core values requires some mechanism to transmit it to future generations. It requires some creativity even to identify the values that apply to a particular situation. For example, it's good to be honest but it's also good to be polite. Which one applies? Or should it be some combination of the two: something that's literally honest and acceptably polite like "that has a very interesting taste—sorry I can't eat more but I had a bad case of the you-know-whats yesterday." That's polite and relatively true. You've only changed one minor historical detail: You weren't sick yesterday but you might be today.

Meaning isn't simply about something that exists, it must be actively—and often very creatively—applied to the situations that arise. If circumstances change, core values will need to be recreated, reworked, recalibrated, reinvented, or simply re-remembered. This very active aspect of meaning-making has also drawn attention from anthropologists. This kind of approach has dangers as well. It is possible, for example, that the emphasis on creativity may preclude a recognition of how limited people's options often are. Even in the explicitly creative areas of the arts, much is often very conventional. Nevertheless, an emphasis on meaning as creation provides a good appreciation of how inventive human beings can be under even the most limiting circumstances. Such an emphasis is also valuable in bringing anthropology into closer alliance with the arts and humanities and thus providing a useful counterbalance to the close relationship of anthropology with the sciences and social sciences.

AN EXAMPLE: THE IDENTITY OF JAPANESE FROM SOUTH AMERICA

It's hard to make much sense of things if you don't know who you are. It's also hard to make sense of other people if you don't know who they are. Identity is thus a crucial piece of meaning about you and the people with whom you interact. It's also an essential piece of information—in some languages you can't even launch into a sentence without figuring out who you are, who is talking with you, and who else may be listening to you. There are many aspects of identity. Some are fleeting (being a freshman) and some durable (being a college graduate). Some are pervasive in their implications (being male or female) and some relatively narrow in their consequences (hair color—well, usually). Some are about you as an individual (you plan to be a lawyer) and some are about "your people." "Your people" raises the issue of group identity. Such identity may be on the basis of kinship or something broader, like nationality or ethnicity. Consider "being Japanese" as an example of such an identity.

"Japanese" is the common designation for people who live in Japan. The people who live in Japan are quite diverse in many ways (by class and region, for example) and include some people who may not even consider themselves Japanese or be considered by other Japanese to be so. There are, for example, people of Chinese and Korean ancestry in Japan and some indigenous people on the country's northern island of Hokkaido. Nevertheless, there is a tendency by Japanese and non-Japanese alike to view the Japanese as a relatively homogenous set of people about whom there is something distinctively Japanese. They are not just a random set of people who happen to live on the islands that are Japan. They are presumed to be bound together by social ties of kinship and shared location, by a shared language, and by shared values that enable them to live together in an orderly way. Some anthropologists have attempted to look at what that core of shared values might be. The results have included emphasis on such things as "saving face," loyalty, and dedication to the group.

This issue of Japanese identity changes, however, when you take the Japanese out of Japan.[2] For example, many Japanese emigrated in the latter part of the nineteenth and early part of the twentieth centuries. Many came to North America, but some went to South America as well. Of those going to South America, the largest group went to Brazil. Once they were in Brazil, there were some identity options. They could still consider themselves Japanese, they could consider themselves Brazilian, or they could pick something in between. Over the generations—as you would expect—they came to rely more on Portuguese than Japanese as a language and thus were at least somewhat "Brazilian" in that sense. However, they tended to marry among themselves and to consider themselves as distinct from the rest of the Brazilian population. Thus being "Japanese" continued to be an important part of their identity.

By the latter part of the twentieth century, there were some 1.3 million people in Brazil who were of Japanese origin, who did not generally speak Japanese, but who nevertheless considered themselves Japanese. At the same time, in Japan, employers were having difficulty finding enough employees and were looking abroad for sources of good workers. They saw these Japanese in Brazil and decided they would be excellent candidates. They were, after all, "Japanese." With these two groups thus recognizing each other as Japanese—and thus as basically the same kind of people—recruiting for workers in Brazil commenced. Ultimately several hundred thousand workers came from Brazil to Japan (especially after changes in Japanese immigration law in 1990). These two sets of Japanese were thus reunited. Since they were both Japanese in identity, things should be fine—or so the reasoning went. However, there were problems. The Japanese from Brazil had rather rudimentary competence in Japanese so there was a language problem. Furthermore, they had absorbed much of Brazilian culture and often acted in ways that didn't seem "Japanese" to the Japanese. To those from Brazil, the Japanese of Japan were, in turn, often unpredictable and rather cold. This question of being Japanese was now in the arena of negotiation. What did it mean to "be Japanese." Since the Brazilians were very much the newcomers and very much the minority, this wasn't much of a contest. Clearly these Brazilians weren't really Japanese and came to be identified as Brazilians as often as Japanese. The issue of Japanese identity as being a shared set of core values had disappeared. Instead the issue was to what degree they might be Japanese—and the Japanese of Japan were deciding that their degree of Japaneseness was relatively low.

Those from Brazil now faced something of an identity dilemma. Were they to redouble their efforts to somehow become fully Japanese in the eyes of their hosts? Were they to return to Brazil? Or were they to stay in Japan but create some new hybrid identity? They were not the same as their hosts in terms of

---

[2]This discussion is drawn from the work of Keiko Yamanaka and Takeyuki Tsuda, but see the work of Ayumi Takenaka for useful comparative information on Japanese in Peru. Articles by all of these appear in *Beyond Boundaries: Selected Papers on Refugees and Immigrants,* Volume 5 (American Anthropological Association, 1997; Ruth Krulfeld and Diane Baxter, editors).

core values and they were unlikely to force their hosts into some broader and more inclusive definition of what "Japanese" might mean. So, instead, they would be Japanese-Brazilian. To create that identity, they reached into their Brazilian heritage to create a new activity for their new semi-Japaneseness. It was time for the *samba*. Soon there were several *samba* parades in different cities, fortifying this newly created hybrid identity of Japanese-Brazilian. The Brazilian part of their identity had another nice boost in 2002 as they watched Brazil win the final game of the 2002 World Cup that was played in Japan.

The example shows the three different ways of looking at the meaning of identity. The *core-values* approach looks toward what helps bind together a set of people with a single identity—in this case, being Japanese. This particular example is helpful in showing the extent to which such assumptions of shared values may be just that: assumptions. Yet it also shows how important such assumptions can be to people. The *arena-of-negotiation* approach is especially appropriate to the returned Japanese from Brazil in their interaction with their hosts. Its strengths lie in indicating the fluidity of meaning and the way that power affects its negotiation. Finally, the *act-of-creation* approach is especially effective in indicating how the returned workers themselves helped create a new hybrid identity. The example also illustrates some other aspects of meaning that will reappear in the coming chapters: for example, the importance of language in creating a shared identity and the way events—like a *samba* parade—can be used both to indicate meaning and to simultaneously create it.

So What Is Human Meaning?

This example of returned Japanese suggests that even for a relatively familiar area of human meaning—figuring out who you are—the nature, construction, and implications of human meaning are complex. There are no simple answers to what something means. The investigation of human meaning can thus become murky, annoying, and fraught with vertigo. That being the case, a few general comments may be helpful as a rough guide. So remember that while meanings may be complex, multiple, and ever-shifting with changing circumstances, there are four relatively reliable themes about the construction and nature of human meaning.[3]

First, human meaning is *open*. There can be new values, or beliefs, or creative acts, or interpretations, or combinations of any of those. Meaning is not closed; there can always be something new and fresh. And people often enjoy that freedom, creativity, and freshness.

---

[3]These four can be in conflict. The search for order, for example, may well have the result of closing down systems of meaning rather than opening them up. The marking of meaning, as another example, may serve either as a means for creativity and openness, or as a mechanism to close down options and create the kind of orthodoxy and orthopraxy noted for religion in Chapter 13.

Second, human meaning is *context-driven*. As will be especially clear in terms of cognition and language, people cannot ignore context even when they want to—or even when they might be better off if they could. Context may not be everything, but human beings have great difficulty ignoring it.

Third, human meaning is *order-seeking*. That search for order can produce useful insights. However, it can also often result in simplifications that get in the way of further insight. Human beings, for example, are prone to thinking in terms of dichotomies ("well, you're either with us or against us"), and often like to further reduce everything to a single factor ("well, it all boils down to . . .").

Fourth, human meaning usually includes some form of *marking*. That's for both practical and expressive reasons. If you figure something out, you don't want to have to figure it out again tomorrow. If you figure out something really important, you might want to create some lasting tribute to it. The specific ways that meaning is marked are numerous, ranging from verbal stories and written texts, to ritual and ceremony, to the linguistic labels we use, to the way we mark our own bodies.

STRUCTURE OF THE CHAPTERS IN PART III

Part III has four chapters that examine the nature of human meaning from somewhat different angles. The first of these, Chapter 15, looks at human cognition. The purpose of that chapter is to reconsider how biology, culture, and environment all affect the way we think about ourselves and the world in which we live. Much of what we think is "out there," for example, is greatly influenced by what's going on inside us as biological entities. Chapter 16 then looks at language, including the basic nature of human language, how languages are structured, and how they affect the way people understand their world. There is considerable irony in any consideration of language since the capacity for language is something we share even though the specific languages we speak keep us apart. Chapter 17 considers the processes by which meaning is developed and maintained—in particular how human meaning is drawn from the physical world and how the physical world is also used as a place to store human meaning. That reciprocal process of drawing meaning from the world, and storing meaning in it, is discussed separately for bodies (they're always with us); places (they're always there even if we aren't); objects (some small and valuable; some large and imposing); and events (like the *samba* parade discussed above). Finally, Chapter 18 explores the world of anthropological action. Anthropologists are people and thus themselves attempt to create a world of meaning. Much of that attempt—very clear even in the early days of Franz Boas—involves applying the anthropological understanding of human society toward simultaneously maintaining the world and improving the condition of people in it.

CHAPTER 15

COGNITION

It is difficult to separate the stories of human cognition and human language that are the focus of the next two chapters. Much of our thought is language-based and much of our language reflects our mental abilities. Even in evolutionary terms, the development of the brain and speech centers are intertwined. Despite the difficulty in separating the topics, this chapter attempts to address cognition while keeping language largely in the background. Language, in turn, will be in the foreground in the next chapter.

This chapter has three main sections. The first is a review of what is known of *the brain* based on the very rapid expansion of research during the last part of the twentieth century. This quick tour of the brain is hardly definitive but provides a reminder of the need to include biology (along with culture and environment) in any anthropological analysis. The second section addresses the distinction between *perception* (what our senses tell us about what's "out there") and *conception* (how we structure that information more abstractly). A few visual illusions will be provided to indicate how our minds mingle issues of perception and conception. As with all human behavior, that mingling of perception and conception has elements of the biological, the cultural, and the environmental. The third section of the chapter focuses on two specific anthropological topics regarding human cognition: the use of *symbols* and the creation of meaning in daily life—what is often called *sense-making*. The first topic conveys something of the structure and durability of human meaning and the latter captures something of the processes through which human meaning is created and recreated. The case studies at the end of the chapter concern how research on artificial intelligence can shed light on the nature of human cognition and how the apparently simple concept of "middle-class" turns out to be rather ambiguous.

THE HUMAN BRAIN

We know that much of what humans are derives from a biological foundation. Upright posture, for example, frees the hands for other work; an opposable thumb provides the potential for that other work to be extraordinarily detailed. Other animals may use tools, but they don't polish arrowheads, attach them to pieces of wood, and shoot them from a bow as they are running across a field. The finely developed human vocal apparatus—including the ability for minute, carefully controlled movements of the throat, mouth, and lungs (to produce air for speech)—is also unique. Other animals can vocalize, but they cannot produce the flow of varied yet regulated sound required for all but the simplest human communication.

Likewise, humans are unique in their range of mental capacities and processes. The mental activity of humans is largely associated with the brain. The brain is not an abstract thinking machine, but living tissue. Nor is the brain an independent and disconnected organ. Nevertheless, "the brain" is usually considered to be that which is encased within the cranium and dedicated to higher order processing of impulses received from other parts of the body. Research in the last few decades has greatly expanded the understanding of exactly which parts of the brain are related to which activities and how the brain does its many jobs.

Consider the development of your brain. As you develop as a fetus, a neural tube emerges out of the primordial folds of your flesh. In that neural tube a new kind of cell forms: the neuron. During the late period of pregnancy, the estimates are that over 250,000 neurons may be created every minute. During that same latter period of pregnancy, the neural tube develops a somewhat bulbous projection on one end that will eventually be the brain. One potential problem is that these neurons are not being created in the same place where they will be needed, so all those thousands and thousands of neurons will be migrating. They will find their destination along a trail that is marked out by what are called *glial* cells. The trail is established by sniffing it out on the basis of trace chemicals. The neurons then clamber along the trail of glial cells. Predictably, some of the neurons get lost along the way. There's some debate about it, but it seems that many of them can fit in even if they go to the wrong place: The auditory neurons, for example, just start acting like visual neurons. Your neurons thus show some ability to adapt to their environment, just as you do to yours.

Once all these neurons are in the right place—or have decided to fake it—the real work begins. The neurons begin to develop extensions, projections, and just plain bumps that will enable them to communicate with other neurons. That communication requires that the neuron do two things. One involves sending out a single tentacle (an axon) that may terminate at the very next cell or may weave its way through the brain and even halfway through the body. The other involves a larger number of smaller tentacles (dendrites) that will receive messages sent from the axons of other neurons. Once all the neurons are in place *and* have traced out the routes by which to connect to each other, you are in business. Those neural networks will provide information from your various senses and provide a mechanism to direct your body to respond to that information. Much, but not all, of that routing will occur through that bulbous region that developed at the end of your prenatal neural tube. Like all mammalian brains, yours has three general parts. The first is a forebrain, which is the seat of your higher and more abstract functions. The second is a midbrain, which is the seat of your more routine functioning. The third is the hindbrain, which is essential to your very biological functioning. Each of these has specific areas that tend to deal with particular tasks, whether it is the visual cortex for watching things or the amygdala for letting you know of danger by automatically putting your entire body on high alert.

The purpose of this review is not to turn you into brain scientists, but only to emphasize the biological context for what human brains can do. Three points are worth stressing. The first is the *complexity* of the brain. Research on the brain, after all, is not demonstrating that the brain is somehow simpler than we thought it was now that we can see its operations so clearly. Instead, we are finding ever greater complexities. Remember that you have billions of neurons. The greatest number are in your brain, but others are snaking around throughout your body. They have trillions of connections. The second point is the *flexibility* of the brain. The notion that there is a place in the brain for each activity would seem sensible, yet the brain in many cases does not act that way. Research on people who have suffered damage to parts of the brain suggests that other parts of the brain can take over the functions of the damaged parts even if it is not normally their job. And remember that not everything is routed through the brain and, of that, not all routed through conscious thought. A great deal is on automatic pilot. The third point is the *processual nature* of the brain. What we think of as the brain is not so much a specific structure in a specific place as a set of connections that extend throughout the body. Those connections are, in part, chemical and, in part, electrical.

These points about complexity, flexibility, and process reflect the fact that the brain is alive. It is not just a machine programmed to do particular kinds of tasks. It not only absorbs information but develops new ways of organizing that information. Some of that matches our usual notions of conscious thought, yet much of it is unconscious, automatic, or more emotional than conceptual.

PERCEPTION AND CONCEPTION

This great advance in research on the human brain is interesting but does not resolve the more subjective issue of how people understand their worlds. Here, more traditional research is still helpful. That research is usually phrased in terms of a distinction between *perception* (the recognition of things "out there") and *conception* (the organization of those perceptions). That distinction follows common usage of the root words *perceive* (which implies you are sensing something that is out there) and *conceive* (which implies a more abstract—and creative—kind of mental activity). Another way to put it is that perception has more to do with the senses themselves (sight, touch, smell, etc.) while conception has more to do with the integration of that information from the senses and the assessment of its implications. As an example, you

Russian grand master Garry Kasparov faces off against IBM's Big Blue Computer. (*I. Uimonen/Corbis/Sygma*)

might perceive a set of long, narrow, yellowish things halfway tucked into a colorful package. Your brain—ever hard at work—identifies these as french fries and considers how these might relate to what your senses are telling you of your hunger (integrating different sensory stimuli). Your brain might also ponder the effect of fast food on global nutrition (a higher level integration of a broad range of information).[1]

THE IMPORTANCE OF CONTEXT

If we compare conceptions and perceptions (or things that are more conceptual versus things that are more perceptual), there are some differences. Although conceptions might be rather free-floating, perceptions are presumably fairly accurate to an objective external reality. It is certainly possible to conceive of things that don't exist but you shouldn't be perceiving things that don't exist. The former is creativity but the latter is hallucination. Thus, your perceptions ought to be relatively accurate. Sometimes, however, they aren't. Consider the simple illusions provided in Figure 15.1. For both the Müller-Lyer and Ponzo illusions, there are two straight parallel lines of equal length. However, they don't look the same length. We thus perceive these lines as being of different lengths even though we have seen these illusions before and know that we are being fooled. Here, our higher, more abstract thinking is more realistic. But

---

[1]It's best to consider perception and conception as on a continuum rather than as an either-or issue. After all, it's not often that you are simply perceiving something without integrating that perception with something else, and it's not often that you are abstractly thinking about something without some connection to what your senses are telling you.

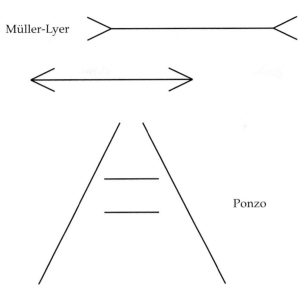

Müller-Lyer

Ponzo

FIGURE 15.1 MÜLLER-LYER AND PONZO ILLUSIONS

why—at the perceptual level—are we fooled by these simple illusions? Some have suggested that the Ponzo illusion works because it looks like train tracks and thus makes us see these two horizontal lines as at different distances. That would suggest cultural and environmental explanations: Our brains have rewired the way we see things due to our previous experiences. However, there is an even simpler point to be made. The lines are not presented alone but with a broader visual context. It would seem that we are incapable of removing unnecessary context even when we ought to, indicating that the importance of context applies even to our most basic physical perceptions. In many situations, that attention to context will give us a broader and richer understanding of what's out there. In cases like these, however, that attention to context stands in the way of solving a very simple problem about the length of two lines.

THE INFLUENCE OF BIOLOGY, EXPERIENCE, AND CULTURE

Consider next Figure 15.2 (on page 194), in which lines of equal length are placed horizontally and vertically. Despite its equal length, the vertical line looks longer. This horizontal/vertical illusion is subject to a range of interpretations. One might, for example, argue that for human beings, any distance "up" is more significant than an equivalent distance on the ground. Climbing directly up a one-mile cliff face is far harder than walking a level mile. Even looking up is harder than looking across. In that sense, the different way height and length are seen reflects our biological adaptation to a world

FIGURE 15.2   HORIZONTAL/VERTICAL ILLUSION

of gravity. Yet it could also be argued that this difference reflects environmental experience. Some research, for example, has suggested that people who live in cities tend to perceive the height as closer to the length than do people who live in more natural environments. In either case, however, "up" is still perceived as "farther" than "across." This is not accurate as to actual distance, but it is certainly accurate to the effort it would take to go the equivalent distance "up" versus "across." Here the perception may be technically inaccurate but it's a good guide to the practical situation.

Finally, consider the Kanizsa illusion in Figure 15.3. Here, the traditional interpretation has been that people tend to see two overlapping triangles and that those triangles, in turn, overlay the small circles. The explanation is that the mind tends to simplify a large number of independent lines into a smaller number of basic geometric shapes. Thus the mind is inherently order-seeking: searching for a simple structure in a complex pattern. These days, however, it's hard to find anyone who doesn't see Pacmen munching their way in from the periphery of the figure.[2] That's a simpler explanation yet and shows clearly the influence of experience and culture on visual perception.

THE WORLD IS FOREST

The mixed influence of biology, culture, and environment on perception is also reflected in real-world situations. Colin Turnbull's discussion of his guide Kenge's first encounter with the open savannah is a good example. Kenge's experience had been in the forest and he had never seen wide-open plains. Initially, he saw elephants in the distance as tiny elephants; he saw a boat on

---

[2]Although the discussion of perception here is of things "out there," perception is very much within the body and conditioned by the senses themselves. Thus, in some reports from people who have gone into trance, people "see" certain kinds of images: dots and jagged lines to start, whorls and tunnels soon after, and eventually usually some distorted images against that whorled background.

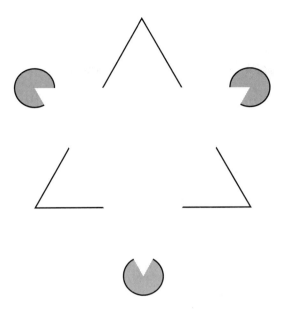

FIGURE 15.3   KANIZSA ILLUSION

the lake in the distance as a tiny piece of wood. He had simply not had prior experience judging objects at great distances. He was correct in perceiving that the elephants and boat were "small," but he had never learned to adjust for such great distances. That was both a perceptual problem (how to accurately judge size at a distance) and a conceptual one (how small could an elephant actually be). But Kenge quickly learned. That perceptual adjustment also had conceptual implications. Kenge had conceived of the world itself as being the forest. The forest was a living presence and generally a positive one. Yet here was a place that was not forest. His solution—as described in the chapter on religion—was to reframe his notion of the forest into something broader that would encompass both forest and savannah. Perception and conception are thus linked; new conceptions will change perceptions; new perceptions will modify conceptions or even create entirely new ones. That linkage of perception and conception lies at the core of anthropology as a method: You can't really understand what's going on somewhere else unless you go there, walk in the shoes of the people, and try to perceive and conceive things as they do.

SYMBOLS AND SENSE-MAKING

What the brain actually does can thus be loosely arranged along a continuum of perception and conception. Perception implies that the brain's work is relatively close to the senses and that the senses—with some interesting exceptions—are relatively objective about what is "out there." Conception implies that the brain's work is more removed from the senses and is thus more general, more abstract, and more independent of the actual moment. Another way to look at this issue is to consider symbols (ideas or objects that contain a general message and thus are relatively conceptual) and sense-making (the process by which meaning is sorted out on a more perceptual basis). Since symbols are the easier part of the discussion, I'll begin with them.

A *symbol* is something that stands for something else. Symbols range from specific and action-oriented to abstract and meaning-oriented. At the more specific end of the continuum are things like a red light, which means to stop. There's no complex web of meaning here; this is a simple practical instruction. Symbols like these are sometimes called *signs*—or sometimes simply *signals*. At the other end of the continuum are more complex symbols that may invoke strong feelings but are not clear about precisely what action is required. A national flag, for example, invokes a range of feelings and thoughts, but it's not necessarily clear what you're supposed to do. Some people restrict the word symbol for this more complex situation, but it's probably best to think of this as a continuum running from relatively simple practical instructions to very abstract and complicated invocations of meaning, with many variations in between.

Symbols vary in their complexity and profundity, but all symbols work in much the same way. Something relatively simple—like a flag, a Valentine heart, a smile, or even a color—stands for something else. Symbols can be highly individual, but they are most effective when they are shared. That sharing occurs on two levels. First, the literal aspect of the symbol itself is shared. For example, a sun, a moon, a flag, or an eagle is a familiar sight. Thus the symbol itself is familiar. A symbol will not be as effective if people have to ask what the symbol itself is. Thus symbols tend to be common objects or representations of them. Second, the meaning of the symbol is also generally shared. That sharing of the meaning is, however, the more complicated part. If we both recognize a picture of an eagle—on a t-shirt perhaps—but you think the eagle is a vicious raptor that just tore apart your cat and I think of it as a soaring, fearless flyer, our use of the symbol isn't going to help our social relationship very much. We share the symbol, but not the meaning of it. Symbols are thus a mechanism to test whether our views are similar and whether we are together. If the symbol is not shared, then our views appear to be different and we are not together. We can stray apart either if one of us doesn't know what an eagle is ("what an idiot") or if we disagree on the meaning of the symbol ("they may fly high but they killed my cat"). On the other hand, if we both recognize the symbol and the meaning of it, we are fully together. Even if we only think we share the meaning, we can still be together. Symbols can thus give a sense of unity by covering up differences.

Symbols show something of what is common to people and serve as ways to demonstrate that commonality. When those symbols *and* their meaning are not shared, however, that demonstrates a lack of commonality. Both those who salute and those who burn a national flag, after all, recognize that the flag is a potent symbol of a country. They just differ on what that means. That agreement or disagreement is achieved very quickly since the symbols don't require great discussion. Symbols are so effective and satisfying because they are so clear and concrete. They pack in much meaning and often with much verve. Would a "don't tread on me" flag, for example, work as well if it pictured a rabbit rather than a rattlesnake? Symbols are appealing because they are compacted pieces of meaning in well-known form. The consideration of symbols is thus a very good research approach to identifying the central values and major points of negotiation within different human societies.

The consideration of human *sense-making,* by contrast, often seems to make things murkier. Sense-making is an honored term in social philosophy, partially because it plays on some different meanings of "sense." We often talk, for example, of "making sense" of things. That implies that things are complex and not terribly clear and we will actually have to do some work to pull them together into a coherent framework. "Sense" also invokes the senses by which we perceive things. Sense-making thus invokes both perception and conception—we are trying to make conceptual sense of what our perceptual senses tell us. While "symbols" convey the appeal of meaning encapsulated in familiar and concrete forms, "sense-making" conveys the complex morass of processes that help us get on with our daily lives.

Understanding human sense-making is something of an ordeal. The human process of sense-making—of making sense of things—is rather messy. It is neither orderly nor very well organized. It is not, then, a rational process where things follow because of clear criteria or cause and effect. On any given day things will vary somewhat, so no master plan is likely to work very well. To refigure the master plan for each new set of events would be forbidding. In order to avoid that constant refiguring, people rely on routines. Something worked last time, it seemed to work okay, so you do it again. You get up and have a cup of coffee, then take a run, clean up and read your e-mail after you check the latest on-line BBC news. If those things don't work, you may try to think through a new routine or, more likely, you find that you are already launched on one. The cup of coffee becomes two cups of coffee, the morning run disappears, BBC gets bumped by the *New York Times* because the load time is too long during major soccer action. If you tried to figure all these things out consciously, you probably couldn't make it through the day. Yet people do make it through the day. Their routines may actually work pretty well—thus requiring little conscious thought. When the routines don't work, people adjust. That adjustment may not require much active attention. Your active mind, the part that does all that conceptual work, may be largely absent as you go about your day. You may function rather better without it.

The net implication is that human thinking may not be very "rational" after all. People seem to perceive things, react to them, and sometimes alter their routines without much of what we normally think of as "thinking." That means there are perceptions and actions without any "thinking" in between. That insight is hard to prove—although the case study at the end of the chapter about artificial intelligence is intriguing. This issue of sense-making is a useful reminder that people aren't simply acting out a script, or performing their expected roles, or implementing some predesigned project. They are interacting with their world, repeating established routines, and creating new ones—often without much thought. They are making sense of things on the run. As they do so, however, they will have some clear reference points in the symbols that they recognize and share with those around them. Those symbols may sometimes tell them what to do (stop! go!) or sometimes simply reassure them that there is some general sense and order to the world—and that they are not alone. Will you please rise for the national anthem?

Case Study
Artificial Intelligence: Perception or Conception?

Much of the thinking about artificial intelligence is framed in a very mechanical, logical way. Machines can be taught to follow a set of directions and—because their memory is vast and their computational speed great—they can follow those directions very accurately and very quickly. On the other hand, machines—at least for the moment—don't seem to "think" in the way we do. They are programmed. They might come up with a program of their own, but would have to be programmed to do that. Someone would have to write down every step along the way. And that's a lot of code. But what if human "thinking" isn't really about that complex and abstract kind of "thinking" but simply a kind of reacting to the environment at a very low level of cognitive complexity? What if, then, machine intelligence could be created on the model of perception/reaction rather than conception/execution? Don't think about it, just do it. Don't create a plan, just develop a routine.

Philip Agre did something of that kind in a virtual environment. He gave the computer the task of placing a set of virtual blocks on top of each other. Rather than writing a step-by-step plan, he instead gave a long list of rules to which the computer could refer. The implications of doing it that way were interesting. Agre measured the actual computer activity required at different stages of the process and found that there was a general pattern of decreasing computer activity as the task progressed. Thus there was initially a high level of activity as the computer ran through the long list of rules to find the ones that applied to the specific situation. But that activity decreased as the computer identified the most relevant rules. Effectively, the computer was establishing a routine based on which rules (of a very large list) seemed to work in this particular virtual environment.

On the basis of this experiment and a later experiment developing a similar approach to playing a computer game, Agre came to believe that the field of artificial intelligence research has lost much by failing to consider how computers might develop the same kinds of routine that people develop. Those routines would not be based on abstract schematic conceptualizations of how things are organized or should be done, but on a set of more general and disorganized rules that can be applied to specific situations as they arise. Many of the most interesting of these rules involve a kind of visual response system. We, for example, are attracted by rapid movement and automatically tend to focus on and watch whatever comes abruptly across our visual field. We do that without thinking through the whole process of why we should or shouldn't be watching whatever flew by. Likewise, Agre programmed his computer to play a game by "watching" objects that moved. This perception/reaction approach worked well enough that Agre's computer played the game better than he did.

Case Study
Who's Middle-Class? African-American Elderly in Chicago

Issues of cognition, of perception and conception, of symbols and sense-making, may seem abstract, but the practical implications can be enormous. Consider some of the ways that people characterize themselves and characterize others. In the contemporary United States, for example, people frequently characterize themselves and others as belonging to supposedly clearly defined racial, ethnic, gender, and sexual orientation categories. One problem with these categories is that many people do not fit into them very precisely. A further problem is that most of these markers of identity, whether chosen by people themselves or ascribed to them by outsiders, depend a great deal on the situation and the particular perspective used.

As an example, consider the meaning of the term "middle-class" in relation to some elderly African-American Chicago residents interviewed by Madelyn Iris and her associates. "Middle-class" is a very widely used term in American society. Its use is generally associated with notions of a good life and the sense that everybody is entitled to such a life. The terms conveys the sense of adequate income, some measure of education, professional or at least white-collar jobs, and a decent environment in which to live. Middle-class people, then, are those who are successful in material terms: They have decent jobs, decent education, and decent neighborhoods in which to live. They are certainly more than simple manual laborers who are in dire financial straits, in crime-ridden neighborhoods, and with limited education.

An elderly African-American man rests his arm on the shoulder of a fellow senior. (*Bruce Ayres/Getty Images, Inc./Stone Allstock*)

These elderly African Americans in Chicago were, according to many of these criteria, *not* recognizably middle-class. Most had been migrants to the Chicago area in the immediate post–World War II era. They saw themselves as "urban pioneers" who had worked the largely blue-collar jobs that they could find. They were, at best, high school graduates—and many had quit school well before completion of high school. They lived in what had become a neighborhood of abandoned properties, gang and drug-influenced streets, and parks too dangerous to visit. How could anyone make sense of these people as "middle-class," given all the educational, occupational, and neighborhoods signs of, at best, a working-class life?

However, there were other characteristics that suggested that these people could and ought to be considered middle-class. Their degree of civic participation remained high despite the decline in the neighborhood. They were active in block clubs, schools, neighborhood committees, and churches. Furthermore, their value structure was quintessentially middle-class. They worked together as couples and as families, pooling different incomes to achieve traditional middle-class goals. They bought their own homes. Perhaps most convincingly, they produced fully middle-class children who did go to college, did get professional or at least white-collar jobs, and did live in quiet, safe neighborhoods. Those nice middle-class neighborhoods, of course, were in the suburbs, far away from where their elderly parents lived.

There are many lessons from this work with Chicago elderly: the vaunted American opportunity to move ahead despite humble origins, the crucial assistance provided by families and kin in that search for success, and the high commitment of people to their local institutions such as schools, churches, and neighborhood groups. One lesson is about human cognition. Words used as simple descriptions—such as "middle-class"—often have complicated meanings and symbolic associations that yield not a single reality, but multiple ones. A typical survey that analyzed the Chicago elderly by income or type of job would doubtless not find these people to be middle-class. Instead they would be "lower-income," "working poor," or perhaps "working class." Yet from an anthropological perspective, these particular elderly seem to be very middle-class in their value structure, in the way they go about their lives, and in the kind of children they raised.

Sources

Cognition is often dealt with in passing in anthropology texts, or as a brief aside to discussions of language or belief systems. Two texts that deal with cognition in more detail—and particularly well, I think—are Emily Shultz and Robert Lavenda's *Cultural Anthropology: A Perspective on the Human Condition* (Mayfield, 1998) and Mari Womack's *Being Human: An Introduction to Cultural Anthropology* (Prentice Hall, 2001). For discussions of the brain, Joseph LeDoux's *Synaptic Self* (Viking, 2002) is a good place to begin. *A Mind So Rare: The Evolution of Human Consciousness* by Merlin Donald (W. W. Norton, 2001) is argumentative but interesting and might be paired with Maurice Bloch's *How We Think They Think: Anthropological Approaches to Cognition, Memory, and Literacy* (Westview, 1998) or Michael Tomasello's *The Cultural Origins of Human Cognition* (Harvard University Press, 1999). The subject of symbols is a richly studied area in anthropology but Victor Turner's *The Forest of Symbols* (Cornell University Press, 1970) and Mary Douglas's *Purity and Danger* (Routledge, 1984) remain solid places to begin. For sense-making, some people may like to track the issue directly to Martin Heidegger or perhaps Alfred Schutz, but Hugh Mehan and Houston Wood's *The Reality of Ethnomethodology* (Kriefer Publishing, 1975) provides a useful introduction to the subject for those of an anthropological or sociological bent.

For the artificial intelligence example, see Philip E. Agre's *Computation and Human Experience* (Cambridge University Press, 1997). His example program seems sensible and he does discuss his findings explicitly in terms of sense-making as identified in phenomenology—so it is an interesting book on those grounds. The information on the Chicago elderly is drawn from Madelyn Iris's "Pillars of the Middle Class Community," *Anthropology Newsletter* (February 1999): 8.

CHAPTER 16

LANGUAGE

This chapter continues the linked stories of thought and language. There is not much thought without language and not much language without thought. Yet one very important difference between the two shapes many of the problems of the world today. While Boas may have argued for the psychic unity of humankind, people speak a wide range of very different languages. This means that whether or not people think along the same lines, the world consists of two kinds of people: those you can understand and those you can't. Thus language both enables communication and makes it difficult—even impossible.

This chapter is in four sections. The first section addresses the general characteristics of human language, especially what we know of its overall potential and how specific languages develop. The second section provides the details of how languages work: their sound systems, word constructions, phrase and sentence structures, and written forms. The third section considers the interaction of language and culture, particularly the way language shapes the way we understand the world. Finally, the fourth section discusses the relationships among language, society, and politics. The case studies at the end of the chapter concern the way time is constructed in the Hopi language and the difficulties in translating works of literature—specifically the tenth-century Japanese novel *The Tale of Genji*.

THE NATURE OF LANGUAGE AND LANGUAGES

There has been a long-running debate about human language and the extent to which it differs from communication among other animals. Research and experiments have shown that other primates—especially gorillas, chimpanzees, and bonobos—can do much of what we can: use arbitrary words to communicate, put those words into structured sentences, and even make up new words. Yet the breadth and depth of human language is unique.

HOCKETT'S CHARACTERISTICS OF LANGUAGE

In a classic discussion of human language compared to the communication systems of animals, Charles Hockett once posited seven key characteristics of language. These continue to provide a good outline of what language enables us to do.

Openness: Languages are not limited in their elements or combinations. New things can be added, new combinations can be created. Language is not a closed system either practically or theoretically. We are limited only by the limits of our creativity.

Displacement: Language does not require that the things being discussed be nearby or viewable. We can talk about the chair in the next room; the site of the first hockey game in Windsor, Nova Scotia; or the remains of a spacecraft on Mars. That's very useful.

Positionality: We can talk about these things (which may not be here) from any particular angle. We can talk about the chair or hockey pond or spacecraft from the front, side, top, from any distance, or under any light conditions. That is also useful. Language enables us to create multidimensional "virtual" worlds through which we can move at will.

Arbitrariness: One of the features that makes language so open is the ability to use sounds and written lines to convey meaning even though they have no intrinsic relationship to that meaning. Although in English cats do "meow" and in Vietnamese helicopters are described by their "wap-wap" sound, we don't have to do that. We can make up anything we want. Hockey could be called "pucks," a chopper could be called a horizontal prop-plane, and a cat's meow could be called a "roar."

Multiplicity of Patterning: One additional feature of this arbitrariness is that we don't even have to have the same system for different parts of a language. We can have very complex declensions for nouns but no conjugation for verbs; we can have a writing system that is not even based on how we talk or we can even (as the Japanese do) have a writing system that has both phonetic and nonphonetic parts to it.

Semanticity: Language even permits us to talk about "things" that aren't really "things" at all. We can, for example, talk about meaning itself. ("Semantics" is the study of meaning.) Such discussions can be difficult, since we're talking about things that we can not directly access with our senses, but it's possible.

Prevarication: As a corollary of the above, language also permits us to talk about things that are not only not "here" but don't exist at all. We can say it's raining when it's not; that something happened that didn't; or that something didn't happen that did. Many people find this a very useful feature of language. Wouldn't it be easier just to say you did something rather than having to do it?

DIVERGENCE AND DURABILITY

Hockett's seven criteria suggest the tremendous potential of human language in general. But how do individual languages develop? There are two very general themes. One is *divergence*. Languages change very fast, and change in ways that tend to lead to a greater number of mutually unintelligible languages. As language speakers spread out from each other with less frequent intercommunication, new *dialects* (variations of a language) develop. Initially they are mutually intelligible, but changes in vocabulary, pronunciation, and grammar gradually render them so different that they become separate languages. This, then, is the first major theme in the history of languages: divergence and mutual unintelligibility. It resembles the biblical story of the Tower of Babel. Maintaining a common language in the face of such divergence has been—at least until the development of mass media—a difficult task.

There is another theme, however, and that is *durability*. Much of the argument about Ebonics (called Black English vernacular, by linguists) is that, although the words from the languages originally spoken by slaves brought to the Americas may have disappeared, the grammatical structures themselves have continued. That durability of grammatical structures is seen more generally in contacts between different languages. If two language groups meet and have some need for communication, a limited utilitarian language often develops, based on the stronger group's language. Such a language is called a trade language or, more technically, a *pidgin*. Pidgins are grammatically simple languages that use limited vocabulary to enable basic communication. Such pidgins can continue for many generations. Yet when people start speaking these pidgins in their own community, fuller grammatical structures develop. The pidgins thus become full languages, what are called *creoles*. Creoles, unlike pidgins, are complete languages with full grammars. Haitian Creole, for example, is a complete language in its own right, not simply a version of French. That is a testament to the durability of underlying grammatical structures in their resistance to French.

KINESICS AND PARALANGUAGE

One further comment about languages is needed before looking at their actual structure. The formal languages under discussion here are not the only form of human communication. Instead, they are part of a broader range of ways

Two Italian men in conversation. (*Paul W. Liebhardt*)

that people communicate. Much of that broader communication involves what we call *kinesics* ("body language" and facial expressions); much involves how we are dressed and adorned; and, at close distances, some of it is olfactory. That broader communication can also be vocal. Laughing and belching convey messages, as do the volume and pace of what we say. Yelling and whispering the same words send very different messages. These nonlinguistic vocalizations are called *paralanguage*. So stand tall (kinesics); clear your throat (paralanguage); and get on with what you have to say.

THE STRUCTURE OF LANGUAGES

There are, it is estimated, some 6,800 languages in the world today. Even if you speak both English and Chinese (Mandarin) and can thus talk to roughly one-half of the people in the world, you are communicating with only a fraction of a percent of the language groups in the world. Each of these languages has a grammar with three main parts: *phonology, morphology*, and *syntax*. Many also have *writing* systems. Each of these is described below.

PHONOLOGY

Phonology refers to the sound system of a language (*~phon* means sound and *~ology* means knowledge about something). Without a sound system it would be impossible to understand what anybody was saying. The number of possible sounds humans can make is very large, so there has to be a system for creating particular recognizable sounds from that range of possibilities. One of the most difficult tasks in learning a new language is exactly this problem: how to recognize the distinct sounds before trying to understand the meanings of those sounds.

The smallest unit of sound that is recognizable in a particular language is called a *phoneme*. The phonemes in languages vary. For example, in English "r" is one phoneme and "l" is a different phoneme. You know they're different phonemes because you can't use them interchangeably without changing a word's meaning. "Lung" is not "rung." Yet in Japanese, a sound somewhere between our "r" and our "l" is a single phoneme. For them, the sounds of an English speaker saying "lung" and "rung" would *not* sound significantly different. As another example, "ah" (pronounced as in "ma") would be a single phoneme in English but in Vietnamese it is potentially six phonemes. Vietnamese is a tonal language and, in the northern dialect, there are the following: a neutral tone "ah," a rising tone "ah," a falling tone "ah," a falling then rising tone "ah," a sharp falling then rising tone "ah," and a sinking, almost glottalized falling tone "ah."[1] We would thus hear six distinct Vietnamese phonemes as only a single phoneme said six times in a row.

MORPHOLOGY

Phonology thus concerns how we recognize out of all possible sounds certain specific phonemes. Morphology (~*morph* for shape or form), in turn, refers to the way meaning is constructed out of these units of sound. The smallest unit of meaning in a language is called a *morpheme*. Thus the English word "dog" includes three phonemes ("d" "aw" "g") but is a single morpheme.[2] (You can take the "g" away and still have a word, but it doesn't have anything to do with a dog.) Morphemes can be either bound or unbound. An *unbound morpheme*, like an unbound dog, can go where it wishes and stand on its own. A *bound morpheme*, by contrast, only has meaning when attached to something else. Thus, in English, the "z" sound indicates a plural: The single "dog" with the addition of the "z" sound becomes "dogs," which has four phonemes ("d" "aw" "g" "z") and two morphemes ("dog" and "multiple-of-them"). Likewise, the three phonemes and single morpheme of "kill" can be indicated as past action by adding the "d" sound and producing "killed" (four phonemes and two morphemes: "kill" and "did-it-already"). In the cases of "dogs" and

---

[1] In English, to the despair of those trying to learn the language, the letter "a" actually represents several different phonemes from the "a" in "ma" and "father" to that in "made." Even the "aw" of dog noted in the text is subject to regional variation.

[2] To continue the English-Vietnamese comparison: In English, "ma" has two phonemes that together constitute one morpheme. That morpheme is an informal reference to one's "mother." In Vietnamese, by contrast, the single phoneme "m" combines with all the different tones of "a" to create six different words depending on the tone. One of those words is also an informal reference to one's mother, but the others include ghost, horse, grave, and rice seedling—which makes proper pronunciation of the tones essential.

"killed," these bound morphemes are called *suffixes* (because they come at the end). There are also *prefixes* ("re"-build, "pre"-cook) and, in some languages, *infixes* (bound morphemes that are inserted in the middle of words).

The results of these morphological constructions are what we call words; these words comprise the *lexicon* of a language. The nature of the words constructed in different languages varies a great deal. Some languages tend toward relatively compact words with mostly unbound morphemes; others construct very elaborate words of combinations of bound and unbound morphemes. Some places of honor for such elaboration go to German for long nouns and Japanese for long verbs. Vietnamese and Chinese, by contrast, use no endings (bound morphemes) for either nouns or verbs and, indeed, are based largely on monosyllabic unbound morphemes.[3] That makes for extraordinary conciseness and—many would argue—an intrinsically concise and poetic nature to those languages.

SYNTAX

Syntax refers to the way these words of various kinds are put together in phrases and sentences. Thus the standard format in English is subject-verb-object as in "I kill the dog." Many other languages use similar constructions: The Vietnamese, for example, would organize that sentence in roughly the same way. Other languages handle things differently. Verbs, for example, can go at the end of the sentence. Thus the object of the action is known before the action itself. There are also more subtle issues of syntax than simple word order. English, for example, requires the use of articles. We cannot have a sentence simply with "dog." Instead it must be a dog, the dog, this dog, or that dog. Nor can we have a sentence without a subject. Those aspects of English often cause problems for non-native speakers. On the other hand, the very lack of such precision in other languages makes them difficult for English speakers. Translators of the classic tenth century Japanese novel, *The Tale of Genji*, for example, note how frequently the subject of a sentence is unstated and often only obliquely implied. Any translation thus requires a full reenvisioning of the ambience of the literary scene rather than a simple translation of what the author put on the page.

WRITING

Finally, languages often have written forms. Hockett's comment about "multiplicity of patterning" is particularly helpful in regard to written language, since it is *not* necessary that the written form of the language necessarily conform to

---

[3]As a technical clarification, the early monosyllabic nature of Chinese and Vietnamese has yielded to frequent use of two-syllable compound nouns even if the word has only a single meaning. That is accomplished either by pairing two words with similar meanings or a regular word with a repeating sound—a kind of "nonsense" word—that is itself without meaning.

the spoken form. English, for example, is written with an alphabet, but is hardly rigorously phonetic—or at least the rules for pronunciation are very complex. Other languages, Spanish and French for example, do a far better job of conformity between the spoken and written language. At the other end of the spectrum is Chinese, which uses characters that usually represent the concept of a word rather than the way it is spoken. The characters for tree, grove of trees, and forest visually convey their message by using representations of one tree, two trees, and three trees respectively. A human leaning against a tree means "to rest," and the combination of images of sun and moon means "clear and bright." One extraordinary advantage of this approach is that people can share an understanding of something in written form, even though they may not speak the same language at all. Thus China could function as a single political entity even though what we call "Chinese" is, in fact, a set of distinct languages by most definitions. Even beyond China, others could use the Chinese writing system. Thus the Japanese, Koreans, and Vietnamese used Chinese characters even though they had their own unrelated spoken languages.

LANGUAGE AND CULTURE

Any language thus includes phonology, morphology, syntax, and, in many cases, a writing system that has its own complexities. Language is an enormous human achievement that permits an impressive breadth and depth of communication among people. One might well argue that it is language that makes people human. Yet if language is so important and people speak such different languages, is it even possible to communicate across linguistic differences? If people do so much of their thinking through language, and they have very different languages, is there even equivalence in their way of thinking? These questions involve the relationship between the language that people use and the entire set of beliefs and behavior that we call their culture.

This relationship between language and culture is especially associated with the names of Edward Sapir and Benjamin Whorf. The former was one of Boas's early students and the latter, in turn, was a student of Sapir. The central question Sapir and Whorf raised was about the relationship between language and the way people perceive the world. Rather unfortunately, this has come to be known as the "Sapir-Whorf Hypothesis." It is hardly a hypothesis in the normal sense, but rather a simple observation that it would be difficult for people to understand their lives and to assess the meanings of their lives outside the conceptual context of their language. The central notion underlying the Sapir-Whorf hypothesis is that the way a language works affects, conditions, constrains, and channels the way people think. That can happen in relation to the words people use: Some people may have more words for some things than other people (kin terms, for example) or the words they use may have different implications (thus "brown" in Chinese and Japanese means "tea color" and thus the North American term "brown-nosing" wouldn't translate very well). Differences in morphology and syntax may also be significant.

ENGLISH

I	killed	a dog
(subject)	(verb/past tense)	(indefinite article/object)

This issue of language and culture thus ranges from complex, philosophical considerations of how language shapes reality to the more practical mechanics of what kinds of words and structures are available in any given language. As a simple, combined example, consider the English sentence "I killed a dog." This simple subject-verb-object sentence is not the only way to get this idea across in English, but it is certainly the standard way to do so. The sentence seems simple and straightforward. It begins with "I," so you know the person talking is the one who is doing something. "Kill" is a verb and because this is English, there is a suffix (bound morpheme at the end of a word) that tells us the action has already taken place. Finally, due to the English use of articles, we know that this is simply "a" dog, not "the" dog, "this" dog or "that" dog. So as this sentence unfolds in English, we know first that the speaker is the subject of the sentence; that the action is a serious one (killing); that the action has already taken place; and, finally, that the object of the killing was some undefined dog.

JAPANESE

watakushi ga	inu o	koroshimashita
(subject/particle)	(object/particle)	(verb in past tense)
(semi-formal)		(semi-formal)

Now consider that same sentence in Japanese. The sentence appears to start in the same way: with the subject. Indeed the subject is not only in the first place but has a special particle after it that indicates it is, indeed, the subject of the sentence.[4] However, *watakushi* is not the only way to say "I." *Watakushi* is a semiformal form, so we know (and the speaker must have determined) that this is *not* an informal setting.[5] Thus, as we launch into the

---

[4]This sentence might also start with *watakushi wa. Wa* is a particle that indicates the topic of the sentence. If this sentence were part of an ongoing conversation, *wa* would probably be used, and, in fact, the subject/topic might also be omitted. See the case study at the end of the chapter for more discussion of indefiniteness in Japanese.

[5]*Watakushi* is technically gender neutral, but women might well use alternative forms such as *atakushi* or *atashi*, which can *not* be used by men.

sentence, we already have some information about the relative formality of the social setting. We are already in a far more socially defined world than we were in English. The second part of the sentence gives the object. As with the subject, there is a particle that tells us very specifically that the dog is indeed the object of the action. So in Japanese, we now have the subject and the object, along with something of the social setting. But we don't yet know what the action is, whether it is good or bad, or whether it is past, present, or future. Finally, along comes the verb. The first part of the verb (*koro . . .*) suggests that it will be some form of the verb *korosu*—so it will be something about killing—and the rest (*. . . shimashita*) tells us that it indeed happened in the past. The verb form also reiterates that this is a semiformal situation (just as *watakushi* at the beginning of the sentence did). Note that only *after* the verb is given do we know that the action was of killing rather than *not* killing. In Japanese, you can thus usually bail out at the end of the sentence—something that is harder to do but not impossible in English: "I killed the dog . . . No way!"

VIETNAMESE

toi	*giet*	*con cho*
(subject)	(verb)	(classifier/object)

Finally consider the sentence in Vietnamese. The basic structure of the sentence is parallel to the English one. The structure is subject/verb/object and there is even something like an article in front of the dog. In this case it's what is called a classifier. In this case the classifier is one used with animals—there are others for books, people, long objects, and so on. Classifiers aside, the sentence would appear to be relatively straightforward. However, there are two hidden complications. One is that the verb does not indicate tense. Thus, unless we know the context, or someone clues us in with additional information, we could listen to this sentence and not know a critical piece of information: Has this happened yet? The other complication is the word *toi*. As with Japanese, this is not a simple substitute for "I." For Vietnamese, the use of *toi* indicates that this is a relatively formal situation between people who have no very personal or established relationship. As with Japanese, then, the very start of the sentence requires an assessment of the overall social situation in which the sentence is being said. If the speaker were among known people, the *toi* would certainly be replaced by *anh, chi, em, con, bac*, or something of the kind. That these alternatives are largely kin terms helps explain much of the warmth that is possible in Vietnamese conversation—a constant reiteration of kin or kin-like reciprocal relations. The use of *toi* avoids all those familial implications and thus a sentence that was neutral in English and formal in Japanese becomes rather cold in Vietnamese.

In this example, one can see how language channels communication and—as the Japanese and Vietnamese examples suggest—forces a recognition of the context in which a sentence is said. It may be possible to translate the basic meaning of a sentence between languages, but it is extremely difficult—and perhaps impossible—to translate the full meaning of that sentence. That suggests (as the Hopi example details below) that people live in worlds that may have very different frameworks of meaning. It also suggests (as the Genji example details after that) that the process of translation can be enormously complex.

LANGUAGE, SOCIETY, AND POLITICS

The discussion so far in this chapter suggests only the beginning of the complexities in how language interacts with culture. After all, any study of language includes not only the general structures that we refer to as *linguistics* but the actual use of language in daily life. Thus, in any particular situation, people choose from among many options in what they say. Others then respond with their own choices. The result may be language that is elegant or crude, verbose or terse, cold or warm. Cumulatively those choices may mean that by the end of the conversation the social world has changed. Perhaps a relatively formal discussion about work that begins in English drifts into a more informal, friendly, or familial talk in Spanish. This interaction between the possibilities represented by the formal language and the social situations in which languages are used is called *sociolinguistics*.

Language also has a very strong relationship to politics. After all, a language affects the way people view the world. That will likely affect the way they view political issues and options. Furthermore, language also marks people as the same as some other people (those who speak that language) and different from yet other people (those who speak some other language). That power of language as a social marker applies even to variations within a language. Few other social markers are so strong. Language, like religion, may even trump race. The African-looking person who speaks perfect Parisian French, the South Asian with a strong Australian accent, or the tanned California-looking person who speaks in clipped British tones, all mark themselves immediately and strongly as being not quite who they originally appeared to be.

Language, like religion, is thus connected very strongly to people's internal lives, to who they think they are, to what they think of other people, and to what other people think of them. A demonstration of linguistic competence may help someone fit into a social group to which they didn't previously belong. That can be useful. By belonging in that new group, however, that same person may be cut off from the old group. That may seem like a reasonable and volitional trade-off when speaking about adults. If the topic is changed from adults to children, this issue of language competence takes on a different tone. Children's education is not the only issue that links language to politics, but it does serve to indicate how strong, volatile, and consequential that connection can be.

AN EXAMPLE: CONTROLLING CHILDREN'S LANGUAGE

It is very hard to teach adults a new language and virtually impossible to make them forget the language (or languages) they already know. Thus for adults, language is largely a given. Children, however, provide a very good battleground for language—as for many other issues. In many colonial situations, for example, it was not possible to do well in life without learning the colonizer's language. To have a future meant to learn English, or French, or Spanish, or German, or Japanese. Parents who might themselves refuse to use the colonizer's language still had to consider the future of their children. In some cases, learning the colonial language was not simply an option for children who wished to move ahead (and their parents who wished them to do so), but a requirement for everybody whatever their future goals. During the period of Japanese colonization of Korea, Korean children attended schools conducted entirely in Japanese. A child who spoke Korean at school would get a beating. As the ultimate linguistic insult, Korean children had to obtain and use Japanese, rather than Korean, names.

Such control of children's language is one of the most effective ways to rupture the ties between them, their parents, and their parents' culture. This was a common strategy not only of colonialism but in the control of indigenous groups—often referred to as internal colonialism. In both North America and Australia, for example, the government set up special English-language boarding schools for indigenous children. These schools removed children physically from their parents and also removed them from their parents' language. It could thus be hoped that when they returned home from school they would abide by the rules and attitudes of the dominant society. With lack of language competence in the "old" ways, there would be nothing left for them but the "new" ways of the dominant society. Rather than killing people, the governments aimed to kill their culture by making sure it was not passed on to future generations.

Echoes of this kind of language policy—and resistance to it—can be seen in the fervor with which issues of language are pursued even today: why many in the United States (and some in Canada) demand a full English-only policy (so that newcomers *will* abide by the core rules and attitudes of the dominant society) and why most immigrant parents in North America agonize over the degree to which their children should learn English (or French in Quebec) and the degree to which they should become fully competent in their parents' language. Bilingualism is the dream for many—but it is a difficult process on the individual level and one with which the United States, unlike Canada, has very little experience.

One final example of this combination of language and politics may help to show both the importance of the subject and the more subtle ways control can be exercised through language policy. When the French colonized Vietnam, they made no particular effort to abolish the Vietnamese language. Indeed, they often supported it as a cultural medium. They understood that education for Vietnamese meant both cultural expression and political action. Thus supporting Vietnamese culture was an attractive way to keep Vietnamese intellectuals out of politics. The colonizers did, of course, emphasize French as the language of the elite and the language necessary for any serious economic or political future. The crucial twist in the language issue in colonial Vietnam, however, lay in how Vietnamese was written. At the time of the French conquest, Vietnamese wrote both in Chinese and in a writing system that mixed different Chinese characters to convey both the meaning and pronunciation of Vietnamese. It was a difficult system and the French could claim practicality, science, and even Vietnamese nationalism on their side in abolishing it. Why should the Vietnamese continue to write their language in Chinese characters? Instead, surely they should use the modern, rational, romanization system formalized (predictably enough) by a French Jesuit missionary, Alexandre de Rhodes. It even came to be called "national language" (*quoc ngu*).

The Vietnamese language survived French colonialism intact, but its use of Chinese characters did not. That might not seem so bad except for two implications of the change. First, the built-in ability to communicate in writing (if not in speech) with Chinese, Japanese, and Koreans, was lost. What better way to control and isolate a colonial people than to cut them off from their region? Second, Vietnamese now found themselves cut off from their own history. The texts from their own long history appeared now in what looked like a foreign language. What better way to control and isolate a colonial people than to cut them off from their history?

Case Study
Language and the Hopi Sense of Time

Benjamin Whorf's major work was with the Hopi. The Hopi currently inhabit an area encased within Navajo territory in Arizona and live mostly in a series of villages along three high mesas. In learning their language, Whorf became intrigued by the grammatical structures of the language and how they affected the way the Hopi understood the universe. He was particularly interested in the way time was handled in Hopi and came to believe it was fundamentally different than in European languages. His argument goes—with some simplification—as follows.

A Hopi elder pauses in the fields. (*Getty Images, Inc./Hulton Archive Photos*)

In English, and in European languages in general, time has three major aspects: the past, the present, and the future. The past consists of events that have already happened and are removed in time from us, the present is this exact moment of time at which we currently exist, and the future consists of a limitless expanse of time where things that don't yet exist will come to exist. That sense of time is built, Whorf would argue, directly into the structure of English. Verbs, for example, have very clear tenses: "I went to Boston" lies in the past; "I am in Montpelier" lies in the present; and "I will be in Montreal" lies in the future (God willing).

Whorf argued that this is a limited, grammatically constrained way of looking at time and contrasted it with the Hopi way. For the Hopi, there are only two kinds of temporal arrangements: what has come to be and what has not yet come to be. Whorf called the things that have already come to be, that which is *manifested*—which means obvious or apparent. Thus for the Hopi, both the past and present have come to be. They are fully manifested. For them, the distinction between past and present is blurred. On the other hand, for the Hopi there are many things that have not yet come to be or, more accurately, have not yet fully come to be. These Whorf called *manifesting*. He argued that the Hopi did not see the future, as we often do, as some new unexplored and unpredictable territory, but rather as a set of things that are already on their way. The future, for them, grows out of the present. The distinguishing feature of the future, one might say, is that it's not yet fully cooked.

Whorf's argument was not simply a philosophical one. He argued that the Hopi way of dealing with time was built into the grammatical structures of the Hopi language. Their language constrained them to view time in this manifested versus manifesting way. Likewise, he would argue, the grammatical structures of English constrain us to view the past, present, and future as quite distinct domains. We must decide—just as in the "I killed a dog" sentence—which tense to use. Without that, we don't even have a grammatically correct sentence. What Whorf suggests is that there is a very different kind of reality embedded in different languages. That idea is a forbidding one in some ways. How can we ever think beyond the confines of our own language? In other ways, however, the idea is liberating. It suggests that in learning different languages, we do indeed have the opportunity to enter different realities—and thus consider the limitations of the reality in which our own language holds us.

Case Study
The Tale of Genji: **Translating a Tenth-Century Japanese Novel**

Japanese is very different from English in its phonology, morphology, syntax, and writing. Thus, translating even a relatively simple sentence from Japanese to English can be difficult. It becomes even more difficult when the writing is more elaborate and seeks to use the full force of the language for literary purposes. Whether in prose or poetry, literary work thrives on the full nuances available in a language and will not hesitate to create new words or grammatical structures if they suit the purpose at hand. This is language at its most open and creative. Thus translating Japanese literature could be expected to be a great challenge.

All that, suggested Ivan Morris (one of the premier translators of Japanese literature) wasn't the worst of it. Looking at *The Tale of Genji*, the tenth-century classic of Heian Japan, he noted that what could reach "nightmare proportions" was the lack of specificity in the language. Proper names were avoided, the subject was often omitted, and such elementary distinctions as past versus present tense, singular versus plural, and male versus female were absent. Sometimes, he noted with much frustration, it is "not even clear if the sentence is positive or negative."

Consider this fragment of a sentence in what Morris presents as a roughly literal translation:

> Recalling all sorts of things what an underhand thing this is to the person/people who joining heart/hearts to a remarkable extent led me . . .

There are problems. We don't know who's recalling what, what was underhanded to whom, and where the leading might be going. As it turns out from the context of the fragment, it is fairly clear that this is a man named Niou. He is on his way to a place called Uji for the purposes of seducing a woman in whom his close friend Kaoru is interested. Thus Morris provides what for us is a much more conventional way of phrasing things.

> Various thoughts occurred to Niou. He recalled how remarkably helpful Kaoru had been in introducing him to Uji in the first place.

That's a very clear translation, but it might be criticized for lacking the flair of what is an acknowledged literary masterpiece. Consider a more florid translation by the great Arthur Whaley:

> It all seemed strangely familiar. Who was he with that second time? Why, of course, with Kaoru; and he became slightly uncomfortable when he remembered all the trouble his friend had taken to bring him and Kozeri together. "I am afraid he would think this rather an odd way of repaying his kindness," Niou said to himself.

Whaley certainly wins the flair award for translating, but also the award for taking liberties. He has filled in all the gaps that a western reader might find with the original and, in the process, has more than doubled the number of words from Morris's translation and turned a fragment of one sentence into four complete sentences.

Whaley provides here, as in many of his classic translations, a very good read indeed. But does that reading convey the tone and sense of the original? There is no final answer to this dilemma of translation. The world that is created in one language according to its rules and opportunities must somehow be disassembled and then reassembled in another language according to that language's rules and opportunities. The translator must be adept in both languages and must have the literary skill to actively recreate the work in the new language. The task is parallel to that of the anthropologist: to try to understand the reality that is another people's existence and to find some way to convey that reality to another culture.

SOURCES

The general discussions of the nature and structure of language are fairly standard and can be supplemented with almost any general full-length anthropology text. A good volume for browsing issues in linguistic anthropology is *Linguistic Anthropology: A Reader* (Blackwell, 2001; Alessandro Duranti, editor). For the issues of language extinction and language preservation, see Daniel Nettle and Suzanne Romaine's *Vanishing Voices: The Extinction of the*

World's Languages (Oxford University Press, 2002) and the *Handbook of Language and Ethnic Identity* (Oxford University Press, 2001; Joshua Fishman, editor). For a broader view of Charles Hockett's views, see his *Language, Mathematics, and Linguistics* (Walter de Gruyter, 1967).

For the example of Hopi, see Benjamin Whorf's *Language, Thought, and Reality: Selected Writings* (MIT Press, 1964; John B. Carroll, editor) and Emily Schultz's more recent reconsideration in *Dialogue at the Margins: Whorf, Bakhtin, and Linguistic Relativity* (University of Wisconsin Press, 1991). For the translation example, see Ivan Morris's stellar description of translational problems in *The World of the Shining Prince* (Kodansha, 1994) and the more recent translations of *The Tale of Genji* by Edward Seidensticker (Alfred A Knopf, 1976) and Royall Tyler (Viking, 2001).

CHAPTER 17

BODIES, PLACES, OBJECTS, AND EVENTS

Much of the meaning of life relates directly to the bodies that we inhabit, the places in which we live and through which we move, the objects that we create and use, and the actual events of our lives. We react to these but also use them as repositories for established meanings and as opportunities to create new meanings. This chapter examines bodies, places, objects, and events as such repositories in which human meaning can be stored and through which human meaning can be remembered, recreated, and modified. For this, it will be helpful to remember the four themes that were noted in the introduction to Part III. Human meanings are *open*. So we must never forget or underestimate human autonomy and creativity. Yet human meaning is also *context-driven*. So we must never forget the importance of context and the frequent inability to ignore it even when it is not relevant. Human meaning is also *order-seeking*. So we must never forget that, although it's a complex world, human meaning aims at something well-ordered. The dangerous corollary is that people often find that order prematurely; openness may be sacrificed both to context (not thinking outside the box) and to order (the pursuit of a quick solution). Finally, human meaning is *marking*: whether that involves an incision on the body, words on tablets of stone, or a giant figure carved out of the rock on a mountain side.

The discussion in this chapter begins with *bodies*. Because they are always with us, bodies are an exceptionally good place to store the meaning of who we are: We do this with how we dress, how we groom ourselves (e.g., where hair should and shouldn't grow), and how we may actually change our bodies through marking (e.g., make-up or tattoos) or even physical alteration (e.g., cosmetic surgery). The chapter's discussion continues with *places*, *objects*, and *events*. Each of these has its own advantages and disadvantages as a repository for meaning and as an arena through which to create and recreate meaning. The first case study at the end of the chapter concerns the vastly increased popularity of tattooing in North America; the second concerns the physical stereotyping of Hutu and Tutsi in Rwanda.

BODIES

The human *body* is a fertile and seminal source of meaning. Much of what we are as human beings derives from what we are as biological entities. But we also modify our bodies so that they reflect what we think is important about us. The body is thus the source of meaning and something on which we impose meaning. The division of society into "men" and "women" is an elementary social classification based on physical differences. Yet human societies often go to great lengths to further accentuate the differences between men and woman in terms of their behavior and their actual bodies. Bodies may be modified by painting, piercing, tattooing, clothing, or surgical change—even to the changing of biological sex itself.

As a simple example, consider physical changes made to people when they reach adulthood. Among the Nuer, for example, the cuts across the forehead (*gar*) signal that a man is an adult. Both male and female circumcision are also frequently used to mark directly on the body that a person is—permanently—an adult. Such marking is often made around the time of puberty and thus the marking of social adulthood matches an actual biological change. This shows the reciprocal way that meaning is both obtained from the body and also placed onto and sometimes into it. Colin Turnbull describes the time at which the Mbuti decided he was in some way one of them. Their way of marking this was to cut lines across his forehead and insert dirt from the forest into those cuts. In that case, the most elementary aspect of the environment (dirt) was mixed with the most elementary element of the body (blood) and permanently sealed together within Turnbull's body. Although not as spiritually elegant a statement, a military tattoo from duty overseas is a similar physical marking that you "were there" and that it was important enough to be permanently marked within your skin.

This reciprocal relationship of drawing meaning from the body and then marking that meaning back on the body is especially clear with sex and sexuality. Existing physical differences between men and women are amplified by clothing and adornment. In the Taliban's Afghanistan, men had beards; women wore *burkas*. In North America, styles are less exclusive, but a buzz cut is male and a skirt female—unless somebody is making a very strong statement about *not* following those conventions. This difference in the way biological sex is rewritten onto the human body shows much of the meaning of gender. Thus, although both male and female circumcision occur in human societies, the results are glaringly different. Male circumcision typically requires only a removal of the foreskin—which some argue has medical benefits—although it may also include some "enhancements" such as putting small stones under the skin of the glans. There is some argument that the result of male circumcision is reduced sensitivity, but the effect is clearly not fatal. Female circumcision, by contrast, involves actual removal of at least part of the clitoris, which does directly affect sexual feeling and response. In some cases it involves complete removal of the clitoris and outer labia and the very sewing together of the vaginal entry. This is hardly a subtle statement: The meaning of male circumcision thus becomes one of sexual activity while that of female circumcision is one of sexual repression. The women's body is changed in a way that makes it clear that her sexuality is to be suppressed and that she herself does not even have control of the access to her own body.

The circumcision example is a severe one. It involves not only a permanent and serious change to the body, but also one that may reflect sharp control by one set of people over another. It is no wonder that many people have fought to make sure the threat of female circumcision to a women—or to her daughter—should be grounds for political asylum. Yet many other kinds of meaning drawn from the body and rewritten onto it are less permanent and of more ambiguous and limited meaning. Body-piercing, for example, may be a stronger statement than tattooing, but it is generally a less permanent one. Both body-piercing and tattooing can be done on public parts of the body (face and hands, for example), on private parts of the body, or on places that may be seen or not seen depending on the social occasion. Japanese *yakuza* (members of organized crime groups) may show nary a tattoo when in a business suit, but a rolled up cuff or loosened shirt collar will show the beginning of full body tattoos.

PLACES

The human body is thus the source of much of the meaning we find in life and of our core identity: male versus female, old versus young, even tall versus short. The body is also a very good place to store that meaning, since it is always with us and always represents us to others: Our bodies are our calling cards. But there are other sources of meaning and repositories for meaning. The *places* through which our bodies move provide another set of opportunities. The environments in which people live are an important objective factor in their lives and they are also a convenient place to "store" information. Different clans may have ancestor or guardian spirits who reside on particular mountains; people may take great pains to locate the graves and tombs of their ancestors in places that are spiritually appropriate yet practically accessible; and nations are likely to be adamant about the meaning of the borders that mark their territory and the memorials they construct to mark the lasting significance of those who came before.

The mixture of dirt and blood in Turnbull's forehead is a compelling one. It was a way to put the place in the person. But if you can't take something of the place with you, then perhaps something of you can remain with the place. One way to rework meaning back into a place is to put something of yourself into it. Two simple bodily fluids you can put into a place are sweat and blood. That sweat and blood can be figurative but can also be literal. Battlefields, for example, are consecrated by the actual blood that flowed there. A house you built yourself may indeed have your actual sweat in it. Imagine the importance of agricultural land to people whose ancestors have worked on that land for generations. The sweat of their ancestors has poured into that land and that place. They have given their lives for the land and their bones lie in graves and tombs in and upon it.

One of the great advantages of place as a repository for meaning is that it endures. You can always return to visit it. The place will normally outlast the people and, in that sense, is a much better repository. What that enduring place conveys is often simply the memory of events. Those events may be as common and personal as where you grew up. But the events may also be epic, widely shared, or of profound meaning, such as the Normandy shores on which the Allies first landed in World War II. These places may be unmarked, marked by only a small sign (Washington slept here; Jacques Cartier landed here), or turned into a full memorial park (as was the epicenter of the first nuclear bomb in Hiroshima, Japan). These places may be relatively natural or very clearly man-made. Carving huge statues out of bare rock has a certain combined appeal. The raw emergence of rock from the earth complements the size of the carving in showing the magnitude and durability of the people's influence—whether it be U.S. presidents at Mount Rushmore, images of the Buddha in Afghanistan, or southern civil war leaders outside Atlanta. It is also possible to incorporate the actual body of somebody into the place. The power of mausoleums comes from this combination. Thus long lines of people queue up to see the actual bodies of Ho Chi Minh in Hanoi and of Mao Zedong in Beijing.

The general importance of place is easy to understand. However, the specific meanings of particular places are more complex. One problem is the variation: Many different kinds of places have different meanings for different people. U.S. civil war battlefields, for example, have a rather different meaning for northerners ("we won and they were wrong") and southerners ("they won but we were right—and fought better"). Places may also have intrinsically mixed meanings: Southern U.S. plantations—including those of Washington and Jefferson—provide messages both of liberty and of slavery. One result is that the meanings of places are often contested. The Vietnam War Memorial, for example, is—all would agree—a place on the mall in Washington, D.C. that concerns the U.S. involvement in Vietnam. The original memorial—the Wall—implies that the meaning of the place is as a memorial in remembrance of all the Americans who died there. In a reaction to that notion of a death memorial, a more traditional statue of soldiers was ultimately erected in remembrance of soldiers who fought. That, in turn, annoyed many of those who had appreciated "the Wall's" somber implication of loss. Similar questions affect the area of the former World Trade Center in

An architect describes plans for re-developing New York City's World Trade Center. (*Kathy Willens/AP Wide World Photos*)

New York City. The importance of the place is clear, but should the rebuilding be as a tribute to the American life force or as a more somber memorial for the dead? Those debates will continue because places serve not only as repositories of meaning but as mechanisms through which to reconsider the meaning of the events they represent.

OBJECTS

Place and body are thus both important sources of meaning and very good repositories for meaning. If there is something of the place in the person (Turnbull's forehead perhaps, or a scar from the Normandy landing), or of the person in the place (Mao's body in his Beijing mausoleum), the combination is even stronger. One major advantage of the body is its mobility; one advantage of place is its stability. *Objects* provide an alternative to both. Like person and place, meaning comes from objects and can, in turn, be stored there. Yet objects have some advantages. They can, unlike places, usually be moved, even if they are very large. They can also be created from scratch. A memorial stone to unknown soldiers may have more effect if their remains are there, but it can be a meaningful reminder even lacking such remains.

Most objects have both practical utility and symbolic importance. Cars are means of transportation and symbols of status. Both the practical utility and the symbolic importance may involve multiple features. Thus a car has utility as a more-or-less efficient, powerful means of getting from one place to another and also as a temporary mini-environment in which people spend large amounts of time. On the symbolic level, cars indicate not only general socioeconomic status but also something of a person's values and lifestyle: big trucks and small trucks, SUVs, sports cars, performance cars, or hybrids to show you're green. Needless to say, cars also provide a mobile personal billboard for smaller objects that advertise one's experiences and values, whether with license plates, bumper stickers, flag decals, or head-bobbing dogs in the back window.

The *kula* valuables from the Trobriand Islands provide a more traditional anthropological example. There is, in the Trobriands, a general system of exchange involving red shell necklaces (*soulava*), which are always exchanged for white shell arm bands (*mwali*). The exchange system follows a general circle in which—looking from the air—the *soulava* move in a clockwise direction and the *mwali* move in a counterclockwise direction. This is, in the terms of the chapter on economics, balanced reciprocity based on different items being exchanged, with an often large delay between the initial gift and the return gift. Furthermore, the necklaces and arm bands are quite valuable, even though their direct practical utility is limited. The value of these objects comes partly from their physical characteristics: Some are bigger, more finely colored, or better shaped. Value also comes from their history as they have moved around this exchange network. A particular necklace may have come from a particularly valued trading partner and have a particularly well-known history—people may even remember when it last came around the full exchange circle. Value has been added to the necklace by the events in which it has participated. The value of each necklace and arm band is partially drawn from its physical nature, partly from the way those physical materials are made into a particular article (necklace or arm band), and partly from the meaning of this article as an item in a comprehensive exchange network. Obtaining such an object demonstrates that you are part of this network and that this network has endured for a very long time.

Some objects in North American society also increase in value as they pass through different hands. Consider an old family Bible. The names of several generations are carefully written on the inside of the front cover. Like the *kula* variables, this object has increased in value because of the many hands that have touched it and the events (births of children) of which it is an official record. For the family this is an invaluable heirloom. For strangers, however, it may well be of little value. Value is in the eye of the beholder. This family Bible has a value that varies depending on whether one is a member of the family or not. It is an object with a history and it is also an object that, because it lists the generations, is itself a history—although abridged—of the family. This object is also a religious text. Here again, the meaning lies in the eyes of the beholder. For fundamentalists, this Bible may—depending on the translation—be viewed as the literal word of God; for others its meaning will be somewhat more metaphorical, will partially overlap with their own religious traditions (Muslims, for example), or perhaps seem odd to those from unrelated traditions (Buddhists and Hindus, for example). Whatever your own view, you would be wise not to spill your coffee on this worn old book. It may be the most valuable and meaningful thing these people have. If these people are refugees, it may be literally the only thing they could bring with them and thus the only object that connects them to their former home. One small object has thus come to incorporate family, God, and homeland.

EVENTS

In terms of human meaning, events serve much as objects do. They both generate meaning and serve as repositories for it. Both vary greatly in nature, in practical significance, and in symbolic importance. A simple daily routine such as eating dinner, for example, has obvious practical importance, but when people eat together it also creates a sense of being together. That meaning of "those who eat together" is a strong one. If such an event has some spiritual content—such as a prayer before eating—the joint image of being together for nutritional and spiritual nourishment is stronger yet. If such events become more elaborate, they may take on all the aspects of ritual described in the chapter on religion. Then the event itself also draws on the potential of the body, the place, and the objects. A wedding, for example, is an event to which people attach great meaning and from which they also draw much meaning. The wedding dress itself is essential. It is a temporary modification of the bride's body and, if inherited from a mother or grandmother, is an object that brings the past into the event. Place is important as well. For those who are even nominally religious, a church or temple setting is essential. Taking pictures captures something of the spirit of the event. Those pictures become objects that carry the meaning of the event through time and across place.

The meaning of events can shift over time. The pictures from that marriage that went bad, for example, lose much of their positive meaning: The original meaning ebbs away. In other cases, meaning may expand. Mohammed Ali was once simply Cassius Clay. His early victories were impressive—even dazzling—as technical accomplishments. Yet the meaning of those victories has changed over time. They are now seen in the light of his religion, his opposition to the Vietnam War, and his battle with Parkinson's disease. Those fights are no longer just the unexpected boxing successes of an upstart Louisville Lip but the opening rounds of a longer, more heroic saga. In turn, any sporting event that includes him—such as an Olympics—brings into that new event the full meaning of his life story.

One sort of event of particular interest to anthropologists involves language. An event that is language-based has particularly rich opportunities for conveying and creating meaning. A couple who write their own vows, for example, are explicitly choosing to create their own meaning to the ceremony rather than simply accepting the traditional wording. Here again is a reciprocal relationship: What they put into those vows will return to them later. It may be enough to remember them or to reread them privately. But they can also recreate them in the original context. Thus there is an evolving North American custom of repeating marital vows later in life. The words of many years ago can be brought to life again. Here, again, is the reciprocal nature of the relationship between people and events: The original vows are themselves a source of meaning and repeating them takes from that meaning but also breathes new life into it. To repeat the event is to renew the meaning of the event.

If one were to imagine a perfect event for this reciprocal inputting and extracting of meaning, it would probably be at a repetitive time in the annual cycle (a solstice or equinox would be nice but a specific date like December 25 would work very well); have some special objects associated with it (gift-wrapped presents, candles and incense, special decorations); have some enjoyable sub-events (lots of food and drink); and provide a chance for people to dress up—or maybe even put on costumes. The event would link individuals with their families and communities and give them an opportunity to tell stories, sing songs, perform plays, and simply play. It would certainly provide links between their everyday lives and their more spiritual lives. Such an event would provide opportunities to draw on the reservoir of meaning from this event in past years, to find ways to renew that meaning in the light of events of the most recent year, and to add to that reservoir with additional memories for the future. The event would—as perhaps the most essential issue of meaning—remind you who you are and to whom you are related.

There are three points to remember overall from this discussion of events and from the previous discussions of bodies, places, and objects. The first is that the relationship of people to all of these is to some degree *reciprocal*. Sometimes the meaning is drawn from them; sometimes it is put into them. The second point is that in this two-way relationship can be seen the basic tension between *openness* and *context* that was introduced earlier in Part III. In all the examples used here, there was some originating context, whether of the real human body, an actual place, or a previous event. Yet there were also new creations from that old material. The third point is that the reciprocal relationship of people with bodies, places, objects, and events serves particularly well the *order-seeking* aspect of human meaning. Even if something has multiple and perhaps conflicting meanings, those meanings can be located in the same body, place, object, or event and ordered to suit the purpose at hand.

Case Study
The Tattoo Renaissance in North America

The human body is an excellent place to mark meaning. There are many ways to do that. Some are external to the body and some internal; some major and some minor; some visible and some invisible. Some are temporary and some permanent. The anthropological record shows all kinds of practices: scarification, piercing, cutting, elongation, branding, reshaping—even what would now be called subdural implants. These practices are sometimes done volitionally by people and sometimes forced on them. Sometimes the result indicates being conventional and sometimes it indicates being unconventional. As a reminder that the meaning of these practices is subject to wide interpretation, it may be helpful to note that Canada and the United States are sometimes categorized as societies that practice genital mutilation. Not of women, but of men. Actually not even of men, but of defenseless male babies. But that's what male circumcision is even though "genital mutilation" doesn't seem to fit very well with either the usual sense of "mutilation" or the combination of medical and religious views that underlie it.

One common means of permanently marking the body is tattooing. Tattoos have the virtue of conveying complex pictorial and written meanings in a very durable and often artistic way. In many parts of the world, a tattoo is a normal part of assuming adult roles. In those societies, *not* having a tattoo would be

Tattoos: abstract and pictorial. (*Stockbyte*)

the unconventional thing. The history of tattooing in the Euro-American tradition is rather different. Although tattooing can be found throughout Western history, its use has tended to be limited to marking people as unusual. Three particular uses can be identified from historical materials. The first is the enforced marking of people. The permanence of a tattoo—or simple brand—was its virtue. A slave would always be marked a slave; a prisoner always marked as a prisoner. That tradition of tattooing remains very much alive today, except that the tattoos are not enforced by the prison authorities but by the inmates themselves. The second use is religious. For example, tattoos from pilgrimages have been found. They appear to involve a very standardized set of symbols that pilgrims would obtain at the site of their pilgrimage. After people returned from the pilgrimages, these tattoos continued to be evidence of their faith and their travel. The third use involves soldiers and sailors. Instead of representing religious pilgrimages, these tattoos represented war or commercial experiences, often in quite distant and exotic parts of the world. It was early voyages to Polynesia, in fact, that began to revolutionize and expand the use of tattoos in Europe. The Polynesians were masters of the art and the word "tattoo" itself derives from a Polynesian word (usually spelled *tatu* or *tatau*).

With the rapid expansion of tattooing in North America over the past several decades, it is no longer clear whether tattooing is conventional or unconventional, whether it continues to represent the kinds of tattooing seen in Euro-American history or simply a new kind of stylistic fashion. Many tattoos do not represent anything factual about the people who have them. Chinese characters don't represent trips to China; hand grenades don't represent military service; prison markings have even filtered into commercial tattoo parlors for the general population. Many contemporary North American tattoos, unlike tattoos known from the broader anthropological record, are thus not "authentic" in the usual sense. They are, notes Susan Benson, "fantasies of permanence, control, and autonomy" that are in contrast to a world characterized by impermanence, lack of control, and lack of autonomy.[1] Whatever their ultimate fate—which now includes some possibility of removal—the tattoo renaissance does suggest the increasing importance of the human body as the primary mechanism through which Euro-American society is fighting many of its personal and social battles. That is clear not only in tattoos but in the pervasive emphasis on fixing the body through exercise, surgery, and genetics. That "corporeal absolutism" (in Benson's terms) is also evidenced in the more extreme versions of body-piercing and self-mutilation that remain at the fringes of conventionality.

---

[1]Susan Benson, "Inscriptions of the Self: Reflections on Tattooing and Piercing in Contemporary Euro-America," in *Written on the Body*, ed. Jane Caplan (Princeton University Press, 2000), pp. 234–254.

Case Study
Hutu and Tutsi in Rwanda

The meaning that is attached to bodies is not always as volitional as the discussion of tattooing suggests. Instead the body is often used as a marker of enforced social divisions of the most damaging kind. Thus it has often been with race. Some apparent physical variation of size or shape, of color or particular feature, is used as a primary social marker. In the United States, for example, the importation of slave labor from Africa brought together two different-looking populations from very different parts of the world. With the necessity for controlling that labor, a justification of racial differences proved all too convenient. Yet even with two disparate populations, a great deal of work was required to keep the racial lines clear. There were many people of mixed racial background who defied easy categorization; there were also both free and slave African Americans. The legal apparatus and social mechanisms used to keep the races apart were difficult and complex, even with two sets of people drawn from very different parts of the world.

Consider, instead, the dynamics of race and ethnicity among two African populations living side by side in Rwanda. The people called Hutu and Tutsi lived together in relative peace, spoke the same language, generally followed the same religion, lived in the same neighborhoods, often worked side by side, and intermarried extensively. Hutu and Tutsi were thus often related to each other by blood and marriage. Yet the two were also considered different. Tutsi were tall, Hutu were short. In origin, Tutsi were later migrants into Rwanda and pastoralist, Hutu were longer established in Rwanda and traditionally horticulturalist. Ultimately the differences overcame the similarities. In 100 days in 1994, Hutu massacred some 800,000 people, largely Tutsi but including some Hutu as well. It was arguably the most efficient killing the world had ever seen. It was also one of the most chilling since the killing was largely done with machetes and often by people who knew the victims personally.

The roots of the Rwandan genocide are multiple, including the withdrawal of international forces from Rwanda at exactly the moment when they were most needed. In longer historical terms, colonial policies helped sharpen the divide between Hutu and Tutsi and post-independence governments also exploited the Hutu/Tutsi divide for their own political purposes. By the time of the genocide there was an active public relations campaign by a radical set of Hutu that fanned the flames and organized the killing. The Tutsi were "cockroaches" and they were to be exterminated.

There was a practical problem, however, for Tutsi and Hutu were not completely separate races that could always be easily told apart. Just to be sure, identity cards were issued that included whether the person was Tutsi or Hutu. Since many people had both Hutu and Tutsi relatives, that formal identity process was itself somewhat arbitrary. Proof of "racial" identity was thus provided by a piece of bureaucratic paper that was often only partly accurate. During the course of the genocide, accounts suggest that killing was also an arbitrary process. Many people were killed because they looked like stereotypical Tutsi. However, people were also killed because their identity cards indicated they were Tutsi—even though sometimes they did not look Tutsi. If the card said "Hutu" but people looked Tutsi, they might be killed anyway. People were also killed because they looked well-off (rich people were assumed to be Tutsi), seemed well-educated (good education was a sign of being Tutsi), acted strangely (they looked guilty or fearful), would not themselves kill others (they must be protecting their own kind), had been accused by somebody of being Tutsi (whether correctly or for spite), or simply had something that the killers wanted.

It is not easy to draw lessons from the Rwandan genocide. It is clear from human history that genocides occur. Rwanda joins the list with Armenia, the Jewish holocaust of World War II, the Hindu/Muslim atrocities that accompanied the partition of India and Pakistan after that war, and, most recently, the Balkans. In all those cases some kind of difference was assumed to be so strong that those on the other side of the divide were entitled only to be slaughtered. In the Rwandan case, the divide was based on a notion of physical differences, yet those physical differences had to be organized bureaucratically (identity cards) and socially (Hutu had to report which of their neighbors were Tutsi). There also was extensive propaganda asserting that Tutsi were a unitary force and that the continued existence of the Tutsi was dangerous to the very survival of the Hutu. In Rwanda—as with race relations in the United States—not even shared Christianity was enough to soften the divide. In the aftermath of the genocide, as Hutu and Tutsi try to find a way to live together again in Rwanda, there has been a noticeable conversion to Islam. Muslims, it is said, did not participate in the killing, unlike the Christian pastors who betrayed people in their own congregations.

SOURCES

There is a wide and scattered literature on the issues covered in this chapter. I have aimed to provide a relatively stabilized view, but just as human beings in general can draw meaning from, and write meaning onto, bodies, places, objects, and events, so too can academics. The body probably takes the brunt of this academic meaning-making. As a sampling, consider browsing in some of the following: *The Political Lives of Dead Bodies* by Katherine Verdery (Columbia University Press, 1999); *Transmen and Ftms: Identities, Bodies, Genders, and Sexualities* by Jason Cromwell (University of Illinois Press, 1999); *Bodies and Pleasures: Foucault and the Politics of Sexual Normalization* by Ladelle

McWhorter (Indiana University Press, 1999); and *Feminist Theory and the Body: A Reader*, edited by Janet Price and Margrit Shildrick (Routledge, 1999). After that, you may well be ready for a walk on the quiet side pondering the durability of place, for which Keith Basso's *Wisdom Sits in Places* (University of New Mexico Press, 1996) provides a wise and steady guide.

Regarding the subject of tattooing, see Victoria L. Pitts's *In the Flesh* (Palgrave, 2003) for a general cultural studies approach to contemporary body modification; Jane Caplan's edited volume *Written on the Body* (Princeton University Press, 2000) for an invaluable historical review of the Euro-American experience with tattooing, and Alfred Gell's *Wrapping in Images* (Oxford University Press, 1993) for his influential discussion of tattooing in Polynesia. For Rwanda, perhaps the best place to start is Philip Gourevitch's *We Wish to Inform You That Tomorrow We Will Be Killed with Our Families* (Farar, Straus, and Giroux, 1998). There is a variety of good film on Rwanda but the 1999 Frontline presentation (and accompanying background Web materials) of *Triumph of Evil* is an especially good companion to Gourevitch's book. Liisa Malkki's *Purity and Exile* (University of Chicago Press, 1995) provides a useful comparative perspective on Burundi, where the Hutu/Tutsi story has played out in a rather different way.

CHAPTER 18

ACTION

The discussion in the previous chapter was about the reciprocal interaction between human beings and their bodies, places, objects, and events. That discussion of the construction of human meaning suggests that people are not simply following a script handed to them. They are both acting on the meanings that they find and elaborating them. This reflects human autonomy and what anthropologists often call *agency*—which means simply that people are acting as agents on their own behalf in their own lives. On the other hand, much of what happens in the construction of meaning is social: It involves other people. Those other people may have greater or lesser power and that power will affect how meaning is constructed. The openness of meaning systems is, after all, always limited by the context. That context includes power differentials and those power differentials are generally based on objective material conditions and who has access to what resources.

A consideration of the construction of meaning thus leads back to consideration of material conditions in the world—who has access to what resources, and what that access to resources yields in terms of relative power. Since anthropologists often work with people who are at the weaker end of the power spectrum, they tend to be particularly sensitive to such power differentials. Although the less powerful have their options for resistance and agency, those options are limited. In many cases, the power differential is so severe that people's lives are at risk. They may die as a result of the direct actions of the more powerful, or they may die of disease and malnutrition as a result of being limited to less food or medical resources. In yet other cases, the dangers may be less life-threatening than identity-destroying. The less powerful may survive but only by becoming a lesser part of somebody's else world—rather than remaining at the center of their own.

The lesson that many anthropologists draw from this is that action is needed to improve material conditions in the world and to foster enough reduction in power differentials so that people are free to pursue their own destinies—to pursue, as Boas had it long ago on Baffin Island, their search for truth and humanity. That search for truth and humanity—that ultimate search for meaning—thus requires decent and equitable access to resources. It is not surprising, then, that many anthropologists are less concerned with the ways that people construct the meanings of their lives than with giving them the basic material for lives on which they can then build that meaning. The result is an anthropological commitment to action.

This final chapter discusses that commitment to action. The discussion is in four parts. The first is a review of the contemporary world and the context it provides for anthropological action. The second is a rough inventory of the principles that guide anthropologists in such action. The third is a consideration of two cautionary tales about how action—even savvy and well-intended action—can have unintended and negative consequences. The fourth is a concluding comment on the likely direction of anthropology in the twenty-first century. The first of the case studies at the end of the chapter concerns the nature of work in modern society and what one anthropologist found about "the last best work." The second example invokes a broader social issue that links North America to the rest of the contemporary world: the plight of refugees.

MANAGING CHANGE IN THE CONTEMPORARY WORLD

As anthropologists enter the twenty-first century, they find a world that is in many ways similar to the one they faced at the beginning of the twentieth century. It is still a world with enormous inequalities within countries and between them. It is still a world where minority peoples are at risk both for their lives and for their ways of living. It is still a world where race is taken seriously—despite a full century of anthropological effort to debunk the notion. It is still a world of hunger and epidemic disease, of war and natural disaster. Yet in other ways the world is very different. Those differences contain good news along with bad. Colonialism is largely gone—although some fear that "globalization" is little more than a new, administratively simpler version of it. The spread of democracy has been impressive—but it is also clear that democracies can themselves be fragile as well as aggressive militarily. Many of the peoples anthropologists feared would disappear are alive and recreating the very lifeways anthropologists took such efforts to record—but others are now in danger of disappearance.

GLOBALIZATION

Globalization has become something of a buzzword at the beginning of a new century. In many ways, the processes to which it refers are not new ones. Much of the world has been "global" for several thousand years. True, the trek along the Silk Road that linked the Mediterranean, South Asia, and East Asia was a slow and laborious passage. But it did not stop the flow of goods and it did not stop the explosive spread of ideas and religious beliefs—especially Buddhism. In more modern times, what could be more "global" than colonialism, a process that brought virtually all parts of the world under the control of a set of countries who had best mastered the potential of industrial production. Even closer in time, what could be more global than a world war? Or the subsequent forty year clash of capitalism and communism that drew into battle even the smallest and most remote of countries?

Nevertheless, the contemporary world does have distinctive features that suggest that globalization may be a good word for describing some objective changes. Some might suggest that the answer lies with speed: the speed of travel, the speed of communication, the speed of production and changes in production, the very speed of change itself. But, again, much of that speed is not new: intercontinental jet travel, instantaneous world phone communication, the overnight sensations caused by Western products (Winston cigarettes, the Beatles), even space travel are now all roughly at their half-century mark. Given that, others might suggest that the distinctiveness of the contemporary scene lies in the combination of speed and volume—not only that some people and goods can rapidly transit the globe but that vast numbers of them can. Certainly the instantaneous transmission of large volumes of data by large numbers of people is something new.

Finally, some people would argue that globalization is less about the extent of global interaction and more about the control of these interactions. While most Europeans and North Americans consider the values of an expanding global economy to be self-evident, others see a new kind of colonialism that may benefit some people but that is sharpening social divisions between richer and poorer countries, and also sharpening social divisions within those countries. Consider the comments of Arundhati Roy, one of the most eloquent critics of the new U.S. role in the world. The "New Imperialism," she remarks, "is upon us. For the first time in history, a single empire with an arsenal of weapons that could obliterate the world in an afternoon has complete, unipolar, economic and military hegemony."[2] All countries in the world, she thus points out, are "caught in the cross-hairs of the American cruise missile and the IMF checkbook."

FORCES OF DESTRUCTION, FORCES OF CREATION

One particularly troublesome change is the degree of destruction and damage in the modern world. Much of that damage is to people and much is directly carried out by people. Genocide has occurred in several parts of the world. The sheer efficiency of the genocide in Rwanda is particularly stunning: Roughly 800,000 people were killed in three months in 1994. Yet the ensuing political and social breakdown in the neighboring Congo, which was to a great degree an aftereffect of the genocide, actually led to far more deaths. One 2001 report suggested about 2.5 million. These included a number of

---

[2]*The Nation*, February 9, 2004, page 11. The article was adapted from her comments at the World Social Forum in Mumbai in January 2004.

massacres, mostly along ethnic lines. But the destruction of people is not only in war. AIDS continues to ravage much of southern Africa, starvation appears periodically in various parts of the world (Ethiopia, North Korea), and the very hazards of industrialism take their toll on people's health (chemical exposure) and their very lives (industrial accidents, especially in mining operations).

There has also been severe damage to other living creatures and to the environment. The destruction of forest lands in highland areas contributes to flooding, as bare soil cannot hold the water from rains. Vietnam, for example, has seen much cutting of forests in its highlands and, in turn, has seen record-breaking floods in virtually every year since the late 1990s. Without forests, the soil itself is not even safe: It is carried off with the water from the hills or swept up by the wind. Dust storms originating in Mongolia can now shut down airports in Korea and deposit soil tainted by pollutants in Japan. In the cities of the world, the process of industrialization takes a heavy toll. The pollution that afflicted European cities is now being reproduced in far more numerous and far larger cities throughout the world. This time, the effects are spread more broadly and raise a significant threat of ecological collapse through both urban and rural pollution.

At the same time as the unleashing of such forces of destruction, the forces of creation are also expanding. While this is sometimes beneficial, it also raises troublesome questions. The increasing human control over our own biology is a particular area of concern. Even a simple medical development like the sonogram can have very sharp social effects. In countries where sons are valued, for example, the ability to "choose" male children (through abortion of female fetuses) has shifted sex ratios at birth toward males. When those males grow up, they will face a shortage of marriage partners. Barring polyandry (which exists but is relatively rare), the men must then either remain bachelors or find women from somewhere else. Some of the current trafficking in women is not into prostitution or other forced labor but into marriage with these men. As the ability to genetically alter and eventually create human beings develops, the dangers are far greater. Even when that ability to control our own biology can be used for good purposes, it is likely to be controlled by the rich and powerful. Those with more power and money could thus not only buy better health care and surgical enhancements to their bodies, but they could buy better-engineered bodies to begin with. They would probably even feel obliged to do so for their children. Finally, after all those years of pretending that human beings are somehow divided into biological races, we might finally be right. There would be biologically different races: a rich one and a poor one.

PEOPLE OUT OF PLACE

For anthropologists, one aspect of globalization that deserves particular note is the increasing disconnection between people and place. Global migration is hardly a new phenomenon, but it does appear to be on the increase, both within countries and between them. Many of these people are forced migrants, either pushed across borders by persecution or displaced within their countries by political conflict and natural disaster. An increasing number of people are trafficked; some, in effect, as indentured servants, others as virtual slaves. Many—including children—are trafficked for the sex trade. What makes this detachment from place even worse is the lessening of the kin ties that would provide a portable social environment for people who are on the move. The social relationships of family buffer people when they are moving and help root them in new localities. In the industrialized countries (from North America to Europe to East Asia) the percentage of people marrying and having children is declining and there is a high level of divorce for those who do marry. This new globalized world thus has large numbers of people who are detached not only from place but from the kin-based relationships that might serve as an alternative to ties of locality.

THREE ANTHROPOLOGICAL GUIDING PRINCIPLES

The partially similar, partially different world of the twenty-first century, with its enhanced biological, environmental, and migration concerns, sets the stage for the kinds of action that anthropologists take. That action is very broad. A recent volume of *Practicing Anthropology*, for example, suggests that anthropologists are in government, the corporate world, nonprofit organizations, and private practice, and that they are working to preserve Appalachian heritage, mitigate the problems of lead paint, protect source water, find better ways for teams to work in government and corporate contexts, improve technology transfer programs, foster debate on female circumcision, preserve forests, and build centers for the homeless. All this anthropological action shares some basic assumptions. Three are worth noting as a core set of guiding principles: preservation, holism, and equality.

PRESERVATION

Since the early days of Boas, North American anthropologists have been committed to preservation. Whether it is the environment, people's lives, or people's lifeways, anthropologists tend to believe that what exists now should be allowed to continue. It is not that the future is to be avoided, that change is bad, or that people's own desires for change should be thwarted. However, a future not built on the past is unlikely to be well-grounded, and change that obliterates the past may be dangerous. Just as the destruction of forests leaves the soil defenseless against the ravages of rain and wind, so the destruction of cultural traditions leaves people with fewer options for the future. Thus anthropologists continue their long, long commitment to preservation. That is a commitment to maintaining the breadth of the human experience and to maintaining its continuity over time. That commitment manifests itself in action that ranges from saving endangered lands and peoples in the Amazon to seeking ways to help immigrants maintain a balance between their original culture and the dictates of life in North America.

One reason for such preservation is that the "old ways" often work pretty well. Low-intensity swidden cultivation, for example, is an efficient and nondestructive way to utilize land that would otherwise be subject to destruction because of a shallow soil layer (as in the tropics) or dangers of run-off (as in mountainous areas). Much traditional healing works very well—partially because of a good pharmacy in the wild that includes roots and herbs that have been the source of much of the best in modern medicine. Many traditional social arrangements also work well. Attempts to rearrange social relationships to control people or even to help them often take very nasty turns. Much of the carnage of the Rwandan genocide of Tutsi by Hutus (and the inverse killing of Hutus by Tutsi in Burundi) can be blamed on colonial policies that underestimated the delicate balancing mechanisms among the various peoples in those countries.

The issue of preservation is not only an academic one. While genocide as an actual organized killing may be fairly rare, the disappearance of entire peoples through disease, starvation, and war is far from uncommon. This is particularly the case for relatively small indigenous groups—like the Yanomami—who are under the combined assault of state power and economic expansion. The story is often an ugly one, as it was in the westward marches of both Canada and the United States. At the very least, governments are likely to want indigenous peoples to settle down, and economic forces will want the resources on their land. Like the Yanomami, indigenous people are all too often near national borders and frequently move back and forth across them. While the size of these groups is often small, they represent a very significant portion of human diversity. Furthermore, in the aggregate, they represent some 300 million people. Their situation has been of special concern to anthropologists since anthropologists are often the only outsiders who know much about them, their histories, their languages, and their cultures.

HOLISM

A second guiding principle for anthropology in action is holism. Like preservation, holism goes back to the very roots of North American anthropology. One aspect of that commitment is the continued attention to the biological, cultural, and environmental aspects of human life. This commitment to holism often puts anthropologists in the position of crossing disciplinary boundaries. Thus many anthropologists are interested in computerization—not because it is something new but because it is yet another in a long list of human tools: things that humans create for practical and symbolic purposes. Those tools— like other objects—also have a reciprocal effect on their creators: We build the tools but the tools change our lives. Many anthropologists also try to reconcile the different areas of traditional healing and modern medicine. Both aim to make the person healthy again: One uses a holistic and usually spiritual approach; the other uses a supposedly objective and scientific approach. Why, anthropologists usually argue, can't we get these two approaches together so that we can heal the complete person: body and spirit, heart and mind.

EQUALITY

A third principle for an anthropology in action is the commitment to equality. The notion of equality derives partly from the evolutionists—who at least wanted to include everybody. It derives even more strongly from Boas and his conviction that we are all equally seekers of truth. This commitment to equality works in several ways. In one way, the commitment is to the equality of all human societies. That is what cultural relativism is all about. In a related way, anthropologists have often worked with people who are minorities within larger societies. Again, the anthropological position is to seek greater equality for them, whether they be ethnic minorities, economically underprivileged groups, or people of varying social or sexual orientations.

March for indigenous rights in Berkeley, California. (*Paul Sakuma/AP Wide World Photos*)

Finally, anthropologists tend to be committed to the equality of individual people. Those different kinds of equality are not always consistent. The idea that all societies are equal runs up against the fact that societies often provide unequal treatment to their members: economically exploiting minorities, depriving women of what we take to be their inalienable rights, and sending young children to work rather than to school. Equality may thus be the most difficult of the anthropological commitments. The notion of equality is not value-free. Without it, however, even the most elementary attempt at anthropological action is likely to fail.

TWO CAUTIONARY TALES

These goals of preservation, holism, and equality are very general ones that anthropologists attempt to apply to a variety of practical efforts throughout the world. It is not always easy to combine all three, but the dangers of not doing so become clear in the two cautionary tales that follow.

SHEEP IN ECUADOR

In Ecuador, a set of people living in the mountains grew sheep. The sheep were hardy, but they were also scrawny with rather poor coats. The wool produced from them was neither abundant nor of very good quality. International development staff thought that a better breed of sheep would make a great difference to these people. That would help preserve their basic life style while the better wool would increase their income. With greater income they could be better integrated into the wider economy and have greater equality in their access to resources of various kinds. The development staff decided that Australian merino sheep, which were also hardy but produced more luxuriant wool, would be a good choice. So they arranged for some of these sheep to be sent to Ecuador. They then tried to talk some of the people into raising these sheep. There would be no cost to them. Initially there was great reluctance, but eventually one adventurous herder decided to try out the sheep. All went well. The sheep were up to the demands of the Ecuadorean mountains and they prospered. A success for development and a success for entrepreneurship? No, not really. One night the people in the valley came and stole the sheep. They were never returned.

RICE IN INDONESIA

The second cautionary tale concerns a new strain of rice that was introduced into Indonesia. It was IR8—one of the best of a wide range of new rice strains developed at the International Rice Institute in the Philippines. The new strain produced far higher yields but also required some changes in how the crop was grown. A project was initiated to help farmers use the new seed. The initial round of the project enlisted students—many from far-off cities—to work with the farmers, helping them to plant the new rice and to apply the necessary fertilizer. The result was an increase in yields that produced at harvest more money for almost everybody. There were some potential problems. The bigger, wealthier landlords, for example, tried to corner the new seed, but those efforts were defeated. Some of the students, it turned out, were politically rather well-connected at home in the capital. So the project was a success for development and a success for cooperative effort. However, in the second round of the project, the students were not included. The distribution of seed and fertilizer was handled through large international companies. This time, the wealthier landlords had better luck at cornering the resources. The bulk of the increase in yield was on their own fields. They were thus able to manipulate prices at harvest time, drive many of the small land-owners into debt, and purchase their land. Result: The rich got richer and the poor got landless.

SOME LESSONS

Both these examples have positive moments. The animals and the crops were improved varieties. They were not simply theoretically better, but were better when tested in the field. In both cases, the projects emphasized the people themselves making the tests—not just being shown or told how the new crop or animal was better. Finally, both projects were based on the practical, financial advantage that would be gained from the new, improved animal or crop. Many attempts to make improvements in people's lives fail to meet these criteria, instead imposing improvements that ought to work but don't (animals die, crops fail) with little attention to the practical motivations of the people involved.

Nevertheless, two well-designed projects went seriously wrong. Much of the problem in both cases was an underestimation of the implications of different environmental adaptations—exactly the issues laid out in Part I of this book. Different adaptations to the environment are associated with differing uses of the land and varying degrees of control over it. One implication of that control is population density. Thus the image of herders in the hills should immediately raise the question of what and who might be down on the plains or in the valleys. Even if the valleys are small, there is likely to be agriculture. The intensity of agricultural land use will be matched by population density. That population density will give the upper hand to the agriculturalists in dealing with these other people in the hills. The upland Indians could do little against the power of those in the valley. The valley dwellers simply saw the new sheep as "too good for the Indians" and took them away.

A somewhat different situation is seen in the Indonesian case. Here, the tension was not between herders and agriculturalists but between some agriculturalists with a great deal of land and some with little or none. Since land is so valuable in agricultural societies, you can expect that people will want to have more of it: It's the only long-term investment. Initially, however, the weaker farmers were politically protected as well as economically assisted. The students were crucial to that political protection. They were outside the local political system but had connections in other places that could be brought to bear on the local system. When they disappeared, that protection disappeared.

These projects thus reflect central tensions in different kinds of environmental adaptation. They also reflect, however, the innate tensions within and among the three anthropological goals of preservation, holism, and equality. Both projects, for example, ultimately failed to include all the people who were involved both directly and indirectly in the development projects. The villagers had no reason not to steal from the herders, and the large landowners had no reason not to appropriate the land of those less well off. The need to integrate those different sets of people, in turn, reflected the overall tension between the goal of preservation and that of equality. What was ultimately preserved in both cases was the *inequality* among the different people involved.

AN ANTHROPOLOGY FOR THE TWENTY-FIRST CENTURY

This tension between preservation and equality is, and will remain, a pervasive problem for anthropology. Attempts at economic development that will increase people's access to the resources of the modern world will continue to be undercut by the reality of differential power. Even the best of efforts are likely to be overtaken by economic and political forces over which anthropologists have little control. One result of that dilemma has probably been positive: a reappraisal of the role of anthropologists. For decades, anthropologists have viewed themselves as cultural brokers—as people who could bridge the differences between cultures to promote mutual understanding and joint progress. That, however, is clearly not enough. Now many anthropologists are considering how they can work as part of larger alliances that can achieve results durable enough to withstand the onslaught of negative political and economic forces. Many anthropologists, for example, have become more involved with nonprofit organizations at the local, national, and international levels. Such organizations are a major force within North America and are becoming more so throughout the world. A network of such nonprofit organizations can be a stabilizing force politically, a powerful means for communication, and a continuing wave of pressure for economic development and human rights.

As anthropologists move forward with that general trend, they will bring their own acute sense of the biological, cultural, and environmental aspects of being human. Their instincts will tell them to balance preservation with development, to look for ways to reanimate and thicken ties of kinship and community, to pursue a workplace that is not so "unnatural," and to help recreate the rootedness of place in a world that so directly threatens it. Some anthropologists will continue their inroads into the nonprofit world; others will continue what have also been significant inroads into the worlds of government and business. Many will teach: Their message will continue to be one of human diversity and human equality. Others will take more independent roles in research and social action. As the two examples below show, those roles may range from discovering what can make a job in modern society fulfilling to how North American society can assist those displaced by violence and discrimination.

Case Study

The Last Best Work: Firefighters in New York City

Miriam Lee Kaprow died of cancer in 1997 at the age of sixty-four. She was a native New Yorker and spent much of her adulthood in ballet and modern dance. An injury pushed her career interests in new directions and she obtained a degree in anthropology when she was in her early forties. Her dissertation research was on Gypsies in Spain, and she continued that interest as a founding member of the American chapter of the Gypsy Lore society. She was fascinated, among other things, by the ways Gypsies resisted the values and organizational structures of the wider society. They contested the identity that the wider and stronger society wished to impose on them. They were and continued to be their own people and, by all accounts, she admired that.

Miriam Kaprow's friends suggest that she—always known as Mimi—was a particularly engaging person, very active professionally, and with two twin devotions: her family and anthropology. She was, as anthropologists should be (and as few of us manage to be as often as we should), filled with energy, innately sociable and attentive to her friends, fully engaged with the people she studied, and a dutiful ethnographer of them. Like many other anthropologists, Mimi also developed new interests over the course of her life. One was firefighters. Firefighters were, she believed, resisters like the Gypsies. What they were resisting was people telling them how to do their job, an extraordinarily hazardous job. The accounts she collected from firefighters suggest not only the general danger but the unpredictability of the danger. It was not so much the fire itself but what different air flows could do to a fire. Simply opening the door to a smoldering room might introduce enough air to turn it into an inferno. A shift in wind might change a fire's direction. Firefighters had to consider not only what a fire was at the moment, but also all the different things it could become. Their lives hung in the balance.

New York City firefighters. (*Bernd Obermann/Corbis/Bettmann*)

To do their job—and to stay alive—required teamwork, but also great independent judgment. Firefighters had little patience with bureaucrats sitting in offices who tried to tell them how to do their job. That horrible risk of the job bought freedom from very much supervision. You were on your own to do your job because in saving lives you were risking your own. For Mimi, that was heroism and it was also what made firefighting the last best work. She noted the dying words of a New York fireman: "It's still the best job in the world." But firefighting was not only dangerous and heroic; it was also fun. Mimi recounted with relish the extent of jokes, pranks, and games among the firefighters: the "scrotum on the head" game that got four firefighters suspended; the way firefighters might wake to find themselves tied to their beds or wake to find their genitals painted (especially appropriate for men getting married); or the masked but naked firefighter who would appear from time to time at fires and—true to legend—remain anonymous despite numerous attempts to unmask him. We don't "go to work," firefighters would say to her, we "go to play."

Here then was that unusual job in the modern, bureaucratic world: a job that you performed independently, using your own judgment and doing it for your own satisfaction. The price paid for that freedom—and that satisfaction—was risk. It was the "red devil." But in that fight with the devil, you at least didn't have a supervisor looking over your shoulder reciting what the manual said you were supposed to do. Your job was your job and you did it. It might save other lives or cost you yours. In the aftermath of 9/11, Mimi Kaprow's earlier comments on the "last best work" resonate ever more strongly.

Case Study
In Search of Refuge: Forced Migration in an Age of Restriction

In the world today, there are some 15–20 million refugees displaced from their home country and about the same number who are displaced but still within their home country. A wide range of governments, international agencies, and nonprofit organizations attempt to address the plight of these forcibly displaced people. Sometimes they set up camps to provide security, shelter, and food—as they have done for decades for Palestinians in the Middle East and Afghans in Pakistan. Sometimes they have intervened in countries to resolve potential refugee crises—as was done in Kosovo. In yet other cases, the lack of reasonable options for returning people to their home country has meant sending them to other countries for resettlement and to begin new lives. North America has been a major destination for such resettled refugees. Both Canada and the United States, after all, have long been immigrant-oriented countries and both have welcomed large numbers of refugees: the United States the greater overall number, Canada the higher per capita numbers.

The plight of refugees, both overseas and when resettled in North America, has been of particular interest to anthropologists. In moral terms, refugees represent the dispossessed and anthropology has a long history of trying to assist the dispossessed. In practical terms, the situation of refugees requires exactly the skills that anthropologists tend to have in balancing the interest and needs of people from different backgrounds and languages. Indeed the very range of backgrounds of refugees has been interesting to anthropologists—whether involving people with whom they are making a new acquaintance or renewing acquaintance with people known from their home country. The involvement of anthropologists in refugee relief and resettlement has been wide-ranging: Some have worked in research and advocacy, others in the nonprofit sector, and some in governmental program management and policy development. Providing the bridge between new arrivals unprepared for life in North America and receiving communities that often know very little about the arrivals is a traditional and generally satisfying anthropological role.

The situation of refugees thus brings together the three anthropological goals of preservation (both of lifeways and of people's very lives), holism (of different cultures and different kinds of organizational efforts), and equality (that refugees resettled in North America indeed have fair and equal access to the resources our societies offer). The situation of refugees also brings North American anthropology back to the consideration of our own societies. Much is at stake. Fears of terrorism, for example, threaten to tip the balance once again from an open welcome of refugees toward a rejection of outsiders of any kind. In the United States, somewhat ironically, the wake of 9/11 has seen proposals for legalization of undocumented migrants but a very sharp decline in the number of refugees accepted.

The specific concern with refugees in North America thus brings anthropologists back to a consideration of North America itself and whether we can preserve the best of our own past while at the same time integrating new sets of people. Anthropologists have provided both positive and negative answers about whether that will be possible. Although there is evidence of generosity and concern toward refugees (and other immigrants), there is also evidence of rejection, avoidance, sometimes hatred, and often simple ignorance. In this area, as in many others, much work is left to be done. It is good work and important work—and anthropologists are likely to be at the center of it.

SOURCES

Most of the material in this chapter falls into the usual category of "applied anthropology." Three general texts to consult are *Applied Anthropology: A Practical Guide* by Erve Chambers (Waveland 1989), *Applied Anthropology: Tools and Perspectives for Contemporary Practice* by Alexander M. Ervin (Allyn & Bacon 1999), and *Applied Anthropology: An Introduction* by John Van Willigen (Bergin and Garvey 2002). The Ecuador and Indonesia examples are drawn from two long texts that have especially useful discussions of applied issues: Marvin Harris and Orna Johnson's *Cultural Anthropology* (Allyn & Bacon, 2000) and Conrad Kottak's *Cultural Anthropology* (McGraw Hill, 2000). Two useful sources for reviewing what anthropologists are currently doing are the journals *Human Organization* (somewhat on the academic side) and *Practicing Anthropology* (very much on the practitioner side). Both are published by the Society for Applied Anthropology.

For the case study on firefighters, see the warm tribute to Miriam Kaprow in the Winter 1999 special issue of the *Anthropology of Work Review*. For refugees, perusing the *Selected Papers* of the American Anthropological Association's Committee on Refugees and Immigrants will give a sense of the breadth of the issue, and the U.S. Committee for Refugees' annual *World Refugee Survey* provides good statistical and program updates. There is also very good film on refugees. One with an international perspective that is relatively hopeful is *The Tree of Our Forefathers*. It details the repatriation of refugees to Mozambique. For resettlement in North America, *aka Don Bonus* may be the most provocative for class use because of its depiction of the hazards refugees face even after resettlement.

GLOSSARY

adjudication   Dispute resolution mechanism based on determinations by a formal authority that has the power to impose a decision.

age   With sex, the most important biological variation in human society. Also, as with sex, its significance varies greatly from society to society.

agriculture   Environmental adaptation in which humans cultivate plants based on specialization in one or a few crops and usually the use of fertilizer, irrigation, and a plow.

animatism   Belief in a pervasive spiritual force that permeates the natural world.

animism   Belief in spirits.

ascending generation   One generation "up"; thus, for you, your parents, aunts, and uncles.

authority   As contrasted with "power," refers to the capacity of people or organizations to tell people what to do, based on their inherent right to do so and perhaps on their perceived wisdom as well.

avunculocal   Type of postmarital residence in which the couple reside together with an uncle, usually the husband's mother's brother from whom he would inherit in a matrilineal society.

axon   A single, often quite long, tentacle by which a neuron sends messages to other cells.

balanced reciprocity   Exchange of goods between individuals that follows a pattern of gift, return-gift, gift in response to the return-gift, etc.

balanda   Australian aboriginal term for nonaborigines. (See the discussion of the Yolngu in Chapter 1.)

bands   Type of political organization based on small, loosely organized groups with only informal leadership.

barbarism   Term used by early evolutionists to designate societies with relatively advanced technology but lacking the refinements (e.g., a writing system) of fully "civilized" people.

berdache   Term usually used for men in Native American tribes who lived as women (transgendered in current terminology). The word itself is European in origin and arrived in North America with the French.

biology   As used in this text, refers to aspects of human beings and their behavior that hinge largely on their unmodified physical nature as opposed to environment or culture.

blended families   Contemporary term used to describe the merging of different family fragments, particularly those resulting from death and divorce.

bound morpheme   A morpheme that cannot stand on its own (e.g., the "z" sound in English that indicates a plural).

broadcasting   System of agriculture in which seed is thrown out ("broadcast") on the soil rather than actually planted in the soil.

byres   Fences or similar structures used to hold animals.

caste   A rigidly imposed system of social differences, often based on occupation but with strong social and cultural implications. Castes are typically not allowed to intermarry and are rigidly stratified.

categories   In contrast to "groups," refers to sets of people who are designated as being the same, whether or not they actually interact with each other.

censorate   Refers to the early Chinese system of having special officials who monitored the work of other government officials.

chiefdoms   Type of political organization based on centralized entities with inherited political offices.

chinampas   Fields in which multiple kinds of fertilizer create very high yields without the use of a plow. Such fields can be traced to the Aztecs but still exist today.

circumcision   In contemporary usage, now refers to a very broad range of alterations of male and female sexual organs, whether soon after birth or much later. Some of these alterations clearly merit the term "genital mutilation"; some (such as the conventional North American male circumcision) seem not to. (See discussion in Chapter 17.)

civil society   Refers to the concept of an organized, engaged citizenry that provides a framework for governance that runs parallel to the formal government. The phrase is usually used in a positive sense, but recent experience with highly militant "civil" organizations (including militias) provides an alternate, less positive view.

clan   A set of kin who belong together because of a believed descent from a common ancestor.

class   Refers to largely economic distinctions within a society, although with pervasive social and political implications. Class membership can be rigidly imposed and inherited; it can also be loosely imposed and subject to change.

class mobility   Refers to the ability to change one's class status. That ability ranges from none (you are what you were born to be), to some (maybe not you but your children can move ahead), to a great deal (you can be anything you want to be).

classifier   A kind of particle used in many languages to indicate what kind of object is being discussed (e.g., an animal, something flat and thin, something round).

cognatic descent   System of reckoning descent that puts together all people descended from the same ancestor.

colonialism   Economic and political system in which some countries or peoples utterly dominate others. To distinguish more recent variants from the classic European and Japanese empires of the nineteenth and early twentieth centuries, hybrid phrases are often used: thus neo-colonialism for recent situations of dominance among nations, and internal colonialism for domination of a set of people (especially indigenous minorities) within a country.

compensation   As contrasted with "punishment," refers to a resolution of disputes that brings things back into balance among the parties.

complexity   One of four themes in human adaptation. Refers to the overall complexity of social arrangements. Usually (but not always) it increases with control over nature and density of settlement.

conception   In contrast to "perception," involves the higher, more abstract aspects of human thinking.

control   One of four themes in human adaptation. Refers to the degree of control over the environment. However, that increased environmental control usually also requires increased social control.

corruption   In this text, refers to the problem of people in government acting in their own interest rather than in the government and society's interest. This is a fundamental problem in all political systems.

Creole   A fully formed language that typically develops from a more limited pidgin (trade language).

cultural genocide   An attempt to exterminate an entire people by obliterating their culture rather than by physically killing them.

cultural relativism   A view that cultures need to be understood on their own terms, rather than on those of the person studying them.

culture   As used in this text, refers to the full range of acquired human characteristics and behavior, versus those that are biologically or environmentally derived.

currency   Anything that can be used as a mechanism of exchange. A currency can range from something like sweet potatoes in a horticultural society, to gold currency in an advanced agricultural society, to bank credits in the contemporary world.

custom   As contrasted with "law," refers to informal, traditional understandings of the way things should be, including how disputes should be resolved.

daughter preference   Parental preference for having daughters.

dendrite   One of a small set of tentacles by which a neuron receives information from another cell.

density   One of four themes in human adaptation. Increased density of people usually has serious social implications that go beyond the environment itself.

descending generation   One generation "down"; thus, for you, your children, nephews, and nieces.

dibble stick   Small stick used to poke holes into the ground, into which seeds are then placed. This is a common tool in horticultural societies.

displacement   In this text, refers to the ability of language to deal with objects that are somewhere else.

diversity   Literal meaning is that people vary, but use of the term is now conventional for describing situations in which human difference is believed to be good.

division of labor   Refers to the way in which different tasks are assigned to different members of a society, whether on the basis of age, gender, education, skill, or other factors.

divorce   General term for any revocation of a marriage arrangement. Individual societies vary in how they define divorce and whether divorce is one thing or many (for example, annulment versus divorce proper in North America).

diyi   Spirits or powers. (See the discussion of the Cibecue Apache in Chapter 13.)

domestication   For anthropologists, generally refers to human control over plants and animals (for example, improved grains, pigs in pens versus wild boars, a larger, faster horse).

DOV   Dried on the vine. A technologically advanced system for automated harvesting of raisin grapes. (See discussion in Chapter 11.)

the Dreaming   Term used to refer to the Australian aboriginal understanding of the past. (See the discussion of the Yolngu in Chapter 1.)

ecology   In this text, refers to a general framework that emphasizes the interaction of human beings and their environments.

ecumenical   Mutually accepting views among different groups, especially different religions.

endogamy   General term that refers to marrying within some group such as a clan, village, or caste.

environment   As used in this text, refers to the external features that condition human behavior, as opposed to biological or cultural factors.

Eskimo kinship terminology   Terminological system based on gender, generation, and nuclearity (i.e., whether relatives are within the immediate nuclear family).

ethnicity   Common system for categorizing diversity. Ethnic labels can be positive or negative, volitional or imposed. They are usually strongest when historical origins, language, and culture are clearly distinctive to a group.

ethnography   The broad study of people's lives and lifeways based on detailed fieldwork. Also, an extended, usually book-length, description of the results of such research.

evolution   A view that, over time, human and other species change based on the differential advantages of new characteristics or behavior.

evolutionism   General theoretical perspective that emphasizes the importance of evolution in human society. Early evolutionism is closely associated with Edward Tylor. (See discussion in Chapter 1.)

exchange   System of circulation of goods based on their economic value. Usually called "market exchange" even though physical markets are not always present.

exogamy   General term that refers to marrying outside a group, such as a clan, village, or caste.

external relations   One of three key responsibilities of any political system: managing the areas and people beyond the limits of the immediate political system.

family   Fairly ambiguous term that often refers to the most immediate kin, but can also refer to the full range of kin, and sometimes to those people considered closest to you whether they are actually related by blood or not. Anthropologists generally use the word "kin" instead.

foraging   Environmental adaptation in which plant and animal food is gathered rather than cultivated or herded. Often also called hunting and gathering.

forebrain   From the front, the first of the three main parts of the mammalian (and human) brain. Used especially for abstract reasoning.

fraternal polyandry   System of marriage in which a women marries two or more brothers.

gar   The marking of male adulthood by cutting a series of lines across the forehead.

garimpeiros   Independent, invading gold miners in the Amazon river basin. (See the discussion of the Yanomami in Chapter 12.)

gender   Technically refers to the social construction of sex but is also now widely used to refer to the combination of the biological and cultural aspects of being male, female, or some other construct (e.g., third and fourth genders among many native American tribes).

generalized reciprocity   Reciprocity in which the exchange is channeled through individuals but largely for group purposes. Compare a wedding (generalized reciprocity) with the exchange of anniversary presents between a couple (balanced reciprocity).

genocide   The attempted extermination of an entire people.

gift-giving   Crucial anthropological notion about how a gift requires a counter-gift ad infinitum. Studying the exchange of gifts provides a very visible map of social relations. (See "reciprocity.")

glial trail   "Trail" marked out in the developing brain by glial cells. Used by neurons as they "migrate" to their final positions.

globalization   Refers to expanding and intensifying economic, political, and cultural interactions in the contemporary world. The word is used both positively (globalization is good for everybody) and negatively (especially that it is a new, even more pernicious kind of colonialism).

gossip   A very useful social sanction widely used in human societies. Especially in close knit societies, it works very well to control people's behavior.

governance   As contrasted with "politics," refers to the ways the work of government is actually carried out.

gowa and *gota*   Apache terms, respectively, for clan and household. (See the discussion of the Cibecue Apache in Chapter 9.)

groups   As contrasted with "categories," refers to sets of people who actually interact with each other in ways that produce some unity among them.

Hawaiian kinship terminology   Terminological system based solely on gender and generation.

"headless" government   Refers to a kin-based political system without formal leadership roles. (See the discussion of the Nuer in Chapter 12.)

heterodoxy   Literally, "other" beliefs, but the term usually conveys a notion of power and of the "other" beliefs being incorrect, dangerous, and perhaps subject to persecution.

heteropraxy Literally, "other" practices or actions, but the term usually conveys a notion of power and that the "other" practices are incorrect and dangerous.

hindbrain The third of the three main parts of the mammalian brain. Tied to basic biological functioning.

historical particularism General theoretical framework that emphasizes the uniqueness of people's histories and the importance of the details (particulars) of their lives. Associated especially with Franz Boas.

holism A view that all aspects of a situation, or of a people's culture, must be understood as a whole, rather than as separate pieces.

horticulture Environmental adaptation in which plants are brought together in gardens, usually also with some animals (such as pigs).

household Refers both to the set of people living together and to the physical structure in which they live.

hunting and gathering Environmental adaptation in which animal and plant food is gathered from the environment. In this text, referred to as "foraging."

hypergamy System of marriage in which the woman marries "up" into a higher status household.

hypogamy System of marriage in which the woman marries "down" into a lower-status household.

illegal immigrants International migrants who either cross the border without authorization or overstay the duration of their visas. Although they are thus "illegal" in their residence, the preferred term is "undocumented."

incarceration Putting people in jails, prisons, or the like. As a sanction, it requires a notably high level of costs, compared with ostracism, gossip, or even direct revenge.

indigenous peoples Refers to those people originally in a particular area who have been displaced, shunted aside, and sometimes destroyed by later arrivals.

individual In contrast to "person," highlights a human being as free-standing, autonomous, and separate from other human beings.

industrialism Environmental adaptation based on extraction of a broad range of resources and the sharp expansion of productive capabilities.

infix A bound morpheme that appears in the middle of a word. (Infixes are common in some languages although not in English.)

infrastructure In this text, refers to the economic, transportation, and communication systems within a political entity.

inheritance Transfer of property or rights, usually after someone dies.

institution Refers to an established activity or relationship (e.g., the institution of marriage) or to a formally incorporated organization (e.g., a governmental institution).

internal order One of three key responsibilities of any political system: ensuring that there is relative peace within the area governed.

Iroquois kinship terminology Terminological system based on gender, generation, and lineality (i.e., whether kin are on the mother's or father's side).

Kanizsa illusion An illusion that demonstrates both perceptual and cultural aspects of human thought.

karma Hindu and Buddhist notion that the relative accumulation of merit affects not only this life but future ones as well.

kindred Kin group that is based on relationships to the individual, thus "ego-oriented." Only siblings can have the same kindred.

kinesics "Body language": the gestures and movements that, together with formal language, create the situational meaning of in-person communication.

kinship The ways in which people are attached to each other by blood and marriage, including both real and "fictive" ties.

kinship terminology Set of words used to designate different kinds of kin. The individual terms and their relationships vary widely in different cultures.

kula   Ceremonial exchange of necklaces (*soulava*) and armbands (*mwali*) in the Tro-briand Islands.

labor migration   Generally refers to the movement of people for work in industrial societies. The movement can be internal to a country (especially from rural to urban areas) or across national borders.

law   As contrasted with "custom," refers to formal, usually written guidelines about how things should be, including how disputes should be resolved.

levirate   System of marriage in which a dead husband is "replaced" by his brother.

lexicon   The words used in a language.

lineage   A group of kin who share the same known descent through an ancestral line, usually of men (patrilineage) or of women (matrilineage).

mana   Polynesian notion of a pervasive force emanating through the world.

manifested and manifesting   Benjamin Whorf's words for the two-part Hopi sense of time that he contrasted to the three-part Euro-American sense of time (i.e., past, present, and future).

market   A physical place where goods can be exchanged. In nonindustrial societies, markets are often periodic (monthly, weekly).

market exchange   System of circulation of goods based on their economic value. Note that "market exchange" is often used to describe economic exchanges even when physical markets may no longer be present.

marriage   General term for any formal linking of nonrelated people into a perma-nent sexual (and usually procreative) relationship. Individual societies vary greatly in how they define marriage.

matriarchy   System in which women (technically mothers) are in charge. Often used incorrectly to refer to matrilineality.

matriclan   Set of kin who believe they are descended from a common ancestor through a line of women.

matrilineage   Group of kin who share the same, known ancestry through a line of women.

matrilineality   Kinship system in which the kin relationships between people are traced through women.

matrilocal   Type of postmarital residence in which the couple reside together with the wife's family. (Technically this is "uxorimatrilocal.")

mediation   Dispute resolution mechanism using intermediaries between the parties, even though the parties themselves must ultimately agree on any resolution the in-termediaries may propose.

midbrain   The second of the three main divisions of the mammalian brain. Used for routine functioning.

mobility   One of four key themes in human adaptation. Unlike control, density, and complexity, mobility does not always change in a linear way: Thus industrialists and foragers share much in the way of mobility, but not very much in terms of control, density, and complexity.

moiety system   A system in which all members of a society belong to one of two mar-riage groups (moieties).

molimo   Trumpet-like musical instrument used by the Mbuti. (See the discussion of the Mbuti in Chapter 1.)

monogamy   System of marriage in which there is only one spouse at a time.

monograph   A specialized, usually book-length, analysis of a particular subject or topic. Tends to be more narrowly focused than an ethnography.

monotheism   Technically, refers to a belief in a single god. Tylor's early notion of a Supreme Being is perhaps more accurate since most so-called monotheistic religions actually believe in a wide range of spiritual entities.

morpheme   The smallest unit of meaning in a language (e.g., "dog" or the "z" sound that makes plurals in English).

morphology   The structure of words in a language.

multiplicity of patterning   In this text, refers to the way different components of a language can be structured in different ways.

mwali   The armbands used in the famed *kula* exchanges in the Trobriand Islands.

nation   Originally meant "a people" and in older documents is used much as the word "ethnic" is used today. In contemporary usage, however, "nation" is often associated with "state" for nation-state. That combined nation-state is a powerful concept: a common people in a shared political system.

negotiation   In this text, refers to a dispute resolution mechanism involving direct discussion among the parties involved.

neolocal   Type of postmarital residence in which the couple reside together at a new location.

neural tube   Earliest development of the brain and spinal cord in the fetus.

nuclear family   A family that includes two genders and two generations, thus mother, father, and child.

one-child policy   Formal policy that parents can have only one child. Implemented in China with considerable success in reining in population growth.

openness   One of the crucial aspects of human language and of human thought.

orthodoxy   Literally "straight" beliefs, but the term usually conveys the forced nature of those "straight" beliefs.

orthopraxy   Literally "straight" practices or actions. As with orthodoxy, the term conveys the notion of control, of some person or group deciding and enforcing those "straight" practices.

ostracism   Expelling a person from his or her family, community, or society. It is a highly effective sanction in small-scale societies where people depend on each other for practical and emotional support.

ownership   A particular concept about the relationship between people and resources that assumes the relationship is singular and total. Thus if you own something, you own all parts of it forever until you die or sell it. Compare that to a more flexible notion of "rights of use" where many different people might be using the same resource at different times and for different purposes.

paralanguage   Vocal parts of communication (yelling, whispering, speed of speech) that, although not technically formal language, nevertheless convey meaning.

pastoralism   Environmental adaptation in which people specialize in one or a few animals (although they also often grow some crops).

patriarchy   System in which men (technically, fathers) are in charge. Often used incorrectly for patrilineality.

patriclan   Set of kin who believe they are descended from a common ancestor through a male line.

patrilineage   Group of kin who share a known descent through a line of men.

patrilineality   System in which the kin relations among people are traced through men.

patrilocal   Type of postmarital residence in which the couple resides together with the husband's family. (Technically this is "viripatrilocal.")

patrinomial   System in which children use (inherit) the names of their fathers.

perception   In contrast to "conception," the physical sensing of the environment.

person   As contrasted to "individual," suggests a human being as enmeshed in a social web, and therefore not fully autonomous and separable.

phoneme   The smallest unit of distinguishable sound in a language (e.g., the "d" or "ow" sounds in English).

phonology   The sound system of a language.

phratry   A group of related clans.

pidgin   A simplified trade language with a rudimentary grammar that develops in multilingual situations. Most (but not all) aspects of the pidgin derive from the economically or politically dominant language.

primus inter pares   "First among equals." Refers to situations in which leaders do not have formal authority over other people.

politics   As contrasted with "governance," refers to the processes by which general goals and policies are chosen.

polyandry   System of marriage in which there can be multiple *husbands* at the same time.

polygamy   System of marriage in which there can be multiple spouses at the same time. Thus polyandry and polygyny are kinds of polygamy.

polygyny   System of marriage in which there can be multiple *wives* at the same time.

polytheism   Belief in multiple gods.

positionality   In this text, refers to the ability of language to "view" an object from any desired position.

postindustrial   Term used to suggest that the basic characteristics of contemporary life are so different from classic or early industrialism that a separate term is needed.

postmarital residence   Refers to the place in which a couple lives after marriage. Decisions about postmarital residence are crucial for the future composition of the household and the nature of the kinship system overall.

power   As contrasted with "authority," refers to the ability to force people to do something against their will, or at least regardless of their own views.

prefix   A bound morpheme that appears at the beginning of a word (e.g., the "re" in revisit in English).

prevarication   A fancy, somewhat more neutral term for lying.

priest   A full-time (usually) religious practitioner whose vision, competence, and authority derive from a formal religious organization. Contrast with "shaman."

property   General term used to refer to any kind of object or place that can be owned. Property can be movable (horse, furniture) or immovable (land).

puktunwali   Pashtun code of hospitality and revenge. (See discussion in Chapter 14.)

punishment   As contrasted with "compensation," refers to a system of extracting pain and property from the "guilty" rather than trying to repair the social relationships between the person who did the "crime" and the person who lost something by that crime.

race   A term that usually implies, without much scientific basis, clear biological distinctions among different, defined sets of people.

reciprocity   System of exchange of goods based on personal connections and mutual trust.

reconciliation   Contemporary term used to refer to efforts to bring together societies that have been fractured by genocide, apartheid, civil war, or other sharp cleavages.

recruitment   In this text, refers to the need of complex political systems to gain competent, reliable people for government work.

redistribution   System of exchange of goods based on the authority of the person or organization managing the exchange.

refugee   In general terms, any person fleeing anything. In formal international law, a person moving across a state border for fear of persecution on the basis of nationality, religion, race, political opinion, or membership in a particular social group.

ridicule   Like gossip, a very useful social sanction in most societies, but particularly in relatively small-scale ones.

rights of use   Contrasts with conventional Euro-American notion of ownership. Instead of a single "owner" with all the rights, different people may have different rights of use or for a limited duration.

ritual   An ordered, repetitive event (or set of events) that is used in establishing and reestablishing spiritual and social connections.

sanctions   Actions taken against people either to change their behavior or simply to punish them for having done something wrong.

Sapir-Whorf hypothesis   Notion that a language influences and possibly determines the nature of thought for people who use that language.

savagery   A term used by early evolutionists for societies with relatively simple technology.

sedentary   Refers to a life-style that does not involve frequent movement beyond the immediate areas of home and fields.

semanticity   In this text, refers to the ability of language to convey abstract meaning.

seniority   Used to differentiate based on many possible characteristics, but in anthropology seniority usually refers to seniority by age. Such seniority is crucial in kinship systems.

sense-making   Refers to the full range of conscious and unconscious thinking by which people make practical sense of their environments. (See discussion in Chapter 15.)

sex   Refers to the biological differences between males and females. Gender (which refers to the social construction of biological sex) is now often used to refer to biological sex as well as the social constructions of gender.

sexual orientation   Culturally conditioned notion of how people are drawn to potential sex partners. Current North American convention involves a list of heterosexual, gay, lesbian, transgendered, bisexual, and "questioning," but cross-cultural data suggest sexual orientations are often rather more overlapping and situational.

shaman   A part-time (usually) religious practitioner whose vision and expertise comes from his or her own personal experiences. Contrast with "priest."

sign   In this text, refers to a relatively simple symbol that has clear practical implications. (But note that the word is sometimes used in a much broader sense.)

signal   In this text, refers to the most elementary of symbols, to something for which a required action is very clear, such as a traffic signal.

skill   As used in this text, refers to varying abilities of any kind. Some skills may be biologically based; many others are environmentally conditioned, and especially in agricultural and industrial societies, many require formal education and training.

social relations   As contrasted to "societal relations," refers to relations that are largely personal among known individuals.

societal relations   As contrasted with "social relations," refers to relations that are not directly personal or among people who are known to each other.

sociolinguistics   Refers to a broad range of topics associated with the intersection of language and social interaction.

solidarity   Refers to the ways in which, and degree to which, people are united with each other. They can be united both because they are the same (e.g., all opponents of the current ruler) or because they are different (e.g., husbands and wives, parents and children).

son preference   Parental preference for sons. This is a crucial demographic issue in strongly patrilineal societies.

sorcery   The ability to control events through means that are at least partly spiritual or supernatural. The emphasis is usually on the sorcerer's control.

sororal polygyny   System of marriage in which a man marries two or more sisters.

sororate   System of marriage in which a dead wife is "replaced" by her sister.

soulava   The necklaces of the famed *kula* exchanges in the Trobriand Islands.

specialization of labor   Refers to any situation in which some people have or develop the ability to do work than others cannot or will not do.

states   Type of political organization based on complex, centralized political entities with defined borders and numerous full-time officials.

stratification   Social system in which differences are organized into vertical layers ("strata"). Those strata may be fairly loosely organized or very rigidly enforced (e.g., caste).

structural functionalism   General theoretical framework that emphasizes the way societies are structured systems, with different aspects of the culture having important functions for the whole. Especially associated with A. R. Radcliffe-Brown and Bronislaw Malinowski.

Sudanese kinship terminology   Terminological system based on the full range of possible kin characteristics, often called "descriptive kinship terminology."

suffix   A bound morpheme that appears at the end of a word (e.g., the "z" sound that indicates plurals in English).

surplus   In this text, used to refer to anything produced beyond what is immediately consumed.

swidden   Technical term for a system of slash-and-burn horticulture.

symbol   Something that stands for something else. In this text, the term covers the full range of possibilities, from a simple direct signal (traffic light) to a broadly cultural and emotional representation (a flag).

syntax   The way phrases and sentences are constructed in a language.

tattoo   Any of a wide range of markings that go into the human skin, and thus are permanent. (See discussion in Chapter 17.)

territoriality   Refers to how people are attached to territory, a combination of how they are linked to territory and the strength of that link.

transgendered   Changed in gender. Actual surgical change would be transsexual.

transplanting   System of agriculture in which seedlings are first grown in one set of fields and then replanted later in the main fields.

tribes   Type of political organization based on well-defined groups structured on kinship.

trust   For anthropology, trust is most crucial in considering reciprocity. Unless the other person can be trusted to produce an equivalent return gift, there is little point in giving that person a gift.

unbound morpheme   A morpheme that can stand on its own (like "dog" in English).

undocumented immigrants   Preferred term for those who are often labeled "illegal immigrants."

unilineal descent   System of reckoning descent that puts together only those people who can trace their descent through a single line.

uxorilocal   Type of postmarital residence in which the couple reside together at the wife's residence.

uxorimatrilocal   Type of postmarital residence in which the couple reside together with the wife's family. Usually termed "matrilocal."

virilocal   Type of postmarital residence in which the couple reside together at the husband's residence.

viripatrilocal   Type of postmarital residence in which the couple reside together with the husband's family. Usually termed "patrilocal."

witchcraft   Involvement in activities that are at least partially "supernatural." In anthropological terms, witches are often contrasted with sorcerers. Sorcerers are people controlling the spirit world for quite human goals, whereas witches are part of the spiritual world and may not even be able to control their activities. North American usage of the term witch is very different, something of a mix of what anthropologists would distinguish as sorcerers, witches, shamans, and priests.